T0272662

SPEAKING OF HARPO

SPEAKING OF HARPO

SUSAN FLEMING MARX

With Robert S. Bader

APPLAUSE
THEATRE & CINEMA BOOKS
Essex, Connecticut

THEATRE & CINEMA BOOKS
An imprint of Globe Pequot, the trade division of
The Rowman & Littlefield Publishing Group, Inc.
4501 Forbes Blvd., Ste. 200
Lanham, MD 20706
www.rowman.com

Distributed by NATIONAL BOOK NETWORK

British Library Cataloguing in Publication Information available

Library of Congress Cataloging-in-Publication Data
Names: Fleming, Susan, 1908–2002, author. | Bader, Robert S., author.
Title: Speaking of Harpo / Susan Fleming Marx with Robert S. Bader.
Description: Guilford, Connecticut : Applause Theater & Cinema Books, an
   imprint of Globe Pequot, the trade division of the Rowman & Littlefield
   Publishing Group, Inc., [2022] | Includes index. | Summary: "The
   autobiography of Harpo Marx's wife, Susan Fleming, tells the story of
   her time as a Broadway showgirl during the Roaring Twenties, her
   struggles as an up-and-coming movie actress in 1930s Hollywood, and her
   twenty-eight-year marriage to Harpo. But her story doesn't end there:
   Susan rediscovered her own identity as a relatively young widow after
   Harpo's death in 1964"— Provided by publisher.
Identifiers: LCCN 2021054409 (print) | LCCN 2021054410 (ebook) | ISBN
   9781493065301 (cloth) | ISBN 9781493067817 (epub)
Subjects: LCSH: Fleming, Susan, 1908–2002. | Marx, Harpo,
   1888-1964—Family. | Motion picture actors and actresses—United
   States—Biography. | Actors' spouses—United States—Biography.
Classification: LCC PN2287.F535 A3 2022 (print) | LCC PN2287.F535 (ebook)
   | DDC 791.4302/8092 [B]—dc23/eng/20220204
LC record available at https://lccn.loc.gov/2021054409
LC ebook record available at https://lccn.loc.gov/2021054410

♾️ The paper used in this publication meets the minimum requirements of American National
Standard for Information Sciences—Permanence of Paper for Printed Library Materials, ANSI/
NISO Z39.48-1992.

Contents

Foreword (Looking Backward)

WHEN I FIRST MET YOUNG ROBERT BADER, IT WAS BECAUSE HE happened to be one of the many young Robert Baders who were pursuing their never-ending love for the Marx Brothers. This band of rapscallions would frequently get in touch with me or my mother, Susan, hoping we could satisfy their Marxian curiosities and fascinations. Robert and the others had many questions, but in particular they wanted to hear anything Susan had to say about my father, Harpo. And maybe his brothers too.

Shortly after our initial meeting, I encountered Robert again. It was on a dark and rainy evening. How's that for old-fashioned intrigue? The place was Frederick, Maryland, where my musical partner, Carrol McLaughlin, and I were on tour doing our comedy concert series for Columbia Artists Management. It was much like vaudeville: one-nighters and on to the next town. Robert and another of those fanatical Marx Brothers fans—this one from Boston, named Matt Hickey—had driven from New York to meet up with another of their Marx-fanatic brethren, Paul Wesolowski, in Pennsylvania. Upon their arrival, this odd trio learned that, for some mysterious reason, the lighting and sound people hadn't shown up. Robert, Matt, and Paul volunteered to fill in. Their complete lack of experience had me envisioning the Marx Brothers destroying *Il Trovatore* in *A Night at the Opera*. But they pulled it off and helped us get through the show—even without any rehearsal. The audience left carrying all the produce they were hoping to heave at us.

Several months later, I encountered Robert again in California. It occurs to me now that he kept popping up at irregular intervals. But he didn't seem to require a restraining order, so I invited him to lunch with my mother. It was in Rancho Mirage, and she had just finished (or given up on) writing her memoirs. Either way, she was ready to put this literary accomplishment to rest in a closet, along with her other artistic dabbling, such as watercolors, oils, and silk screens. "Oh Christ!" she said. "Why would anyone care about my epic masterpiece anyway?" But she decided to have Robert look at it even though she was sure it would be of no interest to anyone else because it was mostly about her. He assured her it would be of great value to Marx Brothers addicts who wanted to know more about Harpo and her life-changing influence on him when he was transformed from a forty-seven-year-old confirmed bachelor into a loving husband and father. Robert also told her that he was very interested in Susan Fleming's pre-Harpo story, reminding her that she had appeared in more than twenty-five films. "They were all junk," she replied in typical Susan Marx fashion.

After Robert read her manuscript, Mom considered his assessment and decided they should collaborate on editing and completing the book. Robert felt it could find a broader audience if it covered Susan's experiences on Broadway and in Hollywood. These elements along with what she'd already written about her life after Harpo, and how she coped with being a relatively young widow, would eventually form the finished book. That she's not here to see it finally completed is probably best for her. She was a very private person, but she had a wonderful story to tell. She wrestled with the idea of sharing her private thoughts with the world, but all things considered, a posthumous publication allows her to hold nothing back and to not have to hear from anyone who doesn't appreciate her occasionally strong opinions. I can almost hear her telling Robert, "That'll be your problem."

Those who knew my mother would agree that she could be articulate about almost any subject. She had a wide variety of interests and had been an avid reader since childhood. But she would clam up if you asked her anything about Susan Marx. She kept her personal feelings to herself—and probably my dad, to some degree. My mother was a role player. As a little girl she pleased her mother and father as Susie Fleming, then on the stage and screen she became Suzanne and then Susan Fleming to please people like Florenz Ziegfeld and Harry Cohn. Her next—and most important—role was Mrs. Harpo Marx, my mother, who lived to please Harpo, my brothers, my sister, and me. Her final and greatest role was Susan Marx—a very special woman I knew as Mom. She finally figured out that she could live for herself and be completely independent. I was blessed by her brilliant presence in my life, just as much as that special fella, Adolph Arthur Harpo Dad Marx was. My mother's story is really a tale of two incredibly different people coming together as the perfect couple. Please enjoy getting to know these two wonderful parents of mine from Susan's unique perspective.

Bill Marx
Rancho Mirage, California
April 2021

Preface: 1964

SEPTEMBER 28, 1964. LOST: TWENTY-EIGHT YEARS. GOLD AND laughter colored. Answers to the name Harpo. Please return to Susan Marx, Palm Springs, California. Just when I thought I had the hang of it, he was gone. I wasn't prepared for it. It felt like I had lost half of myself. Being without him seemed impossible. Lost: One Arm. Lost: One Leg. Lost.

I was suddenly the piece that's left over—a widow. I hated it. That awful emptiness that can't be shared because it's all that's left. My children were kind and rallied with everything but mouth-to-mouth resuscitation. With a wonderful perceptiveness, they demanded attention—their favorite foods, playing games, laughing at their jokes—anything they could dream up to keep me moving. I was numb. My mind wanted to separate from a damaged reality. The telephone rang constantly in sympathy. The world of show business was shattered at the loss of a beloved member of the community and tried to comfort the widow. Red Skelton was crying in Las Vegas, Bob Hope was stunned in Palm Springs, Norman Krasna called from Switzerland, the Irving Berlins reached out from New York . . . All this kindness, all this love, all this nothing.

Harpo's anxiety had started the first year we were married. He had gone for his annual checkup. When he came home, I asked him casually how it had been. He looked at me sadly. "I have hardening of the arteries." I refused to encourage self-pity by being solicitous, so I said, "Do you know any man who hasn't?" He replied, "Sam said it could become serious." I thought, *I'll kill him.* Getting Dr. Sam Hirschfield on the phone, having lost my cool, I snarled, "What the hell do you think you're doing telling a hypochondriac he has hardening of the arteries? Harpo is now convinced he's about to die." A disconcerted Sam said, "I'm sorry. I haven't known Harpo long enough to know how to talk to him. I told him every-thing was fine. The tests showed a slight hardening of the arteries, which is very common in men. Medication isn't necessary, but we could talk diet. Reducing fat and cholesterol is known to retard its advance, and certain oils can even help repair and clear away any problems. Apparently, Harpo only heard 'hardening of the arteries' and panicked. Let me talk to him." Sam tried to tell him he was so healthy he could live another fifty years. If he wanted to live any longer, he could talk to God.

But the damage was done. Harpo's hypochondria only worsened as he got older. When we had only been dating for a couple of years, he'd had surgery to remove a kidney stone, and no amount of reassurance that it was a minor operation could convince him that he wasn't at death's door. He had a remarkably healthy next twenty years, but he was always convinced that a good case of the sniffles could wipe him out. In the mid-1950s he actually suffered a mild heart attack but made a full recov-ery. Harpo's insistence on having his imminent demise taken seriously had kept me in a constant battle against the demoralizing influence of a mortician-like man that brother Gummo had selected as their physician after Dr. Hirschfield somehow died before his star patient.

Our move from Beverly Hills to the desert had limited the clinical consultations to semiannual visits to Los Angeles. Even so, I had rescued him from a couple of different private hospitals where he had allowed himself to be placed for "close observation and needed bed rest!" One time, in exasperation, I had let them have him for a week and then drove into town to take a look. When I walked into his room, a nurse was car-rying a frail little bundle to the john. The bundle looked at me and started to cry. It was up to me. I knew my Harpo. "Nurse, sit him down and leave us alone." A short argument ensued, and she left, ostensibly to report me to someone. I didn't care. Harpo was mine and I knew him better than anyone in the world. He was a believer, and I had to see to it that what he believed would be good for him. Not this. Another week in their hands and he would disappear.

"Okay. Get back into bed and tell me what they've been feeding you." One of the world's most thorough eaters glumly replied, "Liquids." Cripes! "There's a deli down the block. Don't go away, I'll be right back."

Ten minutes later he was gobbling sliced turkey on rye bread with some strong iced tea. "Are you sure this is all right?" he asked, without missing a bite. "I'm sure. Now get dressed." He looked up from his sandwich and asked, "What for?" The look on my face was probably enough to let him know we were leaving, but I told him, "I'm taking you home." He didn't look surprised. He'd had it. There was a moment, as we passed the front desk, when Harpo asked, "Don't we check out?" But I just shoved him out the door. Gummo's doctor might be on his way, and I wanted to be sure he would have to come all the way to Palm Springs to get his patient back. It was a fine ride home. After a severe scolding, a chastened Harpo whipped out his harmonica and for two-and-a-half hours we sang songs and laughed about our daring escape.

Two pleasant years followed under the care of a wonderful man, Dr. George Kaplan of Palm Springs. Dr. Kaplan understood that a heart attack can shatter a person's confidence, and that was the first thing to repair. Medicine would then do what it could to unclog the arteries. We were okay until another mild heart attack interrupted our lives. And then another. Dr. Kaplan told Harpo to limit his activities to nothing more strenuous than golf and painting, both of which he pursued with mixed results. I'm not sure if he had a better handicap as a golfer or a painter, but he occasionally produced a canvas that was the artistic equivalent of a hole in one. But under no circumstances was he to perform publicly anymore. Harpo agreed, and it looked as if we were under control. Except that Harpo occasionally disobeyed doctor's orders when he had a chance to get in front of an audience.

Harpo announced that he was semiretired a couple of times, but he finally made the announcement of his full retirement on January 19, 1963. He was performing at the Pasadena Playhouse with his friend Allan Sherman. Just before the show, he let Allan know it would be his final performance. Harpo and Allan had met in the summer of 1961 when by sheer fate we rented a house in Brentwood next door to the house Allan was renting. Allan was looking for a break in show business, and we were out of the desert heat and close to the cardiologist who was looking after Harpo in the aftermath of his most recent heart attack. Allan's song parodies enchanted Harpo, who became his biggest supporter. (The most supportive thing a person can do for a comedian is stick him in front of Jack Benny, which Harpo did. Jack practically went into convulsions when he heard Allan's songs.) Harpo saw Allan's invitation to appear with him in Santa Monica and Pasadena as an opportunity to bring down the curtain on his fifty-five years in show business. At the end of the second show in Pasadena, Allan told the audience that they had witnessed Harpo's final performance. He was crying. The audience gasped before exploding into a huge ovation. Harpo came back out from the wings and gave a speech filled with big fancy words, a little improvisation, and a few bits of his Bar Mitzvah speech. It was a glorious farewell. But Harpo wasn't quite finished.

In the last year of Harpo's life, we traveled to Seattle, Portland, Denver, and San Francisco so he could give speeches on behalf of the United Jewish Appeal (UJA). In those speeches Harpo discussed our 1963 trip to Israel and his experiences as a victim of anti-Semitism. He expressed hope that the new man in the Vatican, Pope Paul VI, would influence the Christian world to discard any anti-Semitic views it held. Jewish leaders were concerned that anti-Semitism had gained respectability in part because of the controversial behavior of Pope Pius XII during World War II. Many people believed he had turned a blind eye to the Holocaust. Harpo made no judgments. He appeared at these UJA events to promote a message of compassion, optimism, and brotherhood.

Harpo was again reminded of his mortality that spring when a heart attack claimed his dear friend Ben Hecht. It was Ben who had inspired Harpo's work for Israel and Jewish causes. Harpo also performed with the Riverside Symphony at a benefit in which he narrated *Peter and the Wolf*. After nearly fifty years of mostly not speaking on stage, I couldn't shut him up in 1964. His actual final public appearance—once again giving a speech—came at a testimonial dinner for Gus Kettman, the retiring chief of police in Palm Springs, only a few months before that awful day. Harpo always had an angle: "They're benefits. It isn't work."

The period following his first heart attack was the only time I ever found it difficult to be around Harpo. He was driving me mad, acting as though he hadn't actually survived. There was no convincing him that he could enjoy life while making a few accommodations for his health. He was downright depressing. So much so that I took our three youngest children on a trip to the Grand Canyon and sent Harpo to Los Angeles to stay with our oldest son, Bill. Fortunately, Harpo turned things around and saw how lucky he was. To use his words, he was "living on velvet" and he planned to continue doing so. But he could never really shake his hypochondria, which, combined with some actual health concerns, kept me on my toes.

In September of 1964 things would be different. They were going to operate! We had gone to Los Angeles for a few days to celebrate our anniversary with old friends. Gloria Stuart and her husband, Arthur Sheekman, were hosting a small party for us. Without telling me, Harpo let Gummo, who seemed to move with Harpo like a shadow, take him to a heart specialist to see how well he was doing. My idiot boy let him take some tests—aneurysm. Why did he do this when he was in the care of a different doctor? Hypochondria—plus Gummo. I was waiting in the dining room at Hillcrest Country Club for Harpo to join me for lunch when the two of them came in and sprang the news on me. "What do you think, Mom?"

"You are actually asking me for my opinion? I'll tell you what I think. I think you are a lunatic. What's the matter? Does it bore you to be well?" Gummo and Harpo were talking about arterial transplants, which were in the pioneering stage at the time. I said, "If you're so anxious to be back in a hospital, we will go to Texas to see the pioneer himself, Dr. DeBakey." But Gummo, our family expert on the medical world, said, "Not necessary at all. We have some highly skilled surgeons here in Los Angeles, and you will get VIP treatment at Mount Sinai Hospital." What could I say? Let them operate on Gummo, he might enjoy it more? I knew this was out of my hands, so I did the best I could by acting as if there was nothing to worry about.

Evidently, there was no need to wait. Mount Sinai had just changed the sheets on a private bed and a renowned surgeon was available. So, rather than celebrate our anniversary, we admitted my beloved hypo-chondriac into another hospital—instead of the restaurant of our old friend Dave Chasen. There was an eerie moment in the admitting office when Harpo was asked his full name. He didn't seem to hear, and I had a feeling he was looking back in time. The administrator gently asked him again, and Harpo answered vaguely, "Duer—Arthur Duer." Oh, God. I wanted to grab him and run. Alice Duer Miller, one of his closest friends, had been dead for more than twenty years.

That weekend our daughter, Minnie, and her fiancé, Jerry Eagle, came to the hospital with a cake to represent them at the anniversary party, which now was going to be celebrated differently. They had wanted to have their wedding date the same as ours; something to do with establishing a tradition. But they had accepted Harpo's feeling of urgency and would wait until November, giving him a couple of months for a full recuperation. They had to get back to college, so they kissed him and left. I didn't want to leave, but there was no excuse to stay. Trying to hang on to him, I reminded him firmly, "It's our anniversary. I'll be here with the other kids as soon as they let us in. You be in good shape, or it'll spoil the party."

"OK, Mom. I'm going to take a nap." These would be the last words I'd hear Harpo speak. The next day is history, and none of us ever felt like celebrating an anniversary again. The initial report was that the operation was a success and Harpo's aneurysm had been taken care of. But later that day we learned that the four-hour operation was just too much. Hours after coming out of surgery, Harpo suffered a massive heart attack. He was gone. After breathing a huge sigh of relief earlier in the day, I went numb when I got the news.

We had spent those last seven years living in Palm Springs—or more specifically, Cathedral City—full time after several years of weekends and holidays there. We just never seemed in any hurry to get back to Beverly Hills, so we settled in the desert for good. Harpo continued to work for part of that time, but eventually the performing tapered off in accordance with the advice of the doctors—but never completely stopped. Before long he settled into his new routine and concentrated on nothing more taxing than his golf game, painting, and the burning of an occasional steak. There was also the matter of a book called *Harpo Speaks!*

Harpo was still working and keeping a fairly full schedule when Bernie Geis, a dear friend of ours, prevailed upon him to pen his memoirs. Bernie had started his own publishing firm with the help of a few celebrity friends, such as Art Linkletter and my brother-in-law Groucho.

In fact, Bernie had just made a deal for Groucho's book, *Groucho and Me*. Harpo would be assisted by Rowland Barber, a writer Bernie had recommended. Rowland and Harpo hit it off and got to work. Harpo would sit at the harp in the big bay window and regale Rowland with tales of the Marx Brothers, the Algonquin Round Table, and countless other stories that the kids and I had never heard. It shouldn't come as any surprise that much was left unspoken in our marriage. If I didn't ask, he didn't tell. If he didn't ask, I didn't tell. Naturally this left the children somewhat in the dark about the lives of their parents. Neither one of us asked a lot of questions. Thank goodness for Rowland. My boy had a lot to say.

I hadn't known very much about Harpo's life before I came into it. What became apparent to me as he worked on the book was the fact that Harpo and I had traveled very different roads to arrive in exactly the same place. By the time we met, he and his brothers were big stars, and I was starting to make a name for myself—whether I wanted to or not.

CHAPTER ONE

Don't Tell Anyone You
Were Born in Brooklyn

To my mother's lasting mortification, I was born in Brooklyn, New York. That was not classy. My father and I always felt it was a punishment meted out by the gods to instill humility in her for her intermittent upper-class pretensions. I was never clear about how she acquired this attitude. She was born in Troy, New York, a sleepy little town roughly 150 miles from the lights of Broadway. She grew up in Bethlehem, Pennsylvania, which didn't make things any better for her. Poor Mother—a beautiful, talented, and witty woman, who was born to sing Wagner at the Met, but whose dreams would remain dreams. When the Metropolitan Opera Company did call on Mother, her trips to New York for singing lessons were promptly cut off. "Gulla"—the nickname my Swedish grandparents gave the daughter they named Gunhild vonPhilp—was not allowed to leave Bethlehem for a whore's life. Incidentally, everyone else just called Mother "Bunny."

So, Mother stayed home, went to parties, and waited for her destiny in the person of William Lazier Fleming. Father had been attending Lehigh University in Bethlehem when he met Mother. With his gentle demeanor and strong artistic sensibilities, Father was never really equipped to deal with a strong-willed, frustrated lady like Mother. Orphaned at the age of ten, Father was raised by an aunt and uncle and traveled as far as he could to make his own way in life. When he wrote from Spokane, Washington, where he had taken an engineering job with a mining company, that she should come west and marry him, they compromised. He traveled 2,500 miles from Spokane and Mother made the twelve-mile trek from Bethlehem so they could get a marriage license in Northampton, Pennsylvania, on December 30, 1905. The wedding took place in Mother's house. I wonder if her version of a compromise gave Father any second thoughts. They immediately moved to Sierra City, California, for Father's next mining job. When her time came, as they used to delicately say, she went back East to have her baby. Winter was rough in a desolate mining town, and her baby was due in February. Rather than return to Bethlehem, Mother chose to stay with her sister in Brooklyn. Therefore, the life of Susan Alva Fleming began on February 19, 1908, at 1402 Pacific Street in the Crown Heights section of Brooklyn. Not classy! If only my aunt could have lived on Riverside Drive.

As a mining engineer, and later a stockbroker, my father's jobs moved us from New Jersey to California, to Long Island, to Alaska, to Connecticut, and finally to New York. Our fortunes changed as often as our locale. This hopscotch life made me a shy, introspective child, and I was forced to make constant social adjustments through a kaleidoscope of school rooms. Making friends was nearly impossible, and I spent most of my free time with my nose buried in books. Our years of prosperity were the worst for me. I was given piano and ballet lessons—neither of which I liked. I rebelled against piano early on and got a reprieve until we moved to a large house in Forest Hills, a pleasant suburb of New York City. We lived in the shadow of Forest Hills Tennis Stadium, on a street appropriately named Tennis Place. I was around seven years old when we arrived there.

The years in Forest Hills were our longest and most affluent period. Summers were spent on the eastern tip of Long Island and are remembered with pleasure. Father had found success as a stockbroker. How he arrived at that profession I don't know, but Mother had probably made it clear that she was through with snowy winters in Colorado and Nevada mining towns. She was finally in her element. As the daughter of a Swedish baronet, she could indulge her fancy for coronets embroidered on the linens. At parties I'd be dressed in an embroidered white dress with matching blue bows on top of my head and my rump and then posted at the front door to greet the guests by name. Later I was expected to demonstrate my many talents. "Susan, dear, recite something for the

Rountrees," or "Let the Georges hear you play your new piece," after which the assemblage would say, "Isn't that cute?" and laugh pleasantly. The horror of childhood has never left me. I have some photos of when I was too young to be exhibited, and I looked like a happy enough child, but those taken from age eight on are depressing.

Music lessons resumed because there was a lovely piano in the Forest Hills house. But there was a dent in my musicality, which Mother discovered one day while standing beside me as I practiced. She was attempting to sing the song I was playing, but I wasn't playing in the same key as on the sheet in front of me. It called for an immediate conference. Clearly, I had inherited my father's ability to play by ear, so time and money would no longer be wasted on music teachers. No problem, this would allow time for other cultural activities like ballet—not a likely choice for a girl with weak ankles. Three times a week our chauffeur drove Mother and me into Manhattan to the Chalif School of Dancing. This was a renowned operation from which many finely trained dancers graduated to important ballet troupes. The likes of me were put up with because our mothers contributed handsomely to the support of the school.

It took a calamity to discourage my participation in this cultural adventure. The Chalif School season culminated in a dance recital at Carnegie Hall. We lesser stars were to be allowed to cross the stage individually, entering from the wings from one side and exiting into the wings on the other side. As usual, I was apprehensive, but Mother was delirious with pride, bringing friends in from Long Island for my debut at Carnegie Hall and having me presented (offstage fortunately) with a bouquet of roses, to the great amusement, I'm sure, of all the other mothers. The blood still pounds in my ears when I think of it. Being children, we did not wear tutus, but little, short floppy skirts with bloomers, and dancing slippers instead of hard-toed ballet slippers. I suppose the sight of the children was pretty, but not to me. I was paralyzingly self-conscious and too aware that Mother was experiencing through me the start of a brilliant career that had been denied her. That was quite a load to carry across that vast stage.

We had rehearsed the crossing, so I knew that six leaps would take me across, but when my turn came it was like moving under water. My leaps didn't take me very far. I tried longer steps before leaping, but my bloomers started to complicate things. The first three prayerful steps plus a frantic leap had jolted loose the elastic holding up the legs, and they started to slide down. I had managed to get halfway across the stage when it seemed my skinny little body wasn't going to hold up the rest of the bloomers either. The last I remember of that episode was clutching my bloomers and trying to leap off stage with some pretense of normality. Mother was dressing me in beautiful expensive clothes, but always a size or two too large, hoping I wouldn't grow out of them so quickly. If I was to debut in those bloomers, we should have waited a couple of years. All things considered, my stage debut was not much different from Harpo's. So consumed with stage fright was Harpo, that he wet his pants. But while my traumatic debut came at the tender age of eight, Harpo's came when he was nineteen!

We eventually left Forest Hills and, after several more years of constant relocation, had come full circle, back to Brooklyn. Mother was again in the vicinity of her sister, who had found an apartment for us in a quiet residential area in the Brooklyn Heights neighborhood. The subway provided an easy link to Manhattan, which enabled me to finish high school at prestigious Horace Mann. Our lives now took on an air of permanency. Having no idea where to place me academically, the school tested me for grade placement. It turned out that Father's home tutoring, while in transit, had advanced me to college level. I begged off.

I would have been content to just sit around and read for a couple of years, but Mother saw my cousin Beatrice preparing for her freshman year in college, which was expected to lead to a prosperous career. As this was a bit premature for sixteen-year-old Susan, we would get on with the cultural aspect. It was too late to pursue ballet, but there was still modern dance. Ned Wayburn's School of Dance in New York was well known and easily accessible by subway. (I would learn many years later that my brother-in-law Gummo had been a pupil at the Wayburn School during the early vaudeville days of the Marx Brothers. By the time I got there in 1924, Gummo had been out of show business for several years.)

I'm sure Mother didn't know that Wayburn put on the dances for the revues of Florenz Ziegfeld. I certainly didn't. I had never heard of them or him. I was just glad not to have to get up on sore toes again. But my first class was tap and I woke up. I was a natural. I adored tap dancing. I also managed to find a friend, a beautiful little girl named Marion Levy, who would soon be known as Paulette Goddard. We had similar child-hoods. She too had been through numerous relocations, but the reasons were very different. Paulette's parents separated when she was very young and her mother ran off with her, always staying one step ahead of her father. To make ends meet in New York, Paulette's mother pushed her into modeling. She certainly had the looks for the job.

I remember Paulette with great affection, although I never could fathom her emotional upheavals. She was naturally cheerful and fun, but those perfect features with the radiant smile could unaccountably become awash with tears as she sobbed, "I'm so ugly." This might have been a prelude to sharing a troubled heart with her friend, but comforting illusionary pain was not in my line. I'd had enough irrational behavior from my mother. At this point I was looking for emotional peace, not additional drama. Paulette would have to look more closely in a mirror.

Ziegfeld had just opened a private club in Palm Beach, Florida, called Club de Montmartre. It was basically a playground for the rich people spending the season there. He created a new show called *Palm Beach Nights* to play in the club. There wasn't any theme to the show. It was simply another edition of *The Ziegfeld Follies*, but he couldn't call it that because he was embroiled in a legal fight with his partners in the *Follies*. The star was Claire Luce, a wonderful dancer, and the cast included Morton Downey and Cliff Edwards, better known as Ukulele Ike, years before he provided the voice of Jiminy Cricket in *Pinocchio*. Wayburn encouraged Paulette and me to show up for the chorus tryout. Mother was fearful of a final breach with Grandma, who had stifled her own chance at a performing career. But her daughter might have the career denied to her. So, tap shoes in hand, we went to the theatre.

Paulette was okayed promptly, but I wasn't feeling well and was my usual, listless self. Ziegfeld didn't want any part of me, but Wayburn insisted I was his best dancer and he wanted me. I was in, but really because it wasn't all that big a deal who was in the chorus. The chorus provided pace for the show, but the showgirls were Ziegfeld's stars. It was his joy to glorify all six feet of them, lavishing money on decorating their lovely bodies with incredible costumes of towering headdresses and jeweled gowns in which they sensuously paraded about the stage. The great showman hired the finest talents in music and comedy, but he was impatient when the principals took time away from his girls. They were what his spectacles were all about, and his well-dressed audience agreed. They could be enraptured by the tableaus Ziegfeld staged, which we would laugh at now, but then beauty was worshipped.

The strenuous rehearsals got my adrenaline going. I was no longer just a kid taking dancing lessons. I was a pro. Somehow or other I wasn't listless anymore. There's a lot to be said for regular exercise and irregular hours. I had a purpose and was making what seemed to me an enormous salary to pursue it. In no time at all there, I was in a Spanish costume clicking my heels on the floor of a nightclub in the most glamorous playground in the country, Palm Beach. The show would spend ten weeks there. On opening night, January 14, 1926, a card came to me in the chorus dressing room with some orchids (which I had never seen before) and an invitation to supper. If this eager swain was surprised when Mother came along, he never showed it. He was good looking, dark, and suave. A combination I hadn't seen a lot of around the high schools. He must have been in his forties. He took Mother and me to fashionable restaurants and other pleasant places for lunches. I was fascinated. Then one day Mr. Ziegfeld called me into his office and in his fatherly fashion shattered my pride in being attractive to older men. All he said was, "Do you know that man is married?" Although there hadn't been any loving overtures, I had assumed he was interested, and I was dazzled by his sophistication into thinking life with him could be exciting and romantic. Now he seemed secondhand and tarnished, and I was embarrassed, seventeen and immature. That's gulping time. But nothing to linger over.

I was told there would be a New York production of the show and that I should expect to be in it. Mother was ecstatic and couldn't wait to get back and move us out of Brooklyn. I was surprised to make the cut. Paulette was never in doubt. Before the show opened in New York, we spent a week in Atlantic City, where the show was called *Ziegfeld's Palm Beach Girls*. The more sophisticated theatre people took notice of the fact that we had a nice little dance revue, but nothing resembling a Broadway show. Ziegfeld took care of that in a hurry, and we were soon ready to open. There wasn't anything much about the show that was memorable, but I can still picture Claire Luce popping out of a silver globe during the opening number. There was some controversy about the title because Paramount had just released a new Bebe Daniels film called *The Palm Beach Girl*. Ziegfeld again changed the name of the show to *No Foolin'* just before the Broadway opening, which took place on June 24, 1926. A few weeks later the show had yet another name: *Ziegfeld's American Revue*. He was getting closer to calling the show what it really was: *The Ziegfeld Follies*. For some inexplicable reason, Ziegfeld also decided to change my name. I would now be *Suzanne* Fleming—at least occasionally. I never called myself Suzanne, and it took a few years to shake it.

Was this the start of a career? Who cares? I was on Broadway. Newly arrived from Mars. I was a Ziegfeld Girl—or at least I would have been if not for the height requirement, which limited me to the chorus. And not a peep out of Grandma. Suddenly our family started to follow the new direction of a daughter who unexpectedly found herself in show business. We moved into an apartment on West 55th Street, and I reported to work at the Globe Theatre at Broadway and 46th Street every day until we closed in September. It made no impression on me at the time, but Harpo and his brothers were knocking 'em dead in *The Cocoanuts* just a few blocks away. I had only a vague knowledge of the Marx Brothers, but a producer friend of mine was acquainted with Harpo and ran into him on the street while I was with him. I only remember his hair protruding wildly from under his hat. We were introduced and quickly went our separate ways—a near miss.

Among the more interesting people I met in my first days as a Ziegfeld Girl was an artist named James Ben Ali Haggin III—or just Ben Ali to his friends. He was a portrait painter as well as an occasional stage designer for Ziegfeld. His grandfather was a wealthy attorney, art collector, and rancher, and it was rumored that Ben Ali had inherited several million dollars. He was very sweet and was married to an actress named Helen Roche. He would design and stage musical tableaus for the Ziegfeld shows, and one July afternoon, during our Broadway run, Ben

Ali dragged all of us chorus girls from the show out to the Paramount Studio in Astoria to film one of these numbers for a new Adolphe Menjou movie that was in production. What happened next still amazes me. Fortunately, Mother was very diligent in collecting and saving newspaper clippings, so it'll be better to just let the *New York Telegram* of July 28, 1926, tell the story.

> Thanks to a Ben Ali Haggin tableau in *Ziegfeld's American Revue* and to Adolph Menjou's discerning eye, Susan Fleming has been cast for a leading role in Menjou's starring picture, *The Ace of Cads*, in production at the Paramount Long Island Studio. That the part is an important one is shown by the fact that first Lois Moran and then Clara Bow were cast for it. When other pictures kept them from playing the part, a search for a suitable ingenue to be Alice Joyce's daughter resulted. The Paramount casting office files were scanned, and a score of girls were interviewed and screen-tested. None suited Menjou and director Luther Reed, who in the meantime had started work on scenes in which the girl does not appear.
>
> Then early this week fourteen chorus girls from the Ziegfeld revue came to the studio to be photographed in a Ben Ali Haggin tableau. The entire studio staff looked them over. Menjou joined the onlookers, scanned the faces carefully and crooked a forefinger at Susan Fleming. Wide-eyed, she came to him and was led to Reed. "Here's the girl; let's give her a test." The test was made, and Miss Fleming was selected for the role.

There had to be at least a half-dozen girls in that chorus with a burning ambition to act. I was not one of them. Mostly I was surprised that Paulette wasn't chosen. Before I could even process what was happening, I had shot a scene for my test and been taken by some Paramount people on a tour of dress shops to be outfitted with a very expensive wardrobe for my movie debut. For the next several days, Mother was busily clipping items from every paper in town about the young girl plucked from the chorus by Adolphe Menjou. Some of the papers ran a photo of me taken that day. It all seemed grand except for the fact that no one was particularly concerned that I had no acting experience. It was not suggested that I be given leave from the show, so I worked from six o'clock in the morning until five in the afternoon in Astoria, then eight o'clock in the evening until eleven in the theatre. I had no way of knowing that Harpo had worked in a film called *Too Many Kisses* at the very same studio the previous year. He had lived this exact same roller-coaster life while starring in *I'll Say She Is* on Broadway—another near miss, I suppose.

Youth was on my side and, in the parlance of the press agents, I was now a rising star. Pretty perceptive to see all that talent in one sullen look into a camera. I stumbled through my scenes each day and then rushed back to Manhattan to be on stage at the Globe. Had I not been so nervous about acting, I might have taken a moment to be excited about the whole thing. When *The Ace of Cads* eventually premiered, I was billed behind Menjou, Alice Joyce, Norman Trevor, and Philip Strange. When it played in Hartford, banners were stretched across the street in front of the theatre, proclaiming "Hometown Girl Makes Good." We had lived in Hartford only briefly, and it had been several years before, but apparently, I had been held in the bosom of the city—in spite of the fact that in the eighth grade I was turned down for the drama club there. I hope they regretted not having recognized my talents.

Mother, Father, and I saw it at the Rivoli Theatre in Times Square. I'm inclined to agree with the critic from the *New York Sun* who called the film, "one of the dullest photoplays on record." I've since learned that *The Ace of Cads* is now a lost film. Well, thank heaven for small miracles! I'd shudder to think of anyone actually seeing me in this thing.

CHAPTER TWO

The Lights of Broadway

*T*HE *ACE OF CADS* DID NOT SET THE WORLD ON FIRE AND, AFTER some silly publicity about Adolphe Menjou's fairy-tale discovery of Suzanne Fleming, Paramount quickly forgot about me. With movie stardom seemingly out of the way, I returned to the chorus at the Globe Theatre—momentarily the envy of the other girls. From the lowly ranks of the chorus, Paulette and I watched the nightly parade of orchids and the mounting tide of diamond bracelets being showered on the statuesque Ziegfeld Girls. We listened to the laughter and saw it as a game being played by clever, lighthearted women turning the tables on the satyrs of the night, picking them clean and gaily dancing off to other waiting prey. We wanted to play too. I saw myself as Max Beerbohm's *Zuleika Dobson*, trifling with men's affections and leaving a trail of suicidal suitors. This resulted in us being summoned to Mr. Ziegfeld's office. We must have seemed appropriately contrite, and coaxed prettily, as the dear man was so amused by the two shortest showgirls in town (five-feet, three-inches) that he actually expanded our roles. We would be used as stage decoration instead of just dancing. We were thrilled to have been raised to such dazzling heights. We would now be in the sights of Broadway's foremost trophy hunters. We were teenagers, but the world was ours.

Just days after *No Foolin'* closed at the Globe in September 1926, I said goodbye to Paulette and my friends from the chorus as they left for the road tour of the show that was finally allowed to use its proper name, *The Ziegfeld Follies*. So, the truth is that no matter what you've read, Paulette and I were not actually in *The Ziegfeld Follies* together. She was;

I wasn't. As for the road tour, Mother was having none of that. If I had gone, she would have come with me and that would have been difficult if not mortifying. The Roaring Twenties didn't roar much when Mother was around. When Paulette came home from the tour, we vacationed in Miami together. When we got back to New York in April 1927, there were openings in the chorus in Ziegfeld's new show, *Rio Rita*, which had opened on Broadway at the Ziegfeld Theatre in February. Ziegfeld was sentimental enough to hire both of us. I was surprised to learn that my name would remain Suzanne Fleming because the papers were still buzzing on about the Menjou story and it was good for publicity. I was even more surprised a few weeks later when Paulette abruptly left *Rio Rita*. She took a job in another show. I actually felt a little hurt. Of course, she was not obligated to stay at my side, but I honestly thought she would.

Paulette's new show was a colossal failure and never even opened. But she had adjusted to the Broadway lifestyle much better than I had. She met and soon landed one of those wealthy older swains that were sending the orchids and diamonds backstage. Edgar William James, the son of a wealthy North Carolina lumber tycoon, was eighteen years older than Paulette. By Broadway marriage standards he was rather young for the swain role. He made some vague rumblings about being in the movie business, but I don't believe he really was. Mother and I took the train up to see them get married in Rye, New York, on June 28, 1927. Mother asked an odd question that I should have been more interested in but wasn't. "Do you think his family knows she's Jewish?" I didn't think of this again until many years later, when Mother made a similar remark that caused me a lot of pain. I said goodbye to Paulette as the bride and groom promptly moved to North Carolina. Paulette away from the stage didn't seem right, and it wasn't. The marriage didn't last, and she got out of North Carolina in a hurry.

Back on stage in *Rio Rita* without my best friend, I started to worry. Paulette paid off for Ziegfeld. She was naturally showy and gorgeous in a shimmering sheath of gold paillettes. But I had a problem. Now that I was on exhibition, I became self-conscious to the point of paranoia. I couldn't enjoy the exposure. I wondered if I had gotten the opportunity because I seemed to be attached to Paulette at the hip. I skulked behind the scenery whenever the opportunity afforded until an irritated Ziegfeld had me put on a chair and told to stay there, or it was back to the chorus. As a chorine I had been able to laugh and dance and enjoy the activity within the group; but it seemed silly and affected to hold a pose and smile condescendingly over the heads of the audience. I settled for a sulky look, emulating the popular John Held Jr. drawings of the era, the supercilious look of the worldly woman—or in the parlance of the day, the flapper.

I adjusted to my new role and somehow managed to remain a favorite of Ziegfeld's. Just before Paulette's wedding, I had been one of four girls selected by him to represent *Rio Rita* in the big celebration and parade when New York City welcomed Charles Lindbergh after his famous flight to Paris. Every girl in the show wanted to meet Lindbergh. Actually, every person in New York wanted to meet him. It didn't mean much to me, and when it was over, I assured my envious castmates that I spent the afternoon on a parade float in the hot sun waving to the crowd. I didn't get within fifty feet of Lucky Lindy.

As expected, my upgraded status on stage improved my social status backstage. It didn't bring me diamonds, but I never had to feel the humiliation of arriving at the stage door without my own spray of orchids. There were plenty to go around. I look back and wonder at the frenzied revelry of that short period. Like all young people needing a social cluster for security, I wanted so much to be a part of it, but I didn't belong. Having grown up always in the company of parents and constantly on the move, I had never achieved easy communication with strangers. Instead, I developed a social ineptitude that prevented me from acquiring the tools that would have helped me enter this new world of flirtatious superficiality.

If there ever was a time for parental guidance, this was it. But Mother was as naive as I was. An unsophisticated small-town girl, she had experienced only youthful flirtations, but she should have recognized that I didn't have anything but innocence to protect me. I must have retained my virtue because I didn't know what it was. Sexuality was unknown to me, and to even allow the accepted "petting" with these mainly elderly gents repelled me. The mores of this subculture called for gifts as evidence of the gratitude felt in being allowed the company of glittering ladies.

Having no judgment (only the example of the world I was moving in), I accepted the pressure to take home anything that would indicate my presence had been valued. However, being untouchable, I wasn't big game, so I was picking up scraps. The Roaring Twenties are fondly remembered as a madly glamorous period, but it wasn't really. The unrestrained drinking bared the fangs of the dinner-suited men as they prowled the stage doors. Expensive supper parties were the prelude for amorous play. Out of the incredible shower of largesse, my lone souvenir is a gold mesh bag, not attesting to the admiration of an ardent suitor, only a favor tucked into a napkin at a large dinner party. Later, the girls—only Ziegfeld, of course—were given the choice of jewelry or cash as a warm-up for the evening's extracurricular activities. By this point in the evening, I was safely at home telling Mother how innocent the whole thing was.

It was at one of these parties that I received an offer that I could casually mention backstage in the dressing rooms where I was still being treated with condescension by ladies who were picking pockets with both hands. At that party there must have been a moment when our seventy-year-old host decided everyone was loose enough to start trading and offered me a pearl necklace as a reward for sharing his bed. That seemed to me a high price indeed. The noses of the bracelet collectors would be turned down permanently. The only problem was, who would believe me without the necklace as evidence? I really thought about that offer a lot. Not that I longed for a pearl necklace. It was of no interest to me at all, but that someone put such a high value on my virtue was astonishing. This was worth taking up with a young friend whom I liked more than most. Explaining why a man would want to pay such a lot for something that was not given with love, he pointed out that men are collectors just as much as women. "He is a terribly rich man to whom the price of a necklace, even of oriental pearls, is negligible. The value is what you would place on the jewels at your financial level, not his. Take a good look at what you'd be selling. Have you been holding out for commercial reasons, or have you not found the right time to give it away?" That seemed to clear it up, so I still have only the gold mesh bag.

The glamorous world I was now a part of hadn't undone the years of shyness and social ineptitude. Once, in the elevator of our apartment house, a vaguely familiar young man smiled at me and said, "My name is Henry Robinson, do you remember me?" Overwhelmed by a total flashback to my childhood in Forest Hills—when a smile from Henry had me walking on air—I doubt that I said anything intelligible. Then it was his floor, and he was gone. I hoped he knew I was glamorous. It might overcome the obvious impression that I was the same tongue-tied, self-conscious ten-year-old whose mother forced her to exhibit modest talents to the polite smiles of other mothers with equally untalented daughters. Some things never changed, and I seemed to be one of them.

The summer of 1927 was rolling on when I became aware of a new show about to go into rehearsal. Chorus girls and bit players came and went from *Rio Rita*, and I was very much aware that my job in the show didn't amount to much. I could be replaced by any pretty girl off the street who was capable of sitting in a chair. And I always felt that Ziegfeld put me in *Rio Rita* because he considered me to be an extension of Paulette. I'm not sure what made me think I could act, but I accompanied a friend from *Rio Rita* to an audition. It was the heyday of the musicals, and the only shows that could rival *The Ziegfeld Follies* were *George White's Scandals* and *Earl Carrol's Vanities*. It turned out that this new show was being produced by George White, and before I could remind myself that I didn't know anything about acting, I had landed a speaking part in the show. There was a big increase in pay, and I had to learn my lines. The show was called *Manhattan Mary* and the news that I would be leaving *Rio Rita* did not cause Florenz Ziegfeld even a moment of concern. Find another pretty girl to sit in Susan's chair. No problem.

Manhattan Mary turned out to be something of a big deal. Ed Wynn was the star and he had already been to Hollywood to start a movie career. To get him back to Broadway the papers were reporting that George White was paying him $7,500 a week. Needless to say, my salary was probably what Ed Wynn tipped a doorman. I was growing accustomed to the Broadway drill. We rehearsed for around a month and then left for the out-of-town tryouts—hitting Atlantic City, Philadelphia, Pittsburgh, and Newark before opening on Broadway at the Apollo Theater on September 26, 1927. The show was successful enough to last on Broadway until May of 1928. After a summer break, *Manhattan Mary* would go on tour in the fall. As I had when *No Foolin'* hit the road, I stayed home when the show headed out.

The press agent for *Manhattan Mary* managed to get me into the newspapers pretty regularly, and I was posing for a lot of photos, which I was never especially comfortable doing. Somehow, I came to the attention of Alfred Cheney Johnston, a very well-known photographer who was doing a fashion shoot for the Lord & Taylor department store. He had photographed me before, but I was so insignificant in the Ziegfeld shows that he didn't remember me. Johnston was Ziegfeld's favorite photographer, and he frequently did shoots with the girls in the various shows. What no one knew at the time was that he was in the habit of getting the girls to pose nude. I had heard this from a couple of the girls in *Rio Rita*, so I was not shocked when he asked at the end of our Lord & Taylor shoot. I politely declined and made a quick exit from his studio. If Mother knew about the request, she probably would have ended my career on the spot and moved us back to Bethlehem. At that point I was so shy I had trouble seeing myself nude in the bathroom mirror.

My world in the Roaring Twenties was beyond Mother's comprehension. She was dazzled by the glamour and saw my scraps as evidence of a great fiesta in which, supposedly, I was a thrilled participant. Having learned compliance early, I didn't bother to disabuse her of the vicarious pleasure she was feeling. Reality wasn't going to penetrate the walls of our apartment. My parents' sole social contact was over in Brooklyn at my aunt and uncle's. That was the general scene, but it wasn't all ugly. I had three or four young male friends who just liked having me around. With no pressure from them, we attended nice Sunday luncheon parties on houseboats. There were also the Mayfair dances held at the Ritz Hotel where mainly show people played. These were presided over by Mayor Jimmy Walker and the truly glamorous dancer Betty Compton, who would later become his wife. At this point she was his mistress, and we never saw the current Mrs. Walker at the dances. The Ritz was the setting for the memorable night of my twentieth birthday. My beau of the moment had arranged, unbeknownst to me, for nine of his friends to greet my arrival in a stag line and escort me down the red-carpeted staircase to our table in the ballroom. It was an entrance befitting one of

Mother's glamorous and expensive dresses, which she had remodeled for me—a knee-length rose velvet number with floor-length side panels of silver lamé. The rest of the evening is lost in antiquity, but the memory of that dress going down those stairs will be with me forever. We did things in style then.

Manhattan Mary was out on tour without me, so not being in a show, I took some acting classes and did a lot of reading. There's a funny clipping in my scrapbook from the September 1928 issue of *Picture Play* that reads, "Susan Fleming left the screen after only one picture, *The Ace of Cads*, and has dropped out of sight." I suppose I had, but I wasn't too concerned. I never thought of the movies as a possibility anyway. In February 1929 Mother, Father, and I took a lovely boat trip to Bermuda—just in case I'd tired of older men chasing me around. I didn't miss the Broadway life at all, but there came a point when we started to miss my income. The Stock Market Crash of 1929 was still months away, but Father was already coming to grips with the grim future of a stockbroker as panic began to set in. I needed to get back to work. Having already been in a George White show, it didn't take much for me to land a part in *George White's Scandals* that summer. After two weeks of tryouts in Newark and Boston, the show was set to open on Broadway at the Apollo Theater on September 23, 1929.

There's a good reason why shows play out of town before opening on Broadway. *George White's Scandals* was running very long in Newark and Boston, and one of the things they cut to get ready for Broadway was me. If I had been in the chorus, I probably would have made the cut, but with a minor featured part I was in a less secure position. So, I closed in Boston. It didn't really mean much to me, and the truth is they made a good decision. I wasn't very good. I saw the other people who were cut weeping when they got the news, but I couldn't imagine shedding a single tear over this sort of thing. Five weeks later the market crashed, and Black Tuesday ushered in the Great Depression. Father's job was gone, and only then did the reality of my situation became worrisome. We were suddenly an unemployed family of three and any job prospects rested firmly with me. I'd been checking the theatrical want ads and it was clear that I had a better chance of landing a job in a musical than in an office. I went to auditions, but the many unemployed actresses who could actually act presented a problem. In the summer of 1930, I read for a small part in a show that was coming to Broadway. Not surprisingly, the director and coauthor of *Once in a Lifetime* had no recollection of my unsuccessful audition several years later, when we had become friends. By the time I read for George S. Kaufman, he had written *The Cocoanuts* and *Animal Crackers* for the Marx Brothers.

Fortunately, fate took over and changed my life. Eddie Buzzell is a name known to fans of the Marx Brothers because he directed two of their films at M-G-M. But years before that Eddie was an actor in vaudeville and on Broadway. He even did a little acting in movies. He was married to Ona Munson, whom I'd gotten to know when she was starring nightly as the title character in *Manhattan Mary*. (I was surprised to learn that Ona was married because she seemed more than professionally interested in several of the girls in the cast.) Eddie worked at Columbia Pictures in Hollywood, writing, acting, and directing. He also scouted talent and was sent to New York by studio chief Harry Cohn to find some pretty girls from the Broadway shows to put under contract. The less expensive the better. Columbia was known as one of the more frugal Hollywood studios. Eddie placed an advertisement for an open casting call.

I arrived at Eddie Buzzell's casting call and saw several of the girls from the *Scandals*. There must have been a hundred girls there. Having been in *Manhattan Mary* and *No Foolin'* certainly helped my case, and I was one of two girls that Eddie selected. The other lucky one was Loretta Sayers, a beautiful young woman with absolutely no acting experience. My lack of acting ability could go completely unnoticed if I stuck close to Loretta. Eddie made an offer and before I knew it, the Fleming family was headed for Hollywood. This had nothing to do with me having any desire to be in the movies. I needed a job. Or more accurately, the Fleming family needed a job, and Father's chances of finding a position as a stockbroker seemed far more ridiculous than the idea of Susan Fleming making movies in Hollywood.

CHAPTER THREE
Hollywood, Here I Come

THE CRUMBLING, YELLOWED PAGES OF MY SCRAPBOOK TELL OF unusual beauty, but nowhere is there mention of unusual talent. Hype was the governing factor in a career that could be made or broken at the whim of a gossip columnist or studio executive. *The Ace of Cads* was ancient history—so ancient in fact, that it was a silent film! By 1931 silent movies seemed about as current as the Civil War. My chance in the movies had clearly come and gone. Four years of mostly forgettable stage work in bit parts and the chorus was not the road to stardom. Yet, there I was on the train to Hollywood more than a year after my last performance in *George White's Scandals*—my Broadway swan song that didn't even take me to Broadway. The studio publicity machine went to work in a hurry. The papers carried the news that Broadway's Susan Fleming was on her way to Hollywood, where stardom was inevitable.

Variety announced that I had arrived the previous week in their February 18 issue. This would not be worth mentioning had they not announced in the next issue that "Harpo Marx landed here Tuesday." Neither of us knew about this remarkable coincidence at the time. We'd had that near miss in New York, and now this. Our paths were destined to cross. Almost as soon as I'd arrived, the studio helped find Mother, Father, and me a beautiful apartment in a newly constructed Mediterranean building at 1330 North Harper Avenue in West Hollywood. I signed what the press called "a long-term contract" and went to work for Columbia Pictures. In truth it was a one-year contract, but the studio could renew it if I had any potential. I soon found myself in an acting class along with Loretta Sayers, who seemed to be with me at every step of the process. She was even on the train from New York with us. My limited acting experience was probably as much a hindrance for me as Loretta's total lack of acting experience was for her. She didn't have much trouble doing exactly what she was told. I muddled through as usual.

Eddie Buzzell informed me that the time had come for me to meet the head of the studio. I was surprised it was allowed, but Mother accompanied me to my first meeting with Harry Cohn. I'd soon learn that he was perhaps the most detested man in Hollywood. He had plans for his newest discovery that were most assuredly not cinematic. His interest must have cooled when he could never find me without Mother close by. She was an attractive young-looking forty-six at the time, and I'm sure Cohn did not rule out the possibility of making a run at Mother. After a while Cohn was calling her Bunny and rolling his eyes when he saw her. It was obvious to me that my stay at Columbia would be a short one.

My first days at the studio were taken up with more acting classes and publicity photo shoots that seemed ridiculous to me. Susan exercising, Susan cooking a turkey, Susan playing tennis. Oh, and of course the always popular, Susan modeling a dress. I finally went before the cameras for a small part in a short subject called "Kings or Better." Eddie was appearing in a series of one-reelers called "Eddie Buzzell's Bedtime Stories for Grownups," and this was the latest entry. It went well enough that I was cast in a very small part in a feature. Other than the title, I remember absolutely nothing about *Lover Come Back*. According to the review in my scrapbook, it was a "dull little specimen of the dime-a-dozen school of motion pictures." I can't take much of the blame for that. There were eight actors billed above me—including Loretta Sayers. I probably had just a few lines in a scene or two.

In a matter of days, I was on the set of another film in a tiny role with very little to do. This one was called *Arizona*. It was also called *Men Are Like That*. But it was a stinker under any title. It starred a very young John Wayne, who had graduated from bit parts and extra work in silent films to recently starring in *The Big Trail* at Fox. He had played football at the University of Southern California, and I recall him mentioning how his football buddies ribbed him about being in a sissy job like acting. But he was well on his way to stardom. He just looked like a movie star. He was so tall that the director had a wooden box on the set for the other actors to stand on if they had to talk to Wayne in a tight shot. The female lead in the picture was Laura La Plante, who had been a big star in the silent days. People whispered about why she had to take work at Columbia— a significant step down from where she had been only a few years before. Her career was floundering, and she would not last in pictures much longer. It wasn't necessarily the coming of sound. She spoke perfectly well. She just fell out of fashion. Maybe people didn't want to be reminded of silent movies. It was a cautionary tale for me. Even if I made it in the movies, it could all go away in the blink of an eye. But I was moving up the ladder little by little. In this picture I had slightly more to do than Loretta Sayers who, like me, was uncredited.

My next assignment was a detective story with Jack Holt, who had been a star in silent westerns but seemed to be doing just fine in talkies. I had a little more to do in *A Dangerous Affair* and saw my billing move up and away from the bit players. But there was a little intrigue involved. Harry Cohn was no less interested in some extracurricular activities with his newest discovery. And I kept showing up with Mother at my side whenever he summoned me. Perhaps Cohn was trying to negotiate his way into bed with me because I was next cast as John Wayne's romantic interest in *The Range Feud*, a mediocre Buck Jones western. Whatever the reason, I suddenly had my first lead role. Nothing against the Duke, but my most vivid recollection of this film is that I had to ride a horse.

I didn't really get to know Wayne when we made *Arizona*. My part was so small I was probably only on the set for a few days. But on *The Range Feud*, we spent a considerable amount of time together. His star was starting to rise, but he didn't seem comfortable in front of the camera. This much we had in common. I never got used to the fussing over hair and makeup and found the whole process to be a big bore. I got the feeling that Wayne saw himself as an athlete and this movie stuff was just embarrassing to him. *The Range Feud* didn't stand much of a chance with two stars who would rather have been elsewhere, but I guess John Wayne managed to get comfortable because he stayed in the business for about fifty years. I, on the other hand, was about to start blazing a path straight out of the movie business. *The Range Feud* would be my last picture at Columbia.

It was decided that my one-year contract with Columbia would not be renewed. Cohn ran out my contract by getting me (and Mother) out of his sight and having me work at other studios. Columbia loaned me to RKO, where I had a small part in something called *Ladies of the Jury*. As soon as my work on the film was done, I was loaned to Fox for another miniscule part in *Careless Lady*. It would be difficult to find two less distinguished films. Maybe Cohn wanted to see if another studio executive could get past Mother. I wondered if the beautiful young women getting the starring roles at Columbia had all been to bed with Harry Cohn. I was now unemployed in a town with no opportunities for chorus girls. That one-year contract was starting to look like the sum total of my Hollywood career. I wasn't especially upset about that, but there was the small matter of making a living. I was still supporting my parents.

Almost immediately, fate stepped in. I was somehow invited to a party thrown by Samuel Goldwyn. I don't think I even knew this party had a guest of honor, but when I arrived, I had to laugh. I'd been taken to a party honoring Harry Cohn, the man who had just fired me! For dinner I was seated next to Harpo Marx. I'm not sure we immediately remembered our chance meeting on Broadway a few years prior, but when he turned from laughing with Fannie Brice to smile pleasantly, although indifferently, at me, he seemed to recognize me. Prettiness had never attracted Harpo but whatever I said made him laugh. It should have been etched in stone, but neither of us could ever recall exactly what I said to him. It must have been good. We became inseparable.

Our inseparability didn't exactly happen overnight, however. A week after the party, I received a call from someone named Rachel Linden, saying she was Harpo's secretary. She was calling to remind me that I was expected for lunch the following Sunday at Harpo's house. I thanked her but hanging up I couldn't remember anything being said about Sunday lunch. Apparently, I had been put on a list of people who, if they showed up, were welcome. Was this how Hollywood treated its guests? I wasn't flattered and spent that Sunday at the beach club my parents had joined with one of my favorite friends, Tim Holt. I should point out that Tim wasn't yet a film star. In fact, he was about twelve years old, but I knew him from the beach club as the son of Jack Holt, the star of one of my insignificant Columbia efforts.

When I got home, Mother said that Harpo himself had called and was very pleasant, saying that he looked forward to seeing me again and hoped that I would be free to come to lunch the following Sunday. Joseph, his chauffeur, could pick me up and return me undamaged before or after dinner. This was different. The next day, Mother, saying she was my secretary, called his secretary and said I would be delighted. Sunday came, and the door to the wonderful world of Harpo opened to me, changing my life forever. Harpo was living at the famous Garden of Allah, a residential hotel with a bunch of private two-story bungalows and villas on Sunset Boulevard in West Hollywood. He needn't have sent the chauffeur. I could have walked there. It took around a minute to drive from our house on North Harper to Harpo's. With a big grin Harpo introduced me to J. C., a huge white smiling dog who was followed by a small army of four-footed kibitzers, no doubt crowding around to see what new fish he'd caught. These amenities taken care of, Harpo said, "Come and meet some of the regulars."

What a happy surprise. This was no power garden. Just friends in high good humor, lounging at the pool and playing some tennis. Lunch was served at an extended dining table, where they indulged in their favorite sport, conversation, well into the dinner hour. Most of the guests that day and in the coming years were familiar to me—not personally, but rather through their writings. Many of the top novelists and playwrights of the day were coming and going in Hollywood at the urgent request of the studios—not because of some benevolent desire to save the film industry, but for the obscene amounts of money they were offered.

Among those raising their spirits at Harpo's in those days and in the years to come were Ben Hecht, Marc Connelly, F. Scott Fitzgerald, Robert Sherwood, Lillian Hellman, H. G. Wells, George S. Kaufman, Dorothy Parker, Robert Benchley, and Herman Mankiewicz. The list of the lustrous was long and offbeat. Even Aldous Huxley showed up. Harpo attracted offbeat people, but he himself was not offbeat. He was unusual in another way. He was abnormally sane. Harpo was therapeutic. His evaluation of anything started with the present. Mistakes of the past were never considered. Ben Hecht captured the essence of Harpo beautifully in his book *A Child of the Century*: "Harpo had the gift of relaxing anyone who looked at him. Harpo was many other things, but his peacefulness was the quality most remarkable in him. There are many exciting personalities to be found who can stimulate you, but I have come on few who make you feel content, as if some human sunlight were warming you."

Harpo's closest, most beloved friend at this time was Charlie Lederer, a talented young writer who had recently collaborated with Hecht on the screenplay for *The Front Page*—which coincidentally starred the man who started my film career, Adolph Menjou. Charlie was joyous, funny, idealistic, and irrepressible—and he was always in trouble with studio executives. Egomaniacs were a constant target of Charlie's needle, and you couldn't find a big shot at any studio who wasn't an egomaniac. But Charlie always seemed to keep his job somehow. It sure didn't hurt that his aunt was Marion Davies, the mistress of William Randolph Hearst. Even the biggest studio executive didn't risk alienating the Hearst empire. But the crazy thing about Charlie was that among friends, Hearst was his favorite target.

The exact opposite of Lederer, Oscar Levant was surly, moody, and despairing. He clung to Harpo like a life raft. Living in a hotel where he didn't have the use of a piano, this brilliant musician could be found most days at Harpo's piano exercising his fingers with *Time* magazine or a novel propped up on the music stand. Harpo had an uncritical fondness for troubled nonconformists and since there wasn't a more troubled nonconformist in the world than Oscar, Harpo loved him. In spite of his enormous talent, wit, and intelligence, Oscar was hypersensitive, insecure, and always ready to strike with a verbal assault. M-G-M had brought Oscar out to Hollywood from New York, where he was a renowned concert artist, famous for his interpretations of the compositions of his close friend George Gershwin. He appeared in several classic M-G-M musicals—often portraying his own neurotic self. He was clearly at the top of his field, but Oscar was puzzling. His desperate need for acceptance was painfully obvious. He was also a little paranoid and seemed to have a pill for every mood or occasion. If Harpo found any of Oscar's quirks the least bit troubling, he never said so. Oscar became Harpo's constant (and certainly most entertaining) companion.

The cast of characters would change from time to time, due to the transitory nature of the movie industry, but that was the basic crew when the door to Harpo's world opened for me. For the summer of 1932 Harpo rented a beach house in Santa Monica, and the Sunday lunches would often turn into weeklong affairs. It was at the beach house that I had my first meeting with Harpo's father, whom all of the Marx Brothers affectionately called Frenchy. Their mother, Minnie, had died in 1929 so the boys moved Frenchy to California with them in 1931. He seemed a bit lost without Minnie, but he tried to fit into his new role of dashing Hollywood bachelor. Harpo loved to tell the story of the time he spotted Frenchy, impeccably dressed, strolling out of the front gate of Tom Mix's huge estate, which must have had fifty "no trespassing" signs posted on it. He asked Frenchy what he was doing, to which Frenchy replied in his thick accent, "I was taking a walk in the park."

He was a charming man, and I could see where Harpo got the twinkle in his eye. Frenchy loved to tell stories of the brothers' early vaudeville days as much as they did. He could often be seen squiring various young women around Hollywood, and he loved going to the set at Paramount to watch his sons work. He alternated between living with Harpo and Zeppo in those days. A few months after I met him, Frenchy suffered his second heart attack. He quickly became very ill and developed other health problems. The following spring Frenchy died, and the brothers all traveled to New York to lay their father to rest next to their mother. Seeing Harpo and his brothers celebrate Frenchy's life gave me an education about their early years. Harpo hadn't said much about his beginnings, but as the brothers told their favorite Frenchy stories, I picked up a lot of information. And I laughed. Oh, how I laughed. I wished I could have known Frenchy longer.

At about this time Harpo, Oscar, Charlie, and I became a foursome. Looking back at this strange relationship, I've concluded that the three of us were in need of stability and focused on Harpo, who had plenty to go around and didn't mind sharing. My need for stability might have had something to do with my sudden unemployment, but that soon took care of itself. Herman Mankiewicz, one of the Sunday lunch regulars, cast me in his latest Paramount production, *Million Dollar Legs*, alongside W. C. Fields and Jack Oakie. I had heard that *Million Dollar Legs* was originally conceived as a vehicle for the Marx Brothers, but that they had turned it down. This served as a reminder that while I was horseback riding around the Columbia lot with John Wayne, Harpo and his brothers were big stars over at Paramount. Weeklong lunches on the beach were fine for Harpo. The Marx Brothers made one picture a year and had plenty of time for fun. Not me. As a contract player I reported to work whether or not there was to be any shooting that required my presence. Playtime for me was restricted to the weekends.

I suddenly had a one-picture deal with Paramount based solely on meeting Mank at Harpo's beach house. I doubt he had even seen any of the films I'd been in. (Unless he was some sort of cinematic masochist.) My part in *Million Dollar Legs* was a substantial one, and I didn't have to jump into bed with anyone to get it. Maybe there was hope. The film was conceived around the summer Olympics in Los Angeles, which all of us in Harpo's circle attended. While Mank would become much more famous for the screenplay to *Citizen Kane*, I would become known, almost exclusively, for my work in *Million Dollar Legs*. It's one of the few pictures I appeared in that still gets shown from time to time.

I met W. C. Fields my first day on the set, and he was very courteous in welcoming me. He was nothing like the curmudgeonly characters in his films. He was polite and professional with everyone involved in the production and told me to call him Bill when I addressed him as Mr. Fields. He would completely change his demeanor when the director called "action"—as if there was a W. C. Fields switch that would change him instantly from the unassuming Bill that I had just met to the star I had seen in the movies. I had heard that I should expect him to be drunk on the set, but that was not my experience with him. He never seemed intoxicated, but he certainly smelled like he should have been. He was famously quoted as saying, "I drink nothing stronger than gin before breakfast." I'll just say that he was certainly long past breakfast by the time we'd start shooting.

Making *Million Dollar Legs* was much more enjoyable than the pictures I'd made at Columbia, but that probably had more to do with Jack Oakie than anything else. Jack was a dear, sweet man and I adored him. We even dated for a while, but that didn't last very long. He was charming and funny, and I recall a particular moment on the set when he chastised me for riding a bicycle. Actually, he taught me a lesson about the industry. A scene called for me to ride a bicycle, so I did. Jack explained to me that I'd just put a stunt double out of work for the day. Next time I was to say that I couldn't ride a bicycle. That would have been unheard of at Columbia. Harry Cohn had me on a horse and didn't think twice about whether I had ever been on one before.

I never got the hang of Hollywood. It was a strange, impermanent world of hardworking people and highly developed opportunism. Survival depended on employment, and, in a business where every job had a hundred applicants, employment depended on relationships. Casting directors held the keys of the studios, and assistant directors controlled the steady employment of the "favored" among the many thousands of extras and bit players. These men were giving out jobs instead of orchids. My work in *Million Dollar Legs* was well received by critics and audiences, but more importantly, by Paramount. I was rewarded with a new contract and immediately cast alongside Randolph Scott in something called *Heritage of the Desert*. But just as the picture started shooting, I was replaced by Sally Blane. I never found out the reason. I'm allegedly in a crowd shot, probably filmed early on before I lost the part.

Instead, I ended up with a substantial role in *The Book Worm Turns*, a totally forgettable film that was called *He Learned about Women* by the time it was released. But I did get to work with two delightful people, Stuart Erwin and Alison Skipworth. Skippy, as everyone called her, was lovely and very helpful to me. She was a veteran of the London stage and silent pictures and had worked constantly since the talkies came in. She knew what she was doing and understood the machinations of Hollywood. Just watching the manner in which she handled herself in this strange world was quite educational. Some would have called her a tough broad, but she was funny. Comedy came easily to her—or at least she made it seem as though it did. I was nervous about trying to be funny on camera, but Skippy just told me to trust the material. She was around my grandmother's age, but Skippy seemed young and was a great friend to have even if only for a few weeks. Stu Erwin, the lead in the picture, was sweet and he was very kind about getting something close to a decent performance out of me. He'd have a long career and we would remain friends for many years, although we saw each other infrequently.

He Learned about Women inexplicably raised my profile. I was prominently featured in the advertising, and the film got mostly good reviews. But Paramount didn't seem all that interested in capitalizing on any of this, and I spent several weeks doing silly photo shoots and not being cast in anything. I suspect my lack of acting skill was becoming obvious to the studio. In the spring of 1933, there was an announcement that the George S. Kaufman–Edna Ferber Broadway hit *Dinner at Eight* would be coming to Los Angeles and San Francisco. Harpo's old friend, producer Sam Harris, was involved in the production and, with it looking very unlikely that my Paramount contract would be renewed, I was offered a small part. Harris probably assumed I could act. Maybe Harpo told him I could. Sam was Harpo's houseguest for a few months, so he had plenty of opportunity. The West Coast cast, which featured Louis Calhern, Alice White, and Hedda Hopper, was announced in the press, and at the very bottom of the list was my name. I only remember a couple of rehearsals in which the actors read the play for the director. I must not have made much of an impression because I was out of the cast as quickly as I had joined it. My return to the legitimate stage lasted a few days and never progressed past rehearsals. That's how far being the girlfriend of a big movie star took me.

I gamely carried on at Paramount with a tiny part in *I Love That Man*, starring Edmund Lowe and Nancy Carroll. After starring roles in *Million Dollar Legs* and *He Learned about Women*, I should have been well on my way. And I was. But I was on my way to the unemployment line. I had suddenly regressed to a bit part similar to the ones I had at Columbia. Someone at Paramount finally confirmed that I wasn't much of an actress, and I was released from my contract. But I was rescued from unemployment again, this time by Fox. I managed to stick around there long enough to appear in ten pictures, but strictly in small, insignificant roles. No complaints, though. Playing a secretary and taking dictation on a movie set paid a lot better than really taking dictation. I was content to have a job and wasn't really interested in stardom anyway.

During my stay at Fox, the studio merged with Twentieth Century Pictures to become Twentieth Century Fox. They didn't consult me about the merger, but at least I remained employed. I can't recall exactly how it happened, but during the period before the two studios merged, I was in one picture at Twentieth Century. My only memory of being in *Broadway Thru a Keyhole* is that I felt I had come full circle. I had a bit part as a chorus girl alongside another unknown, Ann Sothern. Lucille Ball also had a bit part in this one way before anyone ever heard of her. We were all struggling at the time, and I'm sure the film was as memorable to them as it was to me. None of us were even credited. But I got a laugh out of being a chorus girl again. This I could handle without acting classes!

The funny thing about the so-called golden age of Hollywood is that people seldom realize that for every great classic that has lived on there are probably a half-dozen stinkers that will never again see the light of day. For my part, I just reported to work on time and knew my lines. How history has treated these films is none of my business. The clippings in my scrapbook indicate that I worked in films with the likes of Lew Ayres, Alice Faye, Spencer Tracy, Claire Trevor, Gilbert Roland, and Eleanor Powell during my three years at Fox. The fact that I have no recollection of most of these stars probably just means that my role was limited to a scene or two, shot when they weren't around. For some reason Fox loaned me to RKO for a couple of pictures. I never understood this. Didn't they have their own contract players who remembered their lines? The only noteworthy thing about *Break of Hearts* is that it enables me to add Katharine Hepburn and Charles Boyer to the list of stars I can barely remember working with. I remember Spencer Tracy mostly for the fact that he happened to be married to my father's cousin. I've learned that one of my Fox endeavors has joined *The Ace of Cads* among the ranks of lost films. While I have no memory of appearing in *Charlie Chan's Courage* with Warner Oland, it's probably not a bad thing that the picture can't be seen. I wish I could say the same for a few of the others.

CHAPTER FOUR

The Winter of My Discontent

I'D BEEN SPENDING A LOT OF MY FREE TIME WITH HARPO AND HIS pals—still mostly Charlie Lederer and Oscar Levant, since if we didn't invite him, he'd sulk and show up anyway. But Ben Hecht and his wife, Rose, were also our constant companions. This group was Harpo's chosen family. He was always in contact with his brothers, but when they weren't working, they would gather infrequently and stay in touch by phone, even though they were mostly living near each other. They also occasionally ran into each other unexpectedly around Hollywood. Six-day bicycle races were all the rage in those days, and the crowd was usually filled with movie stars. It was fun to be there simply for the spectacle, but it was silly, and Harpo and I only went a couple of times. Zeppo was a regular, and he usually had a lot of money riding on those crazy races. Friday was fight night in Hollywood, and it was at a boxing match that I had my first encounter with Chico. Groucho stayed away from these events. He preferred quiet evenings at home, but I think his wife wouldn't have minded the occasional six-day bicycle race. Ruth liked to have fun, and I suspect sitting home watching Groucho read was not that enjoyable.

Harpo had another family on the East Coast, this one also chosen. The Marx Brothers were the toast of Broadway long before I came along, and Harpo had become very close with the people he met during that time. In fact, he'd known Charlie Lederer from New York. Ben Hecht went back even further to the Marx Brothers' vaudeville days, when he was a newspaper reporter in Chicago. Eventually I traveled east with Harpo to meet the rest of the family. In the twenties and thirties, New

York was the intellectual capital of the United States. Hollywood was viewed with contempt as a purveyor of entertainment for the unwashed masses. Those playwrights and dramatists I'd see having lunch at Harpo's would often return to the East and complain of the "cultural desert." Hecht liked to tell stories about how he could churn out a few film scenarios in Hollywood within a week and leave town with a bag of studio money that could last him the rest of the year while he wrote his good stuff. It's difficult to imagine Harpo as part of that scene, but the snobbery of Broadway's golden age, while certainly put forth by his closest and dearest friend, probably never crossed Harpo's mind. Alexander Woollcott, with his literary eminence fortified by an enormously successful radio show, was the most prestigious man of the day.

Aleck had adored Harpo from their first meeting. As New York's leading drama critic, Aleck attended the opening of the Marx Brothers first Broadway show, *I'll Say She Is*. From the stage the boys could see Aleck in his customary second-row seat having the time of his life. His review in the next day's paper called Harpo a great clown and suggested that there should be dancing in the streets to celebrate his arrival. He so singled out Harpo that the review ran under the headline "Harpo Marx and Some Brothers." I'll bet Groucho was thrilled. Aleck went back to see the show again a few nights later and was backstage during the intermission. Chico and Groucho teased about Harpo's "fan club" showing up backstage. The next day at lunch, Aleck presented Harpo as his personal discovery to his chums at the fabled Algonquin Round Table. The Algonquin Hotel on 44th Street was recognized by tradition and location as home to the greats of literature and theatre. Hotelier Frank Case happily provided to Woollcott and his cronies the round table in the center of the dining room. This gathering became famous because of the public display of celebrated personalities all known for their wit; examples of which, I'm sure, the hovering waiters were instructed to gather for the hotel's press agent to turn over to the columnists, as they were quoted daily. It didn't hurt that most of these celebrated wits worked at the top New York newspapers.

Aleck loved celebrities, but they had to be entertaining. To get rid of a bore, he did not leave room for misunderstandings. He was devastating.

Consequently, attendance was pruned or encouraged by this lion-tamer. Among those who could be seen on any given day at the lunch hour enjoying one another were Irving Berlin, Robert Benchley, Will Rogers, Helen Hayes, Dorothy Parker, Deems Taylor, Donald Ogden Stewart, Ruth Gordon, and Edna Ferber—most of whom, to Aleck's chagrin, Harpo already knew. The Marx Brothers had been quite well known to the Broadway community for several years. They had played vaudeville's fabled Palace Theatre on Broadway many times. The legend of them being unknown or obscure when *I'll Say She Is* opened is a figment of someone's imagination.

Pretty soon Woollcott introduced Harpo to the most formidable poker game in New York: the Thanatopsis Literary and Inside Straight Club, which included the high rollers of the literary world. They played at the Algonquin and the members included Benchley, whose work was frequently found in the best humor magazines; Franklin P. Adams, writer of "The Conning Tower"—a must-read column for New Yorkers; Heywood Broun, columnist for the *New York World*; Herbert Bayard Swope, managing editor of the *World*; playwrights George S. Kaufman and Marc Connelly; and Harold Ross, the founder and editor of *The New Yorker*. Harpo was an instant hit, losing modestly and cheerfully. To Woollcott's delight, Harpo was invited to be a permanent pigeon, which easily fit into his schedule as they liked to start the game around midnight. Harpo could show up after *I'll Say She Is* finished, relax with his pals in the middle of the night, and sleep well into the afternoon. This game was also hosted by the Algonquin in some deep recess of the hotel. Harpo was at home in this world of acerbic humor. It was as much a part of his makeup as it was Groucho's, except Harpo's sweet temper could soften Groucho's sharpness. Harpo could be enormously funny, but not at the expense of another.

With Woollcott, Harpo's personal life completely changed. One might have expected Aleck to have chosen Groucho, but the pixie in him related to Harpo. And Groucho was probably too insecure to spend his afternoons in the company of a bunch of very funny literate people. Groucho had numerous writers as friends, but he stayed away from the ones who sat around trying to top each other with witty remarks for the benefit of the newspaper columns. One time, Harpo wondered in what direction his career might have gone had he not been swept up by Woollcott. Would he have become a serious musician? Some of the alternatives had us in hysterics. But that was the fun of being with Harpo. He could laugh at himself, which is a quality not all of the Marx Brothers shared. We eventually concluded that Woollcott hadn't influenced his life but had enriched it. I think Harpo really wondered if he might have had a career at all if his mother hadn't shoved him into a vaudeville act full of unemployed relatives. She didn't do this because any of them showed any talent. She did it as a matter of survival. Show business was the only profession Minnie knew where money could be made by people without talent.

Bound by their natural affinity, Aleck and Harpo traveled the world of *belles lettres* together. From the constant house party on Neshobe Island in the middle of Lake Bomoseen in Vermont to sharing a house in Cannes, on the French Riviera, Aleck and Harpo were a team. Neshobe Island was actually owned by Woollcott and a few other investors but was presided over by him as a club with a vague membership. It was an intellectual feast. Wherever Aleck went he attracted the celebrated. In Cannes it was the English literary crowd: H. G. Wells, Aldous Huxley, George Bernard Shaw, and Somerset Maugham. The glamorous young Prince of Wales was also a favorite Woollcott guest at Cannes. My first trip to Neshobe had me a little on edge, but I was welcomed into the scene very easily. No one challenged me to contribute and, much like Harpo, I listened. If I said something amusing it was a bonus, but I wasn't expected to be anything like these literary giants or celebrities. It was just a group of interesting people having a good time relaxing in one another's company. I would occasionally be asked a question about making movies by some important person who had never suffered through the hours of makeup and lighting tests. Maybe my contribution was convincing Somerset Maugham not to waste his time trying to become a movie star.

At Neshobe we might spend time with businessman and future diplomat Averell Harriman and his amusingly sardonic art gallery–owner wife, Marie, or Irene Castle, who, with her late husband Vernon, had been part of Broadway's most famous dance team. By this time Irene was on her third husband, a very colorful character named Major Frederic McLaughlin, who was the owner of the Chicago Blackhawks hockey team. Curiously, sports figures were always welcome in Woollcott's crowd even though he didn't care much for sports. At least professional sports, because the amateur croquet action at Neshobe was fierce. Alfred Lunt and Lynn Fontaine visited occasionally, as did Ruth Gordon. Intelligent women were a major part of the scene, and Aleck was not threatened by them in the least. George S. Kaufman's wife, Beatrice, a woman of enormous energy and good humor, might arrive with or without her husband. Mainly without, as George was not into parties or crowds. But when he came to the island, he brought his croquet mallets and played cards with a vengeance. Alice Duer Miller, a delightful woman of indeterminate age, was a longtime acquaintance of Woollcott's. She'd eventually wind up in Hollywood writing screenplays. Alice competed recklessly in badminton and cribbage and knew everything about the New York Giants going back thirty years, matching the equally impressive Brooklyn Dodger lore of fellow baseball nut Ethel Barrymore. When the visits of these two grand ladies coincided, they sat out croquet, swapping National League anecdotes. Harpo listened intently, being a devotee of the New York Giants since his upper Manhattan boyhood.

Among Aleck's and my favorites was the enchanting tiny scientist Gustav Eckstein. Gus studied animal life as symbolizing the human condition, moving toward an inevitable self-created disaster. In his books he handled his vision of ultimate tragedy with a light touch, describing animal eccentricities in anthropomorphic terms. He had a particular fondness for a host of canaries he studied. All canaries did not look alike to Gus, and he moved deep into their culture. His book *Canary: The History of a Family* was a thoughtful social commentary, amusingly told by a loving man. Aleck sought him out after reading the book, and Gus was soon part of the gang. Harpo took a keen interest in Gus's canaries, and I once shot some home movie footage of him handling the birds under Gus's watchful eye. George Kaufman and Moss Hart populated their play *The Man Who Came to Dinner* with characters based on Aleck and the gang at Neshobe. Sheridan Whiteside was obviously based on Aleck, and Banjo was a thinly disguised version of Harpo. But most people have no idea that the character of Dr. Metz was based on Gustav Eckstein. In the play the canaries somehow became cockroaches. I guess bugs are funnier than birds—or easier to manage in a theatre.

For several years Harpo and I made an annual trip to Vermont for Aleck's Bad Sports Contests. At first, I couldn't believe the acrimony involved in these games. As the reigning champion of affectionate vituperation, Woollcott set the tone of unrestrained abuse. Indoor games or outdoor games provided the "Fields of Battle" for their snarling competitions. But the main arena was the small croquet course in a clearing of the heavily treed island. The Vermont game bore no resemblance to the stately game introduced to ladies of the Victorian era who tastefully poked a wooden ball across manicured lawns. At Neshobe, croquet was akin to war. Harpo and his chums played with a ferocity that could alienate friends and result in the termination of a visit. Betting had nothing to do with it. Croquet for these people was a blood sport—the elimination of their opponents by Napoleonic maneuvers.

Aleck once thought he'd won by stymieing Harpo's ball behind a tree. But nothing delighted my little Napoleon like a challenge to his creativity. He found an old tire being used as a boat bumper, cut it to fit halfway around the tree, then blithely hit his ball through the trough made by the tire—hitting Aleck's ball at the other end. It was just a matter of finishing off Woollcott by bashing his ball into Lake Bomoseen. Aleck's screams of "illegal" found no sympathy in the hysterical crowd looking on. He had to watch (sulkily) the rest of the weekend as Harpo's victory was celebrated joyously by those who had suffered the crowing of a triumphant Woollcott in past games. Aleck muttered that Harpo was a miserable bastard every time he came within earshot, but this in no way diminished his love for Harpo. This was about their cutthroat croquet rivalry.

The number one indoor sport at Neshobe was a game, possibly of Aleck's own invention, called Murder. Guests drew cards for the roles of district attorney and murderer. The murderer had to murder someone within the next twelve hours by whispering "you're dead" to the victim. Notes or telephone calls were not allowed. The victim was forbidden from moving until they were discovered. In *Harpo Speaks!* Harpo tells of the time he incurred Aleck's wrath by writing a note in lipstick on a roll of toilet paper, which left poor Alice Duer Miller "dead" in the bathroom for hours. Aleck was furious, stating that the murderer must meet the victim face-to-face. Harpo was the prime suspect. The note read, "You Are Ded." Aleck was fairly certain all of his other guests were better spellers than that.

Another time, Harpo kept Ethel Barrymore in the john for two hours by whispering through the door that she was dead. Fortunately for her there were only two bathrooms on the island, or she could have been there all night. Woollcott loved this game, especially when he was the district attorney who would question the suspects to discover the murderer, who was allowed by the rules of the game to lie. Others were expected to be completely truthful. Sometimes innocent suspects would lie to Inspector Woollcott just to infuriate him—and bring howls of laughter to all assembled. This was actually more fun than the game. A frustrated Woollcott was a sight to behold. A good loser he was not, but his friends loved him as much for his childishness as for his witty sophistication. We were fortunate to have shared the riches of his nature.

On at least one occasion the thought of Woollcott and his gang proved too intimidating for a guest. Harpo and I were in New York and on our way to Vermont to spend a couple of weeks with Aleck. We invited Oscar Levant to join us. The trip was mostly by train and then a boat would take us to the island. Levant's mood changed on the train and, as we got closer to Vermont, he was panicking about Woollcott giving him a hard time. Oscar's insecurity had overcome any reason by the time we arrived at the dock. As we dragged him onto the boat, he started demanding that we turn around and head back to New York. He had convinced himself that Aleck and his intellectual friends would insult him the moment he set foot on the island. Arriving at the island, we had a tough time convincing Oscar to get off the boat, but we managed to get him onto the dock for a few tense moments. Oscar demanded to be sailed right back to the train station. He boarded the next train back and never did visit Neshobe Island. He came within a few feet of the island, but we just could not convince him that Aleck was harmless.

A profoundly sentimental man, Aleck was fiercely loyal, and in his tyrannical way he dominated the affections of those he loved. During one of my first visits to Neshobe, at a quiet time, late in the afternoon, when nerves were resting from the labors of competition, Aleck picked up his martini and trumpeted, "Miss Fleming," which he called me even after Harpo and I married, "I wish you to join me on the porch." Gulping my martini, I followed nervously. "Sit down," he commanded from the only chair in sight. I sat on the floor, of course. "I'm going to say something to you and I'm never going to repeat it. It shall never be referred to again. I want you to know I approve of you for Harpo." The *Good Housekeeping* seal of approval wasn't in the same league with that of Woollcott. After all, this was America's foremost critic. Too subdued and speechless to reply, I was grateful to hear dinner being called, which meant Aleck's *real* favorite indoor game would begin, giving me time to regain my composure.

Aleck may have been the self-appointed king of Neshobe Island, but closer to home William Randolph Hearst and his magnificent San Simeon were an entirely different case. Located about two hundred miles north of Hollywood, San Simeon was so isolated that it was like visiting another country. And it was probably something like that for Hearst as well, since he spent most of his time there with his mistress, Marion Davies. Mrs. Hearst was not part of the crowd when celebrities gathered at San Simeon. Harpo had been there a few times as Charlie Lederer's guest, but nothing he told me prepared me for my first visit. It's one thing to be told that the driveway leading to the house was six miles long. It was quite another to actually take the slow drive up the mountain. Friday afternoon we took a train from Glendale to San Luis Obispo, where a waiting limousine took us to Hearst Castle, which wasn't even visible from the entrance to the driveway. Hearst owned the world's largest private zoo, and some of his animals freely roamed the grounds, which made navigating the mountain road somewhat interesting for our driver.

By the time I was finally shown to my room, I was overwhelmed. There was a huge four-poster bed with heavy drapes that could easily accommodate eight people. It looked so much like a movie set that I felt like I should be in costume. From the balcony I could see the pool and several priceless objects of art that Hearst had brought over from Europe. Everyone called the place "the Ranch," but it sure didn't look like one.

I dressed for dinner and was escorted to the game room for the cocktail hour. There were about forty guests milling about—mostly of Marion's choosing. The Hollywood weekends at San Simeon were all organized by Marion. On the other hand, when Hearst was entertaining his political friends, Marion had to clear out to make way for Mrs. Hearst.

The doors to the dining room finally opened and dinner was announced. In a huge baronial hall, with flags flying for every fiefdom in some historic kingdom, there was a single refectory table large enough to easily seat the forty guests as well as any latecomers who might arrive. The table spanned the length of the giant room, with a fireplace at one end and the kitchen at the other. Hearst and Marion faced each other at the center of the table, and their guests flowed from the center to the ends of the room in the order of their importance. I was just grateful not to be sitting at the fireplace end. Odd as it may seem in this incredible ancient dining gallery, the table was set picnic style with the islands of condiments in their original bottles and jars set in the center of the table instead of the flowers one would have expected. It was refreshing to find some element of practicality amid all of this opulence. I thought it was a little odd that no wine bottles were visible, and that the butler served only one glass of wine—no seconds. Occasionally Marion would trot back toward the kitchen, saying something about the sauce needing something more, but the knowing smiles among her friends indicated that it was Marion needing something more. Hearst had implemented the rules about alcohol in the hope that it would keep Marion sober, but San Simeon offered numerous hiding places for Marion's secret stash.

After dinner we all moved to the projection room for a movie, but having just been in one, I begged off and headed to the huge four-poster bed to contemplate this unreal fantasy world. We didn't see much of Hearst except for the dinner hour, when he'd seem to suddenly appear at Marion's side. Marion and her movie colony friends spent the days riding horses and playing bridge, or on the tennis courts or in the pool while Hearst presumably took care of his business interests in some remote part of the castle. Late Sunday morning we'd be taken by horse-drawn coaches to a picnic spot where many tables under a tent glistened with silver and cut-glass goblets. After sandwiches, champagne, and caviar, we'd spend the rest of the afternoon on a four-hour journey back to reality—or in our case, Hollywood.

Any visit to San Simeon was memorable, but one stands out for me. We had gone up for a weekend in October 1933. This was a few years before we got married, and Harpo was still enjoying his status as a confirmed bachelor, terrified of the notion of settling down. He was staying for a few more days, but I was working at Fox and was due back at the studio on Monday morning. Howard Hughes was there that weekend with his plane and offered to fly me home on Sunday afternoon. A couple of days later, Charlie Lederer called from the Ranch to tell me that Harpo, who'd given up alcohol years before, had gotten himself thoroughly and tearfully drunk and had to be put to bed. Charlie wanted my help with his bleary-eyed and panicky hangover patient, but I told him Harpo would have to take care of himself.

I guess Harpo's idea of taking care of himself was to leave town for ten months, because that's exactly what he did. Woollcott had arranged for him to perform in Russia in December. As soon as Harpo sobered up, he came back to Hollywood to pack his bags and say goodbye. Within a few days he was on a train heading for New York. A week later he was on a boat bound for Paris, where he spent some time before leaving for Leningrad and Moscow. I'd be spending the holidays without him. Sara and Herman Mankiewicz invited me to their New Year's Eve party, probably feeling a little sorry for me. Mother suggested I find a new boyfriend.

With Harpo cavorting around Russia, I wasn't quite ready to stop dating other people—no matter how much the notion might have appealed to me. When Howard Hughes called and asked me to be his date for a party at his house, I accepted. He was only twenty-eight years old, but he'd already produced *Hell's Angels* and *Scarface* and had a reputation as something of a boy wonder. He sent a car for me, and I was shown into the library where, to my surprise, I found seven of the sexiest ladies in the film business laughing hysterically. "What's so funny?" I asked Jean Harlow. "The party is now complete," she replied, trying to contain her laughter. "We eight women and Howard." I looked at Ginger Rogers. "What's on his mind?" I asked. "Nothing," she said. "That's Howard." We had dinner—just the nine of us. There was a lot of girl talk and absolutely no smoking—perhaps a precursor to the germ-free environment for which he'd later become infamous. After dinner, at least to my knowledge, we were all taken home. This was around thirty years before his reputation as an eccentric overshadowed everything he'd ever done.

I'm pretty sure there was nothing going on between Ginger and Howard at this point, but they later dated on and off for a few years and he eventually gave her an engagement ring. But Ginger wisely broke it off. Howard was mostly interested in controlling everyone in his life. He dated many of the most glamorous women in Hollywood, but they all ran away from him in the end. He was searching for a wife, and it seems incredible that this wealthy, successful, handsome young man kept coming up empty. But he didn't seem particularly interested in me, which was actually something of a relief. On the other hand, I was starting to wonder if Harpo was suffering from a permanent case of cold feet.

When he returned from Russia, the newspapers couldn't get enough of Harpo. In New York the Broadway columnists spotted him all over town—at Casino de Paree with Charlie Chaplin, in a benefit show with Eddie Cantor, or just hanging around with his buddies from the Algonquin. Several of those folks—led by Heywood Broun—got involved with the National Committee for the Defense of Political Prisoners. (Knowing Broun, he probably started the organization.) This was right up Harpo's alley. He always championed the underdog. Marc Connelly, Dorothy Parker, and Broun convinced him to host a benefit show to raise money for the legal defense of the Scottsboro Boys, nine black Alabama teenagers falsely accused of raping two white women. The show was at the Savoy Ballroom in Harlem, and Harpo appeared with Helen Morgan, Bessie Smith, Mildred Bailey, and Buck & Bubbles. The music was by the orchestras of Fletcher Henderson and Benny Carter. That's a show I'm sorry to have missed.

Harpo kept in touch with letters and phone calls, but he wasn't sure when he'd be coming home. I read in the gossip columns that he may be back in Hollywood soon, but then came reports that the Marx Brothers were in New York negotiating for their return to Broadway. The next call I got was from Florida, where Harpo was playing in a charity baseball game. This was followed by a ten-day trip to Bermuda with Sam Harris,

Lou Holtz, and Joe Schenck. Back in New York the papers reported that Harpo was seen at a couple of Broadway shows accompanied by Helen Hayes, Charles MacArthur, Irving Berlin, and Oscar Levant.

My mother was not only sure that Harpo would never get married, she was also wondering if he'd ever come back to California. I saw her point. With his next letter came the announcement that he'd be spending the summer with Woollcott at Neshobe Island. I tried to hide my disappointment, but Harpo called the day after the letter arrived and invited me to join him for a week. The whole gang was gathering to see Groucho take a straight role in a summer stock production of the Ben Hecht–Charles MacArthur play *Twentieth Century*, in Skowhegan, Maine, not too far from Neshobe. I was still under contract at Fox and had to arrange some vacation time, which didn't pose much of a problem at the studio since I was not really doing much more than extra work by this point.

Harpo stayed in Vermont for another few weeks after I headed home. The trip renewed my confidence in our relationship, and I was pleased to assure Mother that all was fine with me and Harpo. It became tougher to believe that when I saw in a newspaper clipping that Harpo bought a boat from one of the Vermont locals. A photo of him sailing in Lake Bomoseen hit the wire services, and his passenger was a young lady named Sylvia Peterson, who happened to be Miss America of 1934.

CHAPTER FIVE
Exit Miss Fleming

OLLYWOOD AND I WEREN'T HITTING IT OFF AS WELL AS WE could have. I still couldn't get very enthusiastic about the process of movie making. I hated the waiting around and could never get comfortable while the hair and makeup people would fuss over me. People probably thought I was kidding when I'd try to explain that it was just my job and that I only did it for the money. I was suddenly part of a widening circle of friends—primarily because of dating Harpo—and they were mostly famous people from the movie business. I was absolutely the least successful member of the group. While we were all enjoying Neshobe Island and San Simeon, the Depression had really kicked in. It almost seemed like the rich Hollywood crowd was unaware of the suffering of millions of people. That all existed outside of our bubble. I knew I was lucky to have a job. If I thought there was a chance of getting another one, I'd have found something else, but the movie business rolled on while many other things did not.

Shortly after I arrived in Hollywood, Paulette Goddard did too, along with her mother and a healthy divorce settlement from that rich North Carolina lumber baron. Paulette didn't need to work but was determined to become a star. She had already been to Hollywood a few years earlier but didn't get much work. When we reconnected, she was doing bit parts even less important than the ones I was getting. But around the same time that I started dating Harpo, Paulette began a relationship with Charlie Chaplin. Chaplin cast Paulette as the leading lady in his next picture, and the fan magazines were suddenly talking of a rumored engagement. Harpo and I saw them socially a few times and they were frequent guests at San Simeon, but once they began shooting *Modern Times*, Paulette and Charlie became scarce. She was suddenly a hot commodity, and there would eventually be talk that David O. Selznick wanted Paulette to play Scarlett O'Hara in *Gone with the Wind*. But Selznick feared a scandal if word got out that Paulette was living with Charlie without the benefit of a marriage license. It seems laughable now, but this was absolutely shocking behavior at the time and could have ruined their careers. Harpo and I were constant companions again when he got back from Russia, but the idea of living together without marriage seemed like a pretty wild leap to me. And Mother would have none of that. While she was living vicariously through the tiny career I was having, Mother was obviously not as driven as Paulette's mother, who had no trouble turning a blind eye to any impropriety. I think Paulette's mother even lived with her and Charlie for a while.

The Marx Brothers were going through some contract problems at Paramount, and Harpo was worried that his career might come to an unceremonious end once they'd finished up their commitment there. He was in his mid-forties and had enjoyed many years of success. Other stars had disappeared after long careers. Maybe this was it. He had a tendency toward fatalism. He could clearly see disaster on the horizon, but he could also shrug his shoulders and take a nap without any trouble. There was an inner peace in Harpo. He needn't have worried. He would soon find himself working at M-G-M, and the Marx Brothers would make their most successful pictures there for Irving Thalberg. I continued to toil away at Fox, trying to figure out what to do about my romance with a perennial bachelor. By this time, I was no longer dating anyone but Harpo. We were a couple in everyone's eyes. If Harpo was attending an event, people expected me to be there with him. It was just a matter of time, but Harpo was in no hurry. There was also the problem of a romance gone bad from his vaudeville days with a girl coincidentally named Fleming. This was an excuse I could do without. What did that have to do with me?

Harpo mostly kept his feelings to himself, but every now and then he would reveal more than he meant to. I knew he preferred my company to anyone else he'd been seeing, and we were always together—

when he wasn't traveling, performing in Russia, or sailing with Miss America for months at a time. Shortly after he came home from that long trip, we got around to the subject of a young dancer I'd been seeing while he was away. The truth is that we just liked to go dancing together, but several of Harpo's friends let him know that they had seen me with an attractive young man on several Hollywood nightclub dance floors. It was the first time I ever detected any jealousy in Harpo. I started to tell him that I wasn't locked away in a convent while he was out of town. I tried to hold it back, but I just started laughing. He was not amused, but I finally told him that it was true that this handsome young man and I were both very interested in settling down. The only trouble was we were both in the same position. He was also looking for the right man. The sense of relief that came over Harpo was reassuring. He was clearly wrestling with himself about commitment. He had a perfectly happy life as a bachelor, but he was worried about losing me. The explanation about my dance partner made him comfortable enough that we never even got around to the topic of some gossip columns reporting that I had reconnected with an old boyfriend from New York while a certain movie comedian was in Russia.

Harpo's professional situation had worked itself out nicely, and the Marx Brothers' first M-G-M picture, *A Night at the Opera*, was a huge success. Paulette and Charlie were also on a roll. *Modern Times* opened in early 1936, and Harpo pronounced it a masterpiece. He was not alone. Critics loved the film, although it did better at the box office overseas. Groucho, who had enormous respect for Chaplin, also hailed the film as brilliant—and he was not one to dish out praise too freely. After finishing the film, Charlie was desperate for a quiet vacation and tried to slip away with Paulette. But nothing with Charlie could ever be done quietly. They sailed for the Orient and the press seemed to have gone with them. During the trip Paulette and Charlie confirmed their rumored engagement. It was kept secret at the time, but they got married in China. I'd be lying if I said I didn't point this out to Harpo in the form of a hint.

After Frenchy died, Harpo had moved out of the Garden of Allah and leased a home owned by actress Laura Hope Crews, but by 1936 he was looking for something to call his own. A good sign, I thought.

He was about to move into a new house in Beverly Hills as the Marx Brothers were preparing for a short road tour to test scenes from their next film, *A Day at the Races*. This had worked well for them with *A Night at the Opera*, so I would be without Harpo for around four weeks in the summer. In his absence I was supervising the painters and decorators. By this time, I had a feeling that this house was going to be as much mine as his, so I was making decisions. One September afternoon, Harpo showed up at the house and found me dressed in paint-covered rags, holding a paintbrush. He took my hand and led me to a chair. "Sit," he said. Dropping to one knee he then cooed, "Miss Fleming, will you marry me?" My coy, "Mr. Marx, this is so sudden" made him whack me in the leg and bark, "Be serious!"

Just around the time Harpo proposed, Irving Thalberg had suddenly died at the age of thirty-seven. Harpo was almost forty-eight and a hypochondriac. Maybe the bachelor life didn't seem so appealing anymore. So, early in the morning on the day we would be married, he came for me looking exactly like his father, a dapper little Frenchman with gloves and cane. They had belonged to Frenchy. Without the impish grin I wouldn't have known him myself. He looked at me approvingly, as with my hat placed to hide my face and some silent movie makeup, I was equally unidentifiable. Handing me the car keys, he mumbled sheepishly, "Late poker game." With that, my man of few words sagged into the car and fell asleep. Okay with me. He was a terrible driver and sleepiness could land us in a tree.

I headed for Orange County, finding a tiny courthouse almost hidden by orange groves. No problem with the license, but the judge would have nothing to do with us. The clerk was kind and suggested the fire station. If the chief was in, he thought he was deputized for such events. Harpo had no doubt things were going swimmingly. But I was having plenty of doubts. What kind of nut was I taking seriously? Is this going to turn out to be some practical joke? Harpo was famous for them, but they never hurt anyone. The chief was in and could perform the ceremony. He called his wife in as a witness, and we were married—or so he said. As we drove away, I said, "I don't think that was legal. I don't feel anything changed." Harpo stopped the car (he'd sufficiently recovered

46

from the previous night's poker festivities by now) and said the magic words, "Honey, for better or worse, I'm yours forever." The scene was so absurd we both started laughing, and that's the way it would be for twenty-eight years.

The 1936 presidential election was thrilling hopeful Democrats around the country, and Hollywood was no exception. Election night, as the returns were being broadcast, we were celebrating the visits of Alice Duer Miller and Ellin and Irving Berlin with a big dinner party at our new house. By dessert time Roosevelt's reelection seemed assured, and Charlie Lederer proposed a toast. We were all laughing and applauding when he looked at us strangely, saying, "I am not toasting the election of Franklin D. Roosevelt, I am toasting the marriage of Mr. and Mrs. Harpo Marx." Harpo found his own way to announce our marriage to the world. After the election he sent a congratulatory telegram to FDR explaining that we had kept our marriage a secret until after the election "because I didn't want to crowd you off the front page." The wire services got hold of it and before long it was everywhere. The M-G-M publicity department, furious with Harpo for daring to elope without notifying them, quickly set up a photo shoot with the great photographer Ted Allan. *Time* magazine ran one of the photos from that shoot under the heading "Marriage Revealed."

From September 26 until November 3, we were secretly married. Paulette and Charlie had nothing on us! Incidentally, we did elope on September 26, but there was some doubt that our crazy wedding was really legal, so we did it again two days later just in case that fire chief wasn't really authorized. That's how we came up with the anniversary being on September 28. Or, more likely we weren't even sure ourselves because the records do indicate that it was indeed legal on September 26. My apologies to the fire chief for ever doubting him.

Harpo was a very private person. It pleased him to move through crowded streets unrecognized. One time in San Diego, he had been rehearsing with a group of stars for a USO show at the naval base there. Needing a break, he said to Cary Grant, "Let's take a walk and get some air." Cary looked at him in astonishment, saying, "I couldn't take two steps out there, I'd be mobbed." Smiling comfortably Harpo said, "Yeah, without makeup I'm in disguise." Feeling a little sorry for Grant, he trotted off to enjoy his anonymity. Recognition was not something Harpo needed. At least not offstage. He preferred his recognition in the form of applause—but as an entertainer for his performance on stage, never for himself as a person. Harpo's attitude about this didn't always fit in with the publicity plans of the studio.

Conditioned by the theatre, where publicity emphasized the show over the individual performer, Harpo had a distaste for his private life being used to promote his work. None of the Marx Brothers believed it would sell more tickets at the box office, and they refused to cooperate with the more intrusive requests from the publicity people. They played along with the innocuous stunts, but personal lives were certainly off limits. The studios had decided, long before the Marx Brothers came along, that the private lives of their stars were most assuredly for public consumption. They created elaborate fantasy lives for many of them, and the adoring public ate it up. Hollywood columnists Hedda Hopper and Louella Parsons cornered the market on the big money of gossip. Their columns sold newspapers to a new readership, fascinated by the veiled suggestions that Eden had been breached again. Sly rumors were carefully phrased so the reader could let the imagination run wild. "What promising newcomer is keeping what promise to her studio head?" or "Whose wife is consoling the broken heart of what recently dumped leading man?" These items could bring the terror of exposure to several Hollywood figures at any given moment. It was contemptible, but it sold newspapers.

Between these two power-mad women there was heavy competition for exclusivity. No publicity seeker dared a divided loyalty. There were two camps. A thoughtless quotation in the column of one would result in a phone call from the other, with something like, "Dear, I wish you had told me, it would have fit so well with some material I'm putting together. Of course, I can't quote you now." The person knew it was a lie, but the whip had been cracked. This was the atmosphere in Hollywood that inspired Harpo's insistence on the secrecy surrounding our marriage. There would be no gossip scoops on this one. We had outfoxed Hedda and Louella, and Harpo hoped they would have fits over it.

Able to relax with our secret revealed, I went off to play golf with Zeppo's wife, Marion. Years of sharing my father's passion for golf, either on a golf course or in the backyard, had made me a fair-enough golfer to be an enthusiastic competitor among the golfing wives of Hillcrest Country Club. The Marx Brothers were all members, but not necessarily for golf. Golf was secondary to the real pleasure found at lunch time when an area of the vast dining room was closed off to become a men's club.

I was uncomfortable when we golfed with Groucho and his wife at Hillcrest. Groucho thought he was entertaining us with what he considered hilarious jokes at Ruth's expense. I made it clear to her that I sympathized and was on her side. Ruth was a good golfer, but I understood why she would have rather been doing something else. Harpo and I shared a love of golf and played together frequently in those days, but I didn't get a sense that Groucho and Ruth were like-minded golfers. Groucho actually took his golf game seriously, but I suspect he thought a golf outing with the wives was not really a serious game of golf. Harpo was a golfer, in a sense. Unlike your average golfer who buys the books and takes lessons to improve his swing, Harpo's fun was in exploring new ways to get his ball in the hole. This was great for a laugh but kept his handicap in the high twenties. A golf course presented him with challenges beyond the game itself, like putting while balancing on one foot. I don't remember if it was Sam Snead who showed Harpo the croquet style of putting, or if it was Harpo who showed Snead, but Snead used it for many years, whereas Harpo's interest didn't last beyond having a special club made.

Unless it was with me and Ruth, Harpo didn't care to play with Groucho, but then only a few garrulous pals did. Golf was not why Groucho joined Hillcrest. He and his crowd would often concede themselves putts under six feet or hold up the whole golf course with their penchant for idle conversation during a round. The manager could always direct a foursome away from Groucho's group by spotting the cloud of cigar smoke moving slowly along the course. Groucho's main activity at the club was lunch at the comedians' Round Table, usually with Harpo, George Burns, Jack Benny, George Jessel, producer Harry Tugend, and writer Irving Brecher. The personnel changed with out-of-town commitments, but the laughter never did. Harpo was funnier than the public ever knew. The other comedians loved to get him talking, which he certainly had no problem doing at lunch.

Among the comedians who were not his brothers, Harpo was closest to George Burns, and I became quite close to Gracie Allen. Gracie and I were very much alike in that neither of us was particularly interested in celebrities or show business. Gracie was a plain sensible woman, very shy and modest. She just happened to be half of a very popular comedy team. George wrote all of the material for Gracie. He was able to use her wonderful natural qualities in a delightful character he created for her. She had grown up in show business and met George when they were in vaudeville separately. They teamed up in an act and actually got married on stage during a show. Gracie completely understood my desire to get out of the movie business. She would have been perfectly happy to quit and leave the performing to George. But that was not possible because Burns & Allen had a hit radio show. They were too successful for her to retire. I had no such problem. Not many people were waiting for the next Susan Fleming film. George and Gracie were nice unassuming people with good values. We made a very normal foursome. Harpo loved George and Gracie, and we spent a lot of time with them at Hillcrest and around town.

Chico, not a golfer, could usually be found in the card room at Hillcrest, playing poker, bridge, or gin rummy. Chico delighted in playing on the nerves of an ever-present gallery. They'd watch the imaginative play of Chico holding a completed hand until the suspense agitated his audience to the point of alarming his opponent into high discards, at which point Chico would call and go down. The ruse didn't always win, but it served to keep Chico's interest on edge. Chico was not known for his interest in winning money. I think he gambled mostly for the rush it gave him. He loved the self-imposed suspense of losing. I can't recall ever seeing Chico's wife, Betty, at Hillcrest. Perhaps she didn't need to actually witness her husband driving them deeper into debt. Zeppo was a different case. Zeppo was a true gambler, only interested in winning by beating the odds. Hillcrest was his playground. A strenuous golfer in the morning, his action in the clubhouse later was among the devotees of horse racing, team sports, and fights, not for the rooting interest, but for manipulation of the odds. When Zeppo gambled his mission was to put his opponent in the poorhouse.

Many years before major league baseball came to California, the Hillcrest crowd took the Hollywood Stars minor league team to their hearts, flocking to tiny Gilmore Field. It was so intimate that players and fans conversed during the games and became friends. And many of the regulars at the ballpark were minority owners of the team. Bob Cobb, owner of the Brown Derby restaurant, and his wife, actress Gail Patrick, were part of the ownership group, and they enlisted many movie people as small investors. Gary Cooper, Bing Crosby, Barbara Stanwyck, Robert Taylor, William Powell, George Raft, Harry Warner, and Cecil B. DeMille were among the many part-owners of the team. When the Stars finished the 1938 season in seventh place in the eight-team Pacific Coast League, Hillcrest gave them a huge banquet. Winning would have been nice, but we loved the Stars, win or lose. I guess we gave them the big party for not finishing last.

At the ballpark, Zeppo occupied the box next to ours, which was fun until Zep discovered that the bookies sat up in the grandstand, where they could relay changing odds to their eager customers by hand signals. Of course, Zep's rooting interest didn't last past his discovery of the money game. It was only a mild irritant until one electric night the Stars actually had men on base. Our box was shouting with excitement when Harpo murmured, "Keep it down, Zep's betting on the other team." I couldn't believe he meant it. "Your daffy brother was on the Stars through the fourth inning, now he's on the visitors? I'm expected to root for his money, not my team?" Harpo thought about it and then turned to his brother and said, "Zep, cut it out or change your box." He had such serene values. Groucho was always fun to have at the ballpark. When the Stars light-hitting shortstop slammed a double, Groucho commented, "That's the first time I've seen him at second base without his glove."

These thumbnail sketches are only to reveal the extraordinary dissimilarity of brothers raised in a close environment, unpressured by warm, loving parents with a sense of humor. Poverty was not demeaning. It was an absurdity. Life was full of the unexpected. Success depended on your attitude. Four of the brothers accepted their mother's happy cynicism, but Gummo was different. Gummo was without passion. He could usually be seen after golf lunching with doctors, absorbed in medical talk. Consequently, at the drop of a hangnail, Gummo was sought out for recommendation of treatment. Over the years this concerned brother of my hypochondriacal mate was consulted on signs of indisposition by all of his brothers. Why call a doctor when you have a brother who plays golf with a lot of doctors?

Being accepted into this family of eccentrics opened a wonderful world of broad relationships beyond my accustomed unit of three. As Harpo's wife I became a representative of their family. I soon learned to expect the unexpected. This was evident on my second golf outing at Hillcrest with Marion. Not seeing my little white cotton bag with the six clubs, which I had carried around public courses for years when playing with my parents, I asked the caddy if he had my bag. "Oh yes," he said. I looked at the typical heavy leather bag that was being offered and wondered what I was going to do with all the shiny new clubs it carried. Nonplussed, I turned to Marion. "It's a gift from Zeppo," she said. "He says 'welcome to Hillcrest Country Club.' Your little paper bag with the egg-beaters would embarrass any caddy carrying it." Not too sure I was pleased, and feeling ridiculous, we started off. But it took only a few holes to find I was playing better, and who wants to embarrass a caddy or Zeppo?

It wasn't hard to enjoy this new life. Transferring my own modest celebrity to that of wife of a great movie star was not as heady as might be expected. Harpo was a simple, gentle man who avoided sham, chose his own friends, and didn't care whether his socks matched. As we had been a close pair socially for several years, it wasn't too difficult to adapt. Besides the brothers, our group of close friends from the Hillcrest crowd included George Jessel, who was incongruously married to Norma Talmadge, a star of the silent screen and once the Queen of Hollywood. In spite of all the glamour, she was a lovely, warm, funny lady. But she just didn't seem all that thrilled about being married to Jessel. There were whispers about her flagging career and the opportunity he gave her to be on his radio show. For Saturday night dancing and nightclubbing, it could be Philo and Lou Holtz, George Burns and Gracie Allen, and sometimes Jack and Mary Benny. This form of recreation was so unlike Harpo. It must have been George's doing as he and Gracie were enthusiastic dancers. Harpo's concept of dancing was to stand in one spot and sway, creating a roadblock on the small, crowded dance floors. This didn't last long. Harpo rebelled, and we quickly returned to our less graceful pleasures.

The truly glamorous hosts of the colony were the Goldwyns. Sam's remarkable wife, Frances, formerly an actress known as Frances Howard, liked to give an international flavor to her small parties. Harpo and I both had a deep affection for Frances. Harpo especially liked these nights, since there was usually a poker game after dinner. I enjoyed evenings with the Goldwyns for the surprise element. Once, after dinner Joan Crawford—whom I had met only superficially—explained to me in lengthy detail why she had been late. Her two children were ill, so she had to wait at home to give them injections, "something one just doesn't leave to a servant's incompetence." I couldn't help feeling she had planned this unlikely account of her devoted attention to the welfare of her children for the enlightenment of the dinner table, but the talk was too lively to interrupt, so she laid it on me later. An insubstantial chameleon of a woman, Joan played different roles for different social occasions. Another time, leaving a party at Groucho's, attended by the elite of Hollywood, Joan went to each guest, shook hands, and bowed, saying how much she had enjoyed the evening. It took some time to cover the large group, but she held every eye. They all watched Joan make her extraordinary queenly exit, as if the party had been to celebrate her.

Then there was Marlene Dietrich—in brilliant contrast to the disturbing Crawford—a delightfully naughty lady. Bored by having to watch tennis following a Goldwyn Sunday luncheon, she decided to amuse herself. After a quick visit to the dressing room, she returned to a chair visible to the open court (especially the four tennis players) and that was the end of the tennis. Marlene had removed her panties and was crossing and recrossing her legs in a manner distracting to the players, who were all trying to play the net for a closer view.

Frances had made a career of being the acknowledged leading hostess of Hollywood, building the Goldwyn prestige across continents. It was assumed her husband was pleased and grateful. Frances played the role with such apparent ease that one evening after dinner she startled me by saying, "Come upstairs with me while I freshen my makeup. I must talk to you." Uncharacteristically, she looked depressed. In her dressing room she suddenly burst into tears. Frances had written a scenario for a film and proudly showed it to Sam who, without looking at it, tore it apart and threw it into the glowing fireplace. An enraged Sam shouted furiously, "How dare you! You stay out of the studio, that's my business. Yours is here at home." Sensitivity was not Sam's strength. But diplomacy was Frances's. It would never be mentioned again, but his cruel dismissal relegating her to an archaic role didn't just create a momentary humiliation; it had to be a consuming hatred in a proud lady. I hope she got even.

A lovely, bright young friend once said to me, "How lucky you are to have a husband who supports you. Mine doesn't think I do anything right." I didn't know it showed. On the morning of our first anniversary, Harpo presented himself at the breakfast table dressed exactly as he had been the day of our marriage—in full Frenchy outfit with gloves and cane. I could have kicked myself for not putting on the ridiculous getup I wore that day, but my lack of sentimentality somehow allowed me to get rid of it. If he was disappointed Harpo didn't show it. He presented me with a gold link bracelet. On each link was a letter to spell out: "Forever Harpo."

CHAPTER SIX

Billy

THE TIMING OF HARPO'S PROPOSAL HAD BEEN IMPECCABLE. I WAS running out of places to work. I had been at Paramount, Columbia, Fox, RKO, and Twentieth Century. Somehow, I even ended up with a bit part in *The Great Ziegfeld* at M-G-M, which did little more than add William Powell, Myrna Loy, and Luise Rainer to the list of Hollywood luminaries whose names appeared above mine in the credits. It was made while the Marx Brothers were at the studio, so for all I know, Harpo might have suggested someone hire me, but if he did, he never said so. The only sensible thing left after that, it seemed at the time, was to go to work for Warner Bros. My roles in the two pictures I did there merely added the final names to my esteemed list of co-stars: Dick Powell, Joan Blondell, and George Brent. *Gold Diggers of 1937* is a pretty good picture that actually turns up on television now and then, but don't blink or you'll miss me. I only mention *God's Country and the Woman* for the historical fact of it being my swan song in the motion picture industry.

My film career never really mattered to me beyond it being my job. I might as well have worked at a factory—which is essentially what a movie studio is. I was happy to make the transformation from contract player to Mrs. Harpo Marx. When I finally decided that I'd had it with the movies, Harpo simply shrugged and said, "Whatever you say." It didn't matter to him if I made movies or not, and that was a lucky thing because I was not going to have an easy time finding work after having been under contract just about everywhere and never really making it in the movies. I suppose my chances would have been better had stardom in Hollywood been something I desired. Paulette Goddard really wanted to be a star, and she certainly had the talent. Combine drive, talent, and beauty and you've almost got a chance. Add being Charlie Chaplin's girlfriend. That should do it. If I had the talent and desire, Harpo probably could have helped elevate my status in the movies. I just didn't want what Paulette wanted. And of course, there was also the ever-present problem of me not being much of an actress.

Around six months before we got married, Harpo was so nervous about giving up bachelorhood that he actually skipped town for a month. This was a scaled-down version of his lengthy disappearance from Hollywood after the Russia trip. He agreed to go to Paris to promote the upcoming French premiere of *A Night at the Opera*. This was something M-G-M was not expecting any of the Marx Brothers to actually do, but they had to ask. When he found out about it, Harpo jumped at the chance. If you believe what he wrote in *Harpo Speaks!* we got married practically the moment he got back to Hollywood from that trip, but that otherwise wonderful book should not be something by which you set your clocks. In Paris, Harpo met the Spanish surrealist painter Salvador Dali, who had fled there from Spain in the turbulent days leading up to the Spanish Civil War. They became fast friends and agreed to meet again in Hollywood when Dali traveled there, which he did in February 1937.

When Dali and his wife, Gala, arrived at our home, the first thing that became apparent was that there wasn't a common language between the four of us. Actually, that might have been the second thing. It was hard not to notice the harp strung with barbed wire that Dali had shipped to the house. It had knives and forks as tuning pegs, and there was some gauze and a little bottle of iodine attached to it. We all spoke, or at least understood, a little German, and Gala and I did a lot of translating. Harpo knew enough German from his childhood to get by, but Dali pretty much stuck to Spanish and the bits and pieces of English he had picked up. The M-G-M publicity department had our visit with Dali in the newspapers, which seemed to please Dali quite a bit.

Dali was fascinated by the Marx Brothers, and he wanted to do a movie with them, but the treatment he wrote was terribly silly stuff and made no sense at all. The main purpose of Dali's visit was to make a portrait of Harpo. He and Gala came to the house each day for around a week. Harpo would sit in the bay window in the morning and play his harp with the sun shining through. Dali would sit nearby sketching parts of Harpo—a hand, his mouth, an eye, the other eye—and in the end he put it all together. Harpo hung all the beautiful sketches around the house. After Dali left, a photographer from M-G-M came to get a shot of Harpo, fingers all bandaged, playing the barbed wire harp. I asked Harpo what he was going to do with the useless unplayable harp, which was a cheap, beaten-up instrument clearly in the right condition for Dali's gag. He shrugged his shoulders and gave me that look that said he had no idea. What I did next has caused people to look at me as if I were crazy for many years. I put the harp out with the trash. I've been told it would have been worth a great sum of money to an art collector or a museum, but it really and truly was a big piece of junk. It just didn't occur to us that there might be a market for junk that had been created by Dali.

Shortly after I called it quits in the business, so did Marion Davies. Hearst had been determined to make her the biggest star in pictures and sunk a lot of money into her career, but she grew tired of it. She was never comfortable once sound pictures came along because of her stammer. She really worked at hiding it and most people didn't notice, but her heart wasn't in the movie business. She instead began devoting a lot of her time to charitable endeavors. We didn't know it at the time, but Marion would soon use a little of the Hearst clout on Harpo's and my behalf.

No longer going to the studio every day, I started to find our glamorous social life routine. I wondered, *Is this all?* It was fun lunching at Romanoff's with Gracie Allen and friends, followed by a little light shopping, but I wasn't getting anywhere. I don't mean professionally. I never wanted to step in front of a camera again for the rest of my life. It was just that our lifestyle had no depth. I had a few bracelets and a diamond pin, and we partied with internationally famous celebrities, but I never saw the importance of any of this. I wondered, *Why were we married?* Harpo's life had been rich and full without me. I wasn't bringing anything new to it. It seemed to me that people marry to create a wonderful new world of family, and you can't do it without children. I never felt any nervousness at suggesting something to Harpo. If the approach was direct, his reaction was generous. But children—this wasn't just some minor adjustment.

Children was a big one. What would Harpo say to remodeling his perfect life? He could glare at me, saying, "If you're feeling so unfulfilled why don't you take a course in something?"

With my relaxed fellow, one time was never better than another to get approval. So, one morning, heart in mouth, I stood in front of the harp and blurted out, "Children." "What about them?" he asked. "We need some," I gulped. "We do?" He smiled. I could only nod. Without any hesitation he said, "Great, how do we start?" An early hysterectomy had put me out of baby production, so we would go shopping. Dr. Sam Hirschfield, our family doctor, dear friend, and general consultant on just about everything, was called. Sam was the last of the great breed of total medical practitioners. One didn't go to Sam to find out which specialist should be seen. Sam could take care of everything. Happily, Sam took us seriously. He didn't say, "Harpo, you're fifty years old." He said, "How wonderful it would be for a child to live with you." Sam didn't mean financially. He sensed then that some years later, when our funny little daughter was four or five years old, if I awoke in the middle of the night wondering why Harpo wasn't next to me, I would look in her bathroom and find them sitting on the floor playing jacks.

Sam suggested we start with accredited agencies. He would make the first inquiries for us. There were guidelines for parent eligibility in matching family backgrounds, as it was thought it would create a genetic agreement that might influence the ease with which the child and new parents create a relationship. To me it was baloney! There couldn't be greater diversity than exhibited by the Marx family, genetically supplied by just Frenchy and Minnie. But why argue? Play the game or go without. Timing and good fortune were on our side. How else to explain our Billy, waiting for months in a crib in the Children's Home Society? He was barely surviving multiple illnesses until one day a man with a gentle humorous face and a pretty lady were standing at the side of his crib watching a nurse trying to feed him. The nurse told us, "He refuses food." I said, "Let me try." I offered the spoon to the face with the huge brown eyes. He looked at me thoughtfully for a moment and then smiled and opened his mouth. There was a gasp from the nurse. Billy, Harpo, and I knew we were made for one another.

But there was a frustrating delay caused by the Catholic church. Billy's natural mother had been Catholic. Although his natural father was Jewish, the church claimed him and would not release him to a non-Catholic family. Because the child was so ill, we asked to be allowed to send medical care while the subject was being debated. The word came back, "Better he loses his life, than his religion." That did it! Harpo went to Marion Davies and things started moving quickly. I never doubted that the Hearst empire's influence was far reaching, and Marion apparently knew just how to use it. She had been a very generous donor to the St. Augustine Catholic Church, which happened to be right across the street from M-G-M. A few phone calls from Marion and things were arranged. Harpo and I presented ourselves to the priest at St. Augustine. Our story was that I was reclaiming my Catholic faith and Harpo—using the name Arthur to avoid detection—expressed a desire to convert to Catholicism. I suspect the priest knew who Harpo was but played along. This church was practically part of the studio. All of the M-G-M Catholics went there. The priests were even technical advisors on M-G-M films involving the church. Thanks to Marion, we pulled it off and soon had a document proving that we were a Catholic married couple.

The time finally came for us to bring Billy home. I could hardly wait to put this skinny little piece of boy into a high chair and fill him up. He slurped up the first spoonful and pounded his little fists on the tray for more. As I was spooning the "more" into him the first spoonful backed up, but he laughed and kept up his drumming on the tray. While I kept the spoon going, the nanny kept cleaning up until the bowl was empty. He stopped then, and we realized he had made his point. It wasn't only hunger. It was also acceptance and trust. Our relationship had been cemented. We didn't know how ill he was until a little later. A pediatrician was coming to the house twice a day "to watch him closely," even bringing a portable X-ray machine. One day I finally called Dr. Sam to ask, "Doesn't it indicate anything that his breath is putrid?" Sam answered, "Of course. There must be abscesses of the lungs. Bring him in so I can take a look." That same afternoon, verified by his X-ray machine, Sam reported, "Not only does Billy have abscesses in his lungs, but he also has them in his ears. And, I think he also has rickets. We have no treatment, but we do have magic. The air in Arizona is curative. Try it."

It isn't in my nature to hesitate when I respect the direction given. The Phoenix season was coming to a close, but the Arizona Biltmore Hotel was open, and that might give Billy a start on recovery. Almost immediately, Billy, Harpo, and I were on the plane for Arizona. We were pleasantly surprised to run into Oscar Hammerstein II on our first day at the Biltmore. Harpo played songs from *Show Boat* in his daily harp practice sessions, so he was thrilled to see half of the team that wrote "Ol' Man River" and "Can't Help Lovin' Dat Man" at poolside each day. If he was disappointed that Jerome Kern wasn't there, Harpo didn't let on. After a week in Phoenix, two parents waited anxiously in Sam's office to hear the results of the new X-rays. I think Sam was the proudest one in the room when he could announce, "You've got a survivor. Not only have the abscesses cleared up, but there also aren't even the expected signs of scar tissue. The ears are clear of the infection, and he has gained three pounds."

William Woollcott Marx was suddenly a chubby, healthy baby boy. We were now officially "Mom and Pop." We refocused our lifelong self-interests to this wonderful child. Our family had started. Friends sent comic telegrams of congratulations, and we set about spoiling him enthusiastically—not because he had missed a year, but because he was a charmer. He even brought joy to Woollcott's brother William in Baltimore, who wrote how pleased he was that our son carried his name. Actually, Billy had been named for my father, who also was pleased, but what's the difference? They could share the honor. When Aleck finally got to meet Billy in person, he introduced himself as "Unky Acky Wooky," the name by which Billy would continue referring to Woollcott well into adulthood. In a letter to Harpo dated April 13, 1942, Woollcott told of the three greatest honors of his life. After noting that Charlie Chaplin's dedication of *The Gold Rush* and Thornton Wilder's dedication of *Our Town* to him were among them, he wrote, "the other was your giving Billy Marx the middle name of Woollcott."

Harpo took to fatherhood in a way that only he could. For me it often seemed like we'd adopted a little brother for Harpo. When Monday morning would arrive and he'd have to leave for the studio, I had to pull him away from Billy to get him out the door and on his way. After a long day of shooting, Harpo would come home and demand every detail of his son's day. After Irving Thalberg died, Harpo didn't seem to enjoy making movies quite so much. At first it was okay, but as the quality of the scripts suffered, so did Harpo's interest. Going to the studio became a chore. It wasn't just the thought of missing any of little Billy's escapades. I knew exactly how he felt. It had always been that way for me, a lowly contract player with no future in movies. But Harpo was a huge star. The release of a new Marx Brothers movie was always a very big deal. But Groucho also was growing tired of it. Chico would never stop if it were left up to him. The money was too good, and Chico, perpetually broke, could never find a better paying job than a Marx Brothers movie. But they were tired of second-rate studio writers working them into vague plots in a variety of unlikely settings. They decided to make the films they owed M-G-M and then call it quits.

Harpo was excited about his new family life and wanted to fully experience it. But at the same time, Groucho and Chico were dealing with crumbling marriages. From where I sat, they were both lousy husbands. Chico's wife Betty had long suffered as he womanized and gambled his way through life without even a thought about her and their daughter, Maxine. Before Harpo and I were married, Maxine came to me with a story that made my blood boil. She was in high school, probably around sixteen. She was humiliated and embarrassed because her father made a pass at one of her classmates. She couldn't tell her mother. She just needed someone safe to talk to. I didn't even mention that story to Harpo until many years later. Sadly, he did not seem shocked by it. I know he was troubled by Chico's behavior, but his fierce sense of loyalty prevented him from being critical of his brother. In spite of Chico's abhorrent lifestyle, Harpo loved him, and they were always very close.

Groucho's wife Ruth had a very different problem. Groucho was not a womanizer at all, but he embarrassed her in other ways. Ruth was not Groucho's intellectual equal by any means, and he made sure she was aware of this every chance he got. He would make jokes at her expense at dinner parties. She smiled and took the abuse, but she also began drinking to ease the pain. Their teenaged daughter Miriam would ride her bike to our house to seek refuge from the arguing. We started hiring Miriam as a babysitter for Billy—even if we weren't going out. She was around fourteen years old and a sweet but troubled kid. I hadn't thought about certain aspects of joining the Marx family. In addition to becoming Mrs. Harpo Marx, I also became Aunt Susan.

Miriam confided in me that Groucho had taken her to the M-G-M lot and introduced her to a few big movie stars. She was upset because Groucho took her to see Clark Gable and said, "Meet my daughter, Miriam. She has a big crush on you." I assured her that her father meant no harm and didn't understand a young woman's feelings about boys. Her response threw me for a loop, and I realized that being Aunt Susan was not always as simple as hiring a babysitter. Miriam told me she was not attracted to Gable at all. She was embarrassed because she thought she was expected to see Gable in that way. All of her friends certainly did. But Miriam melted when introduced to Katharine Hepburn. Miriam was just starting to come to grips with her sexuality. She was afraid to tell her friends and was sure her parents couldn't stop fighting long enough to notice she was upset. Aunt Susan was safe. I was glad to be available to her for any support I could offer. She had a wonderful sense of humor—like her father. And she became an alcoholic—like her mother. Happily, she would eventually beat alcoholism, while managing to retain that great sense of humor.

Being Aunt Susan wasn't always about the problems of my nieces and nephews. Gummo's son, Bob, liked to ride his bike to our house just to listen to Harpo's morning practice sessions. He came for the music and was not running away from any problems at home. He was a good kid and grew up to be very entrepreneurial. He was successful in several businesses and became a renowned home builder in and around Palm Springs. Bob was the product of the very happy marriage of Gummo and Helen. They wound up with the longest marriage of any of the Marx Brothers. When Helen died in 1976, they were just a couple of months shy of their forty-seventh anniversary.

Groucho and Ruth divorced when Miriam was fifteen years old, and it was a relief for her. She continued spending a lot of time at our house until she went away to school. Chico and Betty didn't have as simple an outcome. Chico moved out of his house and got an apartment with his new girlfriend, Mary DiVitha, who worked as an extra at M-G-M under the name Mary Dee. They met at the studio during the waning days of the Marx Brothers. I didn't judge her for moving in with a married man because Betty spitefully refused to get a divorce even though she had been threatening Chico with one for years. I liked Mary very much and found her to be sweet, funny, and pleasant to be around. I couldn't always say the same for Betty, but I felt sorry for her. Being married to Chico had to be incredibly difficult. If Groucho, Harpo, and Gummo hadn't been managing some of Chico's money, she would have lost the house very quickly once the Marx Brothers wrapped things up at M-G-M.

The Marx Brothers' retirement from movies coincided with a general decline in the business. Radio had taken a big bite out of ticket sales, and audiences were staying home with their feet up and a glass of beer. The first to move was Groucho. He had initially decided to devote more of his time to writing, but after a couple of years out of the limelight, he was thrilled to become the host of *Pabst Blue Ribbon Town* on CBS. He privately joked to Harpo about how far he'd fallen, from being the toast of Broadway to becoming a beer salesman. The show wasn't a big hit, but he kept at it for more than a year. Harpo made a couple of appearances on the show. Chico hit the road with an orchestra that had been put together for him, and he even made a couple of records. At one point, Chico became ill, and Harpo went out on the road to fill in for him on a handful of dates.

Harpo looked at some offers and shrugged. Radio was no place for him. What could he do? His silent movie clown was a fantasy. Without the costume and makeup, who would he be? Talk? Forget it. He felt strongly that suddenly having his character speak would destroy its magical quality and there would be no going back. The William Morris Agency, concerned that one of their clients was unemployed, tried to persuade Harpo to let them put together a nightclub act for him. They promised bookings at top clubs and hotels. But Harpo really wasn't ready to go back to work. He was enjoying a new unstructured life and was in no hurry to commit himself. Harpo just wanted to sit around the pool for a little longer. It was far more enjoyable for him to teach Billy to swim than to be on a train heading to the next show. He'd done that for long enough.

CHAPTER SEVEN

Summer of '41

ARPO'S BLISSFUL SEMIRETIREMENT ENDED, AS ABRUPTLY AS IT began, with a call from Woollcott. It was Aleck, don't forget, who packed my boy off to Russia. Realizing Harpo was talking to him, I became concerned about what sort of mess this could get us into. Aleck had been on tour starring in *The Man Who Came to Dinner* as Sheridan Whiteside, the character based on himself. This makes sense until you factor in that Aleck was not an actor. On Broadway the part was played by Monty Woolley, with restrained sophistication. But Aleck himself was allowed to take the play on the road, convincing Kaufman and Hart that he could play himself, famously stating, "I'm the only actor who can strut sitting down." The play was a marvelous romp and as actor-proof as possible. But with Aleck in the lead, it was sheer exhibitionism. If anyone else had played the role as fussily as Aleck, there would have been a suit for character assassination. As a Broadway critic, Aleck would have skewered his own performance. Out-of-town critics, however, were not about to quibble over the quality of Aleck's acting. They saw him as a literary giant having a lark in a parody of himself.

The Broadway version continued its long run for anyone interested in seeing the show with an actual actor in the lead, while Aleck started his tour with a week in Santa Barbara before his big opening in Los Angeles. The combination of actor ego and Hollywood awe went to Aleck's head. He became convinced the stage was his true calling. Harpo and I attended opening night at the Biltmore Theatre on February 12, 1940, and the audience loved it. The tour moved on to Pasadena, Fresno, and San Francisco, where Woollcott's acting career was temporarily ended by a heart attack. Harpo, the perennial hypochondriac, needed to be reminded that Aleck was not exactly in the habit of taking good care of himself. But for Harpo, it was a stark reminder of his own mortality.

Aleck returned to the show after being out of action for almost a year. He committed himself to a healthier lifestyle, noting that "a man's first heart attack ought to be his last." He was finishing an East Coast run in Boston the following spring when the fateful call came. Aleck had decided to do a summer stock production of a Chinese fantasy called *The Yellow Jacket* in Marblehead, Massachusetts. This was not unusual as summer stock companies had sprung up all along the eastern seaboard. What seemed unusual was his idea that Harpo appear in the production. We were planning to meet up with Aleck at Neshobe Island in July, and Aleck convinced Harpo to make it a working vacation—and promised very little work.

Perhaps out to prove that Aleck's performance in *The Man Who Came to Dinner* wasn't such a big deal, George Kaufman himself decided to star in a summer stock production of the show in New Hope, Pennsylvania. Kaufman would play the Woollcott-inspired Sheridan Whiteside role and Moss Hart would take the Noel Coward–inspired role of Beverly Carlton. Kaufman had done the show a few times on tour when Aleck was ill, but, like Aleck, he was not an actor. These were basically vanity productions. Fortunately, no one thought of having Gus Eckstein play Dr. Metz. But guess who Kaufman wanted to take the Harpo Marx–inspired role of Banjo? Suddenly, my semiretired, unemployed Marx Brother was booked for the summer of 1941. If Woollcott could have Harpo in his vanity production, Kaufman felt he, too, was entitled. We were set to open July 28 at the Bucks County Playhouse and August 11 in Marblehead. And for the first time since his days as a young vaudevillian, Harpo had lines to memorize. Not only was he going back to work, but for *The Man Who Came to Dinner* he was taking a speaking part—something he refused to do when offered lucrative radio work.

As Aleck saw it, Harpo wasn't working, so he didn't have any excuse not to appear in an obscure Chinese play that no one understood. According to Aleck the part in *The Yellow Jacket* was perfect for Harpo; no dialogue, and it would be great fun for all. Susan could roam the antiques shops. I couldn't argue with Aleck on that point. My interest in antiques had grown considerably on our recent trips to the East, and I was always redecorating. With Billy in tow for us to show off to all of our Eastern friends, we hit the road. I was ready to visit every antiques shop from New Hope to Marblehead, but first there was a duty to perform. My grandmother, the formidable and extravagantly named Alva Maria Carolina Hammar Luigi vonPhilp, was alive and well in Bethlehem, just a short drive from New Hope. It's easy to see why, upon her arrival from Stockholm, an American immigration official decided she was simply Alva vonPhilp. My grandfather, Casimir, had died when I was nine years old, so Grandma had been alone for many years. Heaven forbid I should return home and try to explain to Mother why I hadn't paid her a visit. Best to get it over quickly.

Grandma looked the same in her eighties as she had years before. No new wrinkles. Life had done everything it was going to do to her. But I didn't know her. We had a lovely lunch. I asked about her health, and she asked me about my life. She assured me that she had never seen me in a movie. She considered movies a waste of time. But I knew she had at least suffered through *The Ace of Cads* because Mother had taken her to see it. We chatted comfortably and without warmth. And, when it came time for me to leave, she really shook me, announcing that she would drive back with me to meet my husband. Didn't she know he was an actor and Jewish? Had she never been the bigot I had assumed? Wasn't she the inspiration for Mother's occasionally anti-Semitic inferences? What happened to the inflexibility? This is the same woman who had forbidden Mother to pursue a singing career. This hell-raiser had become a gentle old lady, although, arriving at the Kaufman farm, she refused to get out of the car. She wasn't paying a social call on the Kaufmans, she just wanted a look at what I'd married. It delighted me to see that my irresistible one clearly charmed her. Grandma died a few years after that visit, so my last memory of her was a happy one.

The Kaufmans had a lovely old farmhouse in the middle of open fields, with a neglected tennis court, a pool with an ample supply of algae, and an acre of lawn for (you guessed it) croquet. On rolling hills nearby, Moss Hart had his farm in a style more befitting a country gentleman, a role Moss enjoyed playing in the midst of all the luxury his success could buy, including a house full of rare antiques, supplied locally. His hills, wonderfully forested by nursery trucks bearing full-grown trees for his privacy, gave rise to Kaufman's remark, "If God hadn't made a tree, Moss would have." Exploring Bea and George's house, I discovered a veritable museum of Pennsylvania Dutch folk art of the eighteenth and nineteenth centuries. Bea had found these treasures in out-of-the-way antiques shops throughout the state, and without professional guidance. Bea offered to show me the shops and off we went, antiquing in the beautiful Pennsylvania countryside, while the men rehearsed. Each time we took off, Harpo would remind me, "Buy it all, there will never be any more." I tried, but there was so little undamaged. Bea was a good tutor. A chip or fine crack could lower the value by 80 percent. Between croquet games, Bea and I hunted for the very best fine antiques, sorting through a lot of junk in our quest and taking turns at "first choice."

We'd been in our house for almost five years but were still figuring out the decor, so my antique hunting was not without purpose. About a month after we were married, Harpo hit me with "I hate the green and gold taffeta drapes. The dining room chairs are too high and my feet dangle. Either we sell the house, or you do something." The mistake had been in Harpo's choice of decorator. Gilbert Adrian was M-G-M's top costume designer, and he would have been a wonderful choice had I needed a beautiful gown. Adrian and our architect had been brought together, and then Harpo went on tour. I minded my own business. Marion and Zeppo had a much-admired colonial home, so Marion worked with Adrian. I felt like we were in good hands, since Marion and Zeppo once had their Hollywood apartment featured in a photo spread in *Architectural Digest*.

The finished product was lovely. Any movie star would have entered the tastefully decorated rooms with pride—but not Harpo. When the first linen couch was set in place, he looked at me firmly and sat down on it. When he tried to put his feet up, the coffee table was too far away and the couch too big. Clearly, I must have a talk with our decorator. Adrian was pleasant about removing some of the oversized furniture, and he gracefully removed himself from the danger of making any more mistakes—there was a wife in place now—let Susan make them. Our house remained a work in progress for a few years. I sent home several large crates from our Eastern trip, confident that beautiful things fit any style of architecture, especially if they have been chosen for more than their decorative effect. Later, a sense of history was part of my delight in opening the crates when they arrived.

Bea and I dragged Harpo along on one of our excursions. I proudly showed him some furniture I wanted to send home, and he didn't really understand what we were looking at. He wondered about the people who had owned these antiques in the past and why the designs were attractive to us. He liked the primitive artistry of the furniture and said, "I enjoy looking at this stuff, but why am I so comfortable with it?" Looking at me hopefully, he went on to complain, "Beyond George Washington chopping down a cherry tree and Ben Franklin discovering electricity while flying a kite, American history is a blank page to me. You're always reading books. Read me something about American history." I assured him, "You'll fall asleep." He had a practical answer. "Not if you do it before dinner, when I'm hungry and awake."

Harpo had a curious problem that was the envy of any insomniac—especially Groucho. He loved being read to, but the act of putting his head on a cushion sent the signal to his brain that he was ready for sleep. However, he was really serious about getting a history lesson that afternoon, so I reached for Carl Van Doren's biography of Benjamin Franklin, which was among the books conveniently on the shelf of the Kaufman guest quarters, and we started. Then I woke him up for dinner. It wasn't lack of attention; it was instant uncontrolled relaxation. I finished the book on my own before Harpo made it through the first chapter. Standing up during the readings was suggested, but he wasn't quite that serious about his history lesson.

Aside from my efforts to empty the antiques shops, I was glad not to have to attend rehearsals, which are boring to anyone not involved in the production. Also, the one rehearsal I did attend made me nervous. George was taking one hell of a chance. Moss could express the superficiality of the Noel Coward character just by playing himself, but George's perception of Woollcott's abusive charm was a surly, ill humor. Of course, no one dared tell him it takes a professional to project a character. I'm sure he thought if Aleck could get away with it, anyone should be able to. Besides, every actor in the play was on a personal ego trip, so if George was going to be lousy, the rest of the cast might look good by contrast. Harpo barely seemed interested in rehearsing, but it was not my place to counsel my favorite architect of the unexpected against inattention. On opening night, I just took my seat in the audience and watched and waited to see what they would do when Harpo, inevitably, forgot his lines. My Harpo's artistry was physical, the timing of dialogue was something he never had to develop. His lone effort of memorization was the sixteen lines of poet A. E. Housman's "When I Was One-and-Twenty," which had intrigued him with its terse philosophy.

Although Harpo's character was on stage only for five minutes in the third act, in that short time he was able to create havoc. Getting lost in the fast-paced, staccato give-and-take of the two-man dialogue, Harpo threw at George any line he could remember. Now every actor at some time has had the dreaded experience of "going up" in his lines or being in a scene with another actor who has. It is part of an actor's stage craft to know what to do when it happens. But George, the celebrated play-wright and director, wasn't an actor. He was rattled and rapidly became hopelessly lost. He tried to give appropriate answers to the false cues coming at him, hoping they would get Harpo back on track, but that just messed it up more.

Finally, members of the cast waiting in the wings to go on realized this was not a comic scene the two men had rehearsed privately and sent the maid on with a cake—which Harpo promptly ate. Confusion then spread to the property man, who brought down the curtain thinking it was a new ending to the scene. It didn't help much for him to raise it immediately, showing a cast bent double with laughter. George and Moss learned that night that the arts are not interchangeable. Perhaps they saw their play as so skillfully written that it only needed performers who wouldn't bump into the furniture. As a director of many plays, George should have known better, but he was on the other side of the footlights for a change. Like Aleck, George's ego got the best of him. Things smoothed out for the remaining performances—they even got some good notices—but fortunately it was a short run. I have always suspected that Harpo, in the true rebellious Marx spirit, deliberately blew his lines. It was always dangerous to be on stage with my fellow. Aleck had arrived in Bucks County to attend opening night. After the show I asked him if he was reconsidering casting Harpo in *The Yellow Jacket*.

Meanwhile, word came from Marblehead that the theatre was promoting a shining cast, headed by Fay Wray and Alfred Drake, to pantomime the story while the Chorus (Woollcott) explained to the audience what they were doing. The Property Man (Harpo) would shove scenery around and help the actors create the illusion. It was explained to Harpo that in Oriental theatre the Property Man is not only mute, but he is also faceless. Dressed in black with a black cloth over his face, he pretty much functioned as a puppeteer, making it all work but remaining anonymous. Harpo agreed to the pretense of invisibility, but there would be no nonsense about covering his face. Aleck assured Harpo that all his movements were described in the script, so he wouldn't even have to attend more than the last two days of rehearsal. Knowing Harpo's indifference to detail, I asked if he would wear his traditional wig. "Oh," he said, an indication that he hadn't thought about it, but would. That was all until a few nights later when dinner was called. He said, "You all go on in, I'll be right down." In less than a minute he reappeared, wearing a bald hair cover with a huge orange-red braid hanging down his back. "Westmore," he said. There would be no doubt in the audience that the Property Man was Harpo. Subtle? It was Harpo at work, creating an image no one else would think of. The Westmore family, renowned for theatrical makeup and hair pieces, always made Harpo's curly wigs, so it was logical for them to perform the "Orientalizing" of Harpo. To my great relief, Woollcott roared his approval.

Aleck had rented a house for us all in the beautiful seaport town of Marblehead, complete with lobster dinners. It was so wonderful we thought about doing it every summer. It was an interesting understanding Aleck had with the owner, a pleasant elderly New England man, who would be allowed to keep a bedroom for himself in return for cooking and keeping house for our distinguished group. Nice arrangement, right? Not right! I don't know why Aleck got it into his head that the man was not to use the bathroom. There was an embarrassing confrontation when Aleck said to him that he could keep a pot in his room, or go next door, or just control himself! Whatever choice he made, he never braved Woollcott again. Very few people ever did. He was a terror when opposed but adored by those he couldn't intimidate. The strong enjoyed his tantrums; the insecure stayed away. The best part was always watching him making overtures to get back into good graces, like a child who has been naughty. Needless to say, the gentleman in Marblehead would not rent his house to Aleck and his friends ever again.

We arrived in Marblehead during the last week of rehearsals. Harpo watched one rehearsal and then announced he'd never seen anything so boring, and not only was he not going to attend any more rehearsals, but he also wouldn't even watch the play during the run. Woollcott thundered, "How the hell are you going to answer your cues?" Harpo, master of the art of simplification, said simply, "Susan will take care of it." Aleck glared at me. "What's this? What are you . . .?" I had no idea, but I knew Harpo would think of something, so I smiled confidently, shrugged, and said to Aleck, "Don't worry." Hey, maybe it would work—and after a day in the lone antique shop in Marblehead, I was beginning to wonder what to do between lobster dinners anyway.

Working with his brothers on stage, Harpo had been pretty undisciplined. The Marx Brothers stuck to the script when the mood struck them, and they moved around the stage however they wanted to. In films the directors and cameramen put markers on the floor to keep the Marx Brothers in their shots. Harpo back on stage again, in a structured play, was a free soul needing a stage director. This would be simple. I would make large cue cards for the props he would use, place them in the property trunk that stood next to him at the edge of the stage, and leave him on his own. This would have worked if he had looked at the cards, but that meant paying attention to the action, which he refused to do. The best alternative was to go home, but he was having too good a time aggravating Woollcott.

The solution was so ridiculous that it fit the play perfectly. I became the Property Man's Property Man. Harpo was seated on a stool just on stage by the side drape. For each performance I was to stand behind him, screened by the curtain, and whisper his cues. For the first few performances, Harpo was satisfied to sit in his place and pretend to fall asleep as if bored by the play, forcing the actors to think of business to attract his attention. I certainly couldn't reach out from behind the curtain to poke him. After a few complaints he decided to give his role some characterization by smoking a cigarette as he worked with the props. But he'd given up smoking a few years earlier. He'd gone to see Sam Hirschfield about a dry cough and trouble swallowing. Sam noticed a dark spot at the back of Harpo's throat and told him to stop smoking for two weeks and see him again. All of his symptoms and the spot were gone when Sam checked him out again, so Harpo quit smoking permanently. For his smoking effect in *The Yellow Jacket*, Harpo had cigarettes made of chalk in different lengths. Starting out with the king size, he palmed it in what he called an inspired bit of acting to switch to a shorter length. I hadn't quit smoking yet, so he had me complete the illusion by blowing smoke at his chalk cigarette from offstage. This was so silly and his asides to me so hilarious, I was convulsed and coughing most of the time. I think he enjoyed playing to me more than the audience.

Woollcott was so relieved when I seemed to have Harpo under control that he ignored us. He was in heaven. In his Mandarin costume he strutted about and, as it was narrative not dialogue, he was allowed to read his lines from a script he carried around the stage. Harpo had little respect for this artistry and, as Aleck became more and more inflated by his mastery of stage craft, Harpo showed signs of restiveness. It was just a matter of time. One night after having led a nonexistent horse on stage, Harpo decided to clean up after it. Encouraged by the delight of the audience, he pursued a nonexistent fly into unlikely places while the actors sensibly stood immobilized until Harpo would calm down and let them resume the action. Everyone was amused, except Aleck. He was purple with rage, not recognizing what a welcome relief this was to a bewildered audience who thought they had come to see a play about yellow fever in Central America but instead were being horribly bored by a Chinese fantasy.

Aleck felt, as the star, that he ought to gain control. So, instead of waiting it out, he tried to resume reading his script as if Harpo wasn't there. But the audience was making such a racket he couldn't be heard. Finally, he blew up and chased after Harpo trying to bat him with his script. Never before or after has *The Yellow Jacket* been such a hit, especially to all his dear friends who had come up from New York to watch Aleck give them pointers in acting. Lovely, except for the final scene in the dressing room after the show. Aleck flung open the door and blistered the walls with a tirade on professionalism, ethics, and courtesy. He was still screeching when friends started to come backstage, gasping with laughter and insisting the new business should be incorporated into the script. Extravagant compliments were heaped on Woollcott for his forceful portrayal, which appeased him somewhat. But only after Harpo promised to be good the rest of the run were we allowed to go home for supper. *The Yellow Jacket* mercifully closed at the end of that crazy week, and we all headed immediately to Neshobe Island for the rest of the summer—and the relative peace of Aleck's comparatively calm croquet-inspired screaming fits.

CHAPTER EIGHT

The Beverly Hills Population Explosion

BACK HOME IT WAS CLEAR THAT HARPO'S LIFE OF LEISURE WOULD soon drive one, or both, of us crazy. Those two weeks in summer stock—no matter how ridiculous—reminded Harpo of the thrill he got from an audience adoring him. He talked about calling the William Morris Agency to see if that nightclub tour offer was still good, but he didn't actually make the call. Then everything suddenly changed—and not just for us. December 7, 1941—or as FDR called it, "a date which will live in infamy." The war in Europe had been going on for a few years, and Americans were divided on whether or not we should get involved. The Japanese attack on Pearl Harbor quickly brought everyone together.

People such as Walt Disney, Henry Ford, and Charles Lindbergh had been with the America First Committee, dedicated to keeping America out of foreign wars. Harpo and his friends pointed out that a lot of the America First people were not exactly friends of the Jewish people. We had listened to a radio address by Lindbergh and were astonished by his overtly anti-Semitic remarks. America First had also been targeting the movie industry, claiming it produced propaganda to drum up support for America entering the war. Harpo always rooted for the little guy, so the oppressive governments in Germany and Japan naturally bothered him. But what puzzled him was that otherwise good people couldn't see them for what they were.

Very few Hollywood people were with America First, but the involvement of Walt Disney—a man Harpo liked—certainly caused a lot of discussion in our circle. Lillian Gish joined and then resigned—probably after getting a lot of criticism from her friends. Woollcott was no shrinking violet when it came to politics. He warned his radio audience about the rise of Adolf Hitler and fascism in 1935. The topic was controversial enough at the time that the makers of Cream of Wheat, his radio sponsor, canceled Aleck's contract. Harpo assured Aleck that the Marx household switched to the Mother Hubbard brand of hot wheat cereal immediately.

The American entry into the war snapped Hollywood into action. The America First Committee vanished almost overnight. The movie industry went to work for the war effort, mostly selling war bonds and entertaining soldiers. One of our friends took a more hands-on approach. Rose Hecht became a sheet metal worker in an aircraft factory. Harpo eagerly joined the parade of Hollywood celebrities who hit the road visiting bases and selling war bonds. I joined a group of Hollywood wives in making uniforms with my limited abilities as a seamstress. And my long-retired father took a job with Northrop in an aircraft factory. The war had an unusual effect on Hollywood. The community threw off its cover of privacy and opened canteens to entertain servicemen. A soldier could walk into the Hollywood Canteen and be served a soda by a well-known movie star. Stars routinely visited the wounded in hospitals and performed shows there just as often. It was a strangely gracious time when we somehow lost our fear of strangers. That dreadful war created a kinship that opened the doors to our homes and let us invite people we didn't know in for dinner.

Harpo entertained the troops at bases around southern California on a fairly regular basis, but he also went on the road to visit camps and hospitals around the country. It was important work and it reinvigorated him. But he received sad news during his travels. His longtime friend, novelist Alice Duer Miller, confided to Woollcott that she had cancer and would not live much longer. Aleck broke his promise not to tell anyone and wired the news to Harpo and Charlie Lederer, feeling that she was so close with them that she wouldn't object. In between camp shows, Harpo traveled to New York. He and Charlie got there just in time. They visited with her for three days. On the first night Alice fell asleep listening to the Brooklyn Dodgers beating her beloved New York Giants. The next morning, she asked Harpo how the Giants did. He spared her the news of her team's loss and told her the Giants had won. The following day, Alice couldn't speak and communicated by squeezing Harpo's hand. She died that evening. Woollcott remarked to his old friends from the Algonquin, "I'll see Alice before any of you do."

Harpo, always with an eye on his own mortality, was shaken. His old friends were dying. It had been just a year since Sam Harris, the great Broadway producer, died. Sam's numerous hit shows included *The Cocoanuts*, *Animal Crackers*, and *The Man Who Came to Dinner*. Another Algonquin pal, Heywood Broun, had died a couple of years before at the age of fifty-one. He and Harpo were the same age. Broun was one of the unhealthiest people I had ever laid eyes on, but this didn't make Harpo any less worried. There had been plenty of bad news in 1942, and it seemed to keep coming. The great illustrator and painter Neysa McMein, another dear friend of Harpo's, fell down a flight of stairs while sleepwalking and suffered a broken back. She needed several operations and never fully recovered. Woollcott had just been in a Boston hospital for gall bladder surgery, and the frequent medical talk had Harpo thinking about his own mortality. He was ready to plan his own funeral, but my hypochondriac was actually doing just fine.

Woollcott convalesced at Neshobe Island that summer, and soon after Alice's death we made our annual visit. Aleck was devoted to the little nearby town of Castleton, Vermont, and served on the board of directors of their public library. He quietly provided financial support and donated numerous books that had been sent to him to review. But he also got involved with helping young people from the town get scholarships and other opportunities. During our visit Aleck introduced us to a sixteen-year-old boy named Robert Cole who had worked for him that summer doing odd jobs around the island. He was the son of Castleton's head librarian. Aleck convinced Harpo to take Robert on his upcoming tour of military bases in the south. Harpo said he'd be happy to have someone to carry his wig and horn. This was all arranged with the boy's school. It was the sort of thing Woollcott did that no one ever knew about.

Over dinner on our first night, Aleck complained about having to take nitroglycerine pills for his heart and asked Harpo to share every detail of his last moments with Alice. They paid tribute to this grand lady they both adored. We made it a short stay, since Harpo was due to get back on the road. It turned out to be the last time we saw Alexander Woollcott. Harpo spoke to him over the phone a few times during the fall southern tour and made sure to call him on January 19 because failing to remember Aleck's birthday was an unforgivable offense. While touring bases in New England, four days after Aleck turned fifty-six, Harpo learned that his dear friend had died after having a heart attack during a radio broadcast in New York.

I met Harpo in New York, and we attended the memorial service at Columbia University the following week. Three hundred people braved a blizzard to be there. Paul Robeson recited the 23rd Psalm and Ruth Gordon delivered one of several eulogies. Neysa McMein, still recovering from spinal surgery, came in a wheelchair. Bea and George Kaufman, Dorothy Parker, Moss Hart, Katherine Cornell, and Helen Keller were among the mourners. After the service a small group headed to—where else?—the Algonquin. Harpo, on the verge of tears, was ashen and barely said a word. George Kaufman and Dorothy Parker slugged back a few strong cocktails. Bea Kaufman, Moss Hart, and I were crying. The Algonquin Round Table, long a relic of the past, now officially ceased to exist. The only other time I had ever seen Harpo so consumed with grief was when Frenchy died.

A few months after Aleck died, Harpo was back to work for the USO, staying close to home at first, visiting bases and hospitals in southern California. Billy was now a healthy six-year-old and we took him along on several of these trips when he wasn't in school. I began to worry. Having been an only child, I knew it wasn't good for Billy to carry the burden of being the focus of all the attentions and anxieties of his parents. We had been so engrossed with Billy and our new life that we had let too many years slip by. Sibling relationships round out a family. And we were also guilty of spoiling Billy. He would benefit from some of our attention going to someone else. The time had come for us to get on with our family shopping. And Harpo could benefit from an injection of new life into the atmosphere. He was still in the dumps about losing Woollcott.

That summer everything fell into place and before I knew what hit me, I was in an upper berth on a train in Utah with a two-week-old baby staring up at me. There was never a thought of naming this child anything but Alexander. Billy was thrilled by the arrival of his little brother, but more importantly, Harpo was captivated. New life. He desperately needed it, and Alexander Marx had made himself comfortable in Harpo's lap at the perfect time. When Alex joined us, Billy was a six-year-old baseball player. Our poodle, Charlie, suddenly abandoned chasing Billy's errant throws in favor of taking his position alongside Alex's crib. It was Billy's first experience of not getting all the attention. Charlie had answered some ancient instinct and given up leaping the garden wall for a night of bumming around the village and settled himself beside this helpless puppy, to protect it until it could take care of itself.

We settled into our new routine, but by Alex's first birthday it was obvious that he didn't have much in common with his older brother, who was now playing organized baseball in the Cub Scout League and didn't need Charlie to get his ball anymore. Alex needed someone closer to his own age, and I wanted a girl. It didn't seem like it would work out at first. The adoption agency people were more concerned with the genetic background and were trying for a match in that department, so the baby girl I went to see was not made available. They held a conference and then led me to another room to see a new baby who hadn't been processed yet. I couldn't believe my eyes! No one has ever produced a more adorable baby. He was picture perfect—round in every part and smiling happily. This child brought a new element to our odd collection of personalities. From the beginning, James Arthur Marx accepted everything with a gurgle of pleasure. Charlie accepted him as his new charge.

Then things began to speed up. We had just about changed two weeks of Jimmy's diapers (which had to be done quickly, as he could hit a target at three feet) when a phone call came from Gracie Allen. She and George were in New York visiting with her relatives in Poughkeepsie. Gracie had seen a beautiful little two-month-old girl with blazing green eyes who, sadly, had been orphaned that week. Gracie said, "You know the Irish. If you hurry before they close ranks around her, I think I can swing it for you." I said, "Harpo, what do you think?" He just smiled. I said, "Gracie, I've a better idea. Get a nurse and put them on the Super Chief." Irish and blazing green eyes—how could we miss? Four days later, a harried-looking woman and a screaming baby stepped off the train. The little demon didn't stop shrieking (not crying, mind you) until in her pink crib, when she promptly fell asleep. None of this dozing off business for her. Suddenly there was total silence. It was disconcerting. As I was standing there mentally wringing my hands over how I had messed up our marvelous conglomerate of a family, my parents arrived to see their new granddaughter. Leaning over the pink crib, Mother studied this image of sudden peace and said, "Oh, she's beautiful." I looked uncertainly and whispered, "Well, yes, asleep, but wait until she wakes up. This is no frightened baby, this is an angry hellion, and she hates me." Mother reassured me. "Relax. Let her have a nap. Then you may see a different child."

When the nap was over, Harpo was hanging over the crib laughing at me as I advanced carefully. "Wow!" he said. "Gracie was right about the green eyes." Then she laughed and held out her arms—to her grandmother. The two of them formed a lifelong bond with one look. There was no doubt our Minnie Susan Marx had come home. It was preordained that our daughter would be named Minnie. All of the Marx Brothers agreed they'd name their daughters after their mother. Chico's daughter, Maxine. Groucho's Miriam, and later on, Melinda. But as an acknowledgment of the special bond between Harpo and his mother, Minnie was reserved in case Harpo ever had a daughter. And now he had one. Harpo had a permanent smile on his face. And no amount of crying and diaper changing could do anything about it. The sudden expansion of our family necessitated full-time help, and we were lucky to find Agnes Millet, a remarkable tiny Irish woman, complete with tea leaves and second sight. She became a beloved member of the family.

Housing had to be attended to, so for starters we turned the master bedroom into a three-crib nursery where, as soon as she could stand by hanging on to the edge of her crib, Minnie reigned as queen. It became the entertainment center of the house. If Minnie was awake, it was playtime. She had her brothers standing on their heads and somersaulting before they could walk. Her tiny arms embraced us all. She had the most wonderful greeting for those she loved. Entering the nursery was something to look forward to. You knew Minnie would jump up and down in her crib until you were near enough for her to leap in the air, fling her arms around your neck, and clamp her legs around your waist in an all-out hug.

As we added Minnie and Jimmy to our family, Zeppo and Marion were adopting two boys, Tom and Tim. Marion and I would have a lot to talk about, and we were both thrilled to be able to share this experience. Competition was keen between the two families as to whose children exhibited earlier development. Let Tim gain a pound before Alex, the telephone rang. When Minnie got herself up on two feet before Tom, I called Marion. First words showed superior intelligence and we both lied. One major difference, though, was that for all of Harpo's enthusiasm about fatherhood and family, Zeppo went along with the adoptions to placate Marion, who was a great mother and did almost everything herself. I couldn't imagine a situation where Harpo wasn't thrilled by his children. Zeppo treated the notion of fatherhood like a present he had to get for his wife. Marion didn't complain—at least not to me. Playdates for Alex, Jimmy, and Minnie with their cousins Tom and Tim were a free-for-all. And the joy this brought Harpo was never shared by Zeppo, who rarely took part in these baby playdates.

In our wonderfully overprivileged small town of Beverly Hills, the number one danger was swimming pools. Every home had one gaping in the backyard. The community was stunned in 1943 when Lou Costello's one-year-old son fell into the family pool and drowned. We immediately fenced ours in. Certain survival called for swimming ability, the earlier the better. The Costello tragedy had me thinking we couldn't wait until all could walk, as Jimmy might not get off his belly until he decided to go somewhere else. I was inclined to follow the example of a friend who had started all six of her children on swimming lessons before they could walk. It worked for her, but Harpo stopped me cold when he pointed out that heavily chlorinated water is hardly the same comfortable environment as the nourishing liquid of the womb. We were very careful and waited a few years.

Eventually Billy, by this time a fine swimmer, was appointed instructor. After some breathing exercises in the bathtub, Billy said they were ready for the water wings. What a day that was. Harpo called in all the relatives for the big show. Jimmy was a natural. When Billy set him in the water, he took off like a rubber duck. (We shouldn't have been surprised—hadn't he been practicing on the carpet for a year?) Minnie was too excited to pay attention to the difference between kicking in water and running on land, so she had to be tied to a contraption that would let her do her splashing without turning over. And Alex? He didn't trust anyone to help him. Wrapped in two water wings, he made his own cautious way around the pool hanging on to the edge. They learned fast in their own way, and it was a relief when the fence could be taken away.

At about this same time, we decided they were ready for the big one—the subject of adoption. It had been necessary to wait for a reasonable degree of understanding of the English language to explain our family group. We wanted our children to see adoption as an implementation of choice. They must feel chosen before they understand the concept of birth, or their security might vanish. It's not uncommon for adoptive parents to be afraid to tell their children of their adoption until it's too late and the children have learned it from someone else.

"Are you really not my parents?"

"Who are you?"

"Who are my real parents?"

"Where are my real parents?"

"Did you kidnap me?"

"Who am I?"

We knew of a few such tragedies, so we started our hide-and-seek story game before maturity might create questions. Alex was a year older than Minnie and Jimmy, who were about two when we sat everyone on the nursery floor to present our first story of discovery. Starting with Alex, Harpo fancied up a suspenseful search over mountains and rivers, with gestures and faces that had them laughing with delight. It was so successful I aimed him at Jimmy, who was thrilled that his daddy was going to search for him. Then I was allowed to wink at Minnie, who was squealing with excitement. We wove an elaborate story about Poughkeepsie, New York, Aunt Gracie and the Irish relatives who gave their permission for her to live with us. If we ever tried to vary the stories, they would correct us. They had been planted firmly with the first account. It was clear. They had been wanted.

Relieved of our greatest concerns, I let fate take care of the rest. But not Harpo. He was a nervous father. His harp was set in the bay window, a vantage point from which he could survey the outdoor activities while he practiced. One morning he let out a roar. When I came running, he was almost speechless. He could see Minnie balancing herself on the ridge of the garage roof. It struck me funny, but he was frantic. To calm him down I said, "I'll get her down, but don't scare her or she'll fall." By the time I reached the back of the garden, she was down, but I had to pretend to be upset so she would promise her father never to do it again. Harpo ordered a Jungle-Gym for insurance. The garden became such a safe playground that a protective Harpo could look out of his window and smile to see Alex sitting comfortably in his swing ignoring Minnie, who might be hanging by her knees from the rings or shinnying up one of the standards. And Jimmy? He was perfectly happy to lay on his back in the grass and study the mockingbirds filling the air with their crazy laughter.

One day, back when we were still wondering if Jimmy would ever walk, Harpo said, "I'll bet I can make him move." While Jimmy watched, Harpo laid the garden hose on the ground in a wavy pattern and then turned on the water. Naturally, the hose started flopping around as if it were alive. Minnie was dancing with delight, while Alex watched doubtfully from a safe distance. Jimmy? He was on his knees at last, chasing this exciting thing that moved unpredictably by itself. Once the three of them got the hang of it, that hose was their best game that summer. With the grass hard on his knees, Jimmy was making an effort to walk. He had his motivation at last. The childlike part of Harpo was never more in evidence than when he related to the kids on their own level, which he loved to do.

CHAPTER NINE

Palestine's Man in Hollywood

W HILE WE WERE EXPANDING OUR FAMILY, WORLD WAR II WAS moving toward Allied victories in Germany and Japan. And FDR was running for a fourth term in the White House. Harpo's support for Roosevelt was unwavering, even in the face of criticism for him not stepping aside after three terms. Groucho felt strongly that FDR should have stepped aside after two terms and made it clear that he voted for Wendell Willkie in 1940. Willkie was actually a Democrat who switched parties to oppose Roosevelt's third term. Groucho and Harpo were both loyal Democrats, but Groucho voted Republican just that one time. After the election Groucho comforted himself by pointing out that since Willkie had switched parties, he didn't vote for a real Republican. He came back to FDR in 1944 because, like many 1940 Roosevelt detractors, Groucho felt we should not change presidents during a war. Many people, including Harpo, were worried about FDR's health, and there was a lot of talk that winning the election might ultimately be fatal for Roosevelt.

Harpo considered FDR a friend and wrote him occasionally, and the president certainly appreciated Harpo's work for the war effort. California governor Earl Warren (who would become Chief Justice of the Supreme Court years later) gave the keynote speech nominating Thomas Dewey at the 1944 Republican National Convention. After hearing the radio broadcast of the speech, Harpo sent this letter to FDR:

June 30, 1944

My dear Mr. President,

I listened to Governor Warren's address outlining the Republican platform and he stressed three points:

1. Win the war,
2. Bring back the boys,
3. Get them jobs.

I wonder if he thinks the Democratic platform is:

1. Lose the war,
2. Keep the boys over there,
3. Don't give them any jobs.

My best to you always.

> Harpistically yours,
> (Herbert Swope gave me that word.)
> Harpo Marx

To Harpo's delight, a letter from the White House arrived the following week:

July 7, 1944

Dear Harpo,

Thanks for your nice letter of the thirtieth. I'll bet if you tried to, you could play those six lines on your harp beautifully. It was good to hear from you.

> Very sincerely yours,
> Franklin D. Roosevelt

Harpo proudly showed the letter to just about everyone we knew. For the next several months the war news was good, and it was just a matter of time before it would end. But the world was stunned on April 12,

1945, by the news that FDR had died. While it may have seemed sudden, it could not have been unexpected for anyone close to FDR. His illnesses had been kept from the public, and we only learned years later how precarious his health was. His fourth term didn't even last three months. Harpo safely tucked away his cherished letter, which he considered one of his prized possessions. It would be under the new president, Harry S. Truman, that, in rapid succession, the Germans would surrender and two atomic bombs would hasten the Japanese surrender. And just like that the war was over.

Harpo resumed his life of leisure. He still did the occasional benefit or nightclub date but had traded in tours of military camps and hospitals for the joy of four kids running around our house. Those occasional nightclub bookings resulted in some interesting experiences. Playing New Orleans during Mardi Gras was wonderful, but we had a scary situation in Baltimore, at a dive called Walnut Grove that the William Morris Agency must not have checked too carefully. This joint was apparently well known to the musicians' union as a place where it might be difficult to get paid. On opening night union representatives wouldn't allow the musicians to sound a note unless they were paid in advance. Harpo looked at me confidently—like I'd had years of experience in arbitration—and said, "Tell them there's no show unless I get paid too." Who? Me? I was terrified. These men were probably mobsters. But Harpo had put the show in my hands, and I was angry enough to stride to the management office to be told that no one had come in yet. I couldn't think of anything else to do, so I sat down saying, "Fine, I'll wait. There will be no show until someone talks to me." In a few minutes a man arrived to assure me that everything would be fine. In return I assured him Harpo was a union musician—which I had just made him at that moment—and expected the same treatment as the band. After the show we left with the loot carefully wrapped in Harpo's overcoat. I sat in the back of the car clutching the hotel key in a way the driver might mistake for a gun if he glanced in his rearview mirror.

Harpo was content with working only occasionally, but there came a situation that was eerily similar to that time when Woollcott called and dragged Harpo into summer stock. This time the call came from Chico.

All Harpo had to do was say yes, and the Marx Brothers would be back in business. Gummo had made all the arrangements. The joke within the family had always been that Harpo would vote with whichever brother talked to him last. Chico was taking no chances. He kept calling to see if Harpo had changed his mind after tentatively voting for a Marx Brothers reunion. Chico had the most at stake in this because Groucho and Harpo were financially set and didn't need to work as the Marx Brothers. Chico's gambling debts could at least be temporarily covered by his share of a new Marx Brothers movie. But he'd probably lose whatever he stood to earn well in advance of the movie being completed.

Once Harpo confirmed that Groucho had signed on, he let Gummo know he was on board. Before anyone could change their mind, there were script conferences and rehearsals in advance of a two-week tour. As happy as Harpo was being retired, I remembered how the audiences in summer stock, and more recently at the camp shows, had energized him. My boy was still a ham. They would play in San Diego and Oakland to test scenes as they had in the past. Groucho had just remarried, and he was taking his new bride on the tour. The wedding was at our house, and it didn't take long for it to turn into a Marx family sing-along. There was a lot of talk at the wedding about the boys getting back into the movies and hitting the road. Harpo asked if I wanted to come along. It was only two weeks but leaving the kids didn't seem like a good idea to me, even though my parents volunteered to take care of everything if I decided to go. I suggested to Harpo that Groucho agreed to the tour because it was a free honeymoon. He shrugged and gave no indication that I was wrong. Kay was lovely and Groucho got her a small part in the show. She was only a few years older than Groucho's daughter, Miriam. I was tempted to warn her about Groucho's tendency to humiliate those closest to him, but I kept these thoughts to myself. She'd either figure that out for herself or somehow miraculously tame the master insulter. I would be rooting for her.

Harpo thought the script was very good, and the brothers began filming *A Night in Casablanca* full of confidence. Harpo proudly brought the kids to the set and showed them off to every technician and extra. As the shooting wore on, the confidence started to fade, and they couldn't finish the picture fast enough. As quickly as they could, the Marx Brothers retired again. Harpo was happy to resume occasional diaper duty. It was better than an early call to the set. Groucho was suddenly in the same boat, as he and Kay supplied our kids with another cousin when Melinda was born shortly after the release of *A Night in Casablanca*. We had a pretty full schedule of birthday parties in the Marx family in those days.

Among Groucho's wedding guests were Rose and Ben Hecht. By this time Ben was a celebrated playwright, screenwriter, and two-time Academy Award winner. Hecht, along with Woollcott, was among the first prominent people to shine a light on fascism in Europe and the plight of the Jewish people there. Even before the American entry into the war, Hecht joined a committee dedicated to forming a Jewish army in Palestine and ending the League of Nations' mandate for British occupation there. In 1943 he wrote *We Will Never Die*, a celebration of Jewish contributions to civilization from Moses to Einstein. It was staged at Madison Square Garden in New York City and also played in large arenas in Washington, Boston, Philadelphia, and Chicago before we got to see it at the Hollywood Bowl.

The show was designed to drum up support for a free Palestine but was advertised as a mass memorial for the two million Jews slaughtered by the Nazis in Europe. (That number would roughly triple by the end of the war, but that's where we were when Ben Hecht ramped up his efforts.) The great showman Billy Rose produced the show, which was directed by Moss Hart. Director Ernst Lubitsch also helped, and Kurt Weill wrote the music. Many of Hollywood's greatest actors read Hecht's words on stage. Edward G. Robinson, Paul Henreid, John Garfield, Edward Arnold, Akim Tamiroff, Joan Leslie, and Claude Rains were featured at the Hollywood show. Most of the movie industry was there—Jack Warner, Louis B. Mayer, Mervyn LeRoy, and many other studio executives were prominently seated up front. Harpo and I sat in Sam Goldwyn's box, and at several points in the show I could see Harpo and Sam in tears.

Privately, Hecht told Harpo that many of these Jewish movie moguls were reluctant to donate to the cause out of fear of offending the European distributors of their films. But they were happy to show up and have their names in the paper as supporters of a free Palestine. It really didn't make sense. Harpo was greatly moved by Ben's passion and told him of the anti-Semitism he witnessed in Europe and Russia in 1933. Harpo offered to help. He recognized that Ben was really sticking his neck out, and, like Ben, Harpo felt his Jewish heritage very strongly in the face of persecution. Harpo had a very strong humanitarian conscience, and he supported Palestine's efforts for statehood and freedom—but not necessarily through diplomacy.

When Ben became the chairman of the American League for a Free Palestine, Harpo wrote a generous check. Through Ben we met Peter Bergson, the American representative of Irgun Zvai Leumi, the underground Jewish liberation group in Palestine. Bergson was fundraising in Hollywood, and Harpo donated money to such organizations as the Emergency Committee to Save the Jewish People of Europe and the Hebrew Committee of National Liberation. These groups passed the money on to Irgun, which was considered by many to be a terrorist group. To put it mildly, Irgun was controversial. The more socially acceptable Jewish liberation group in Palestine was Haganah. This organization was mostly loyal to the British even though the colonial British government would not allow European Jewish refugees to emigrate to Palestine. Haganah would gradually pull back in its support of the British, but it was not enough for the strong-willed supporters of Irgun.

Harpo and Ben favored Irgun, which was started by men of deep passion with no confidence in achieving freedom through diplomacy. The men of Irgun had numbers branded on their arms in the Nazi death camps. They came to the United States to secretly obtain weapons of war. These men found the world of entertainment especially responsive. We met Menachem Begin, a leader of Irgun, who later became prime minister of Israel. Begin's purpose and character had been steeled in the dreadful prisons of Siberia. Begin described for us the terrible privations designed to destroy the will of prisoners. He told how the intellectuals devised mental games of cards and chess to protect their reason, and he graphically recalled his escape and perilous journey on foot across the frozen wastes of Siberia towards Palestine. This was a man of powerful purpose.

On the other side of Irgun's fight for statehood were the people who supported resettlement of the Jews in Palestine without independence. In the early days of fundraising for resettlement under British rule, Harpo and I attended a dinner in Beverly Hills. We heard conservative Zionists who believed the resettlement of Jews could be handled through diplomatic channels with Great Britain. Harpo, as usual, listened intently, analyzing the questions and answers in his quiet way without taking part. I had nothing to say. I wasn't even very interested in the discussion. International politics was beyond me, but being a devoted Harpo watcher, I enjoyed looking at his face for clues as to how he was reacting. I had no idea whether he was listening with an open mind or if he already knew where he stood. Finally, dinner over, we came to the main event. Our host went around the table asking for pledges. When he came to Harpo, Harpo said yes, he would contribute. Not in the astronomical figures he had heard the great industrialists pledge, but whatever he gave he would also match with a donation to support Irgun. There was a shocked silence. "Diplomacy," he went on to say, "has never stopped any wars that I am aware of. Gentlemen, without Irgun we won't have any Jews to support—only dead settlers." That was my Harpo, trusting his judgment without prevarication. On the way home he explained, "There are some people trying to bet on every horse in the race. It's not logical or good economics to throw money into a whirlpool of indecision. If they want a Jewish state, that's what they should say with their money." That was a long statement for a pantomimist—who had actually just donated money to two organizations with drastically different philosophies.

Obviously, money for the support of Irgun couldn't be raised publicly. The United States hadn't decided where they stood, but it was clearly not with the underground group, Irgun. Harpo and Hecht reasoned that if planes needed to defend the settlers were to go to the underground, then the money should come from the underworld. At that time the boss of the local underworld in Los Angeles was Mickey Cohen, a sentimental little man who could be reduced to tears by a well-worded plea for help. Mickey's public business was a haberdashery shop in Hollywood, and that's where Harpo went to introduce himself and talk about the urgent need to get planes across the ocean. Harpo reported back that Cohen, through his tears, had expressed his delight in being called on and immediately put in motion plans for an evening at Slapsie Maxie's, a Hollywood nightclub. Slapsie Maxie was actually Maxie Rosenbloom, an ex-boxer turned movie actor. He specialized in playing dim-witted or punch-drunk characters. Cohen was also an ex-boxer, and he was very affectionate toward Maxie and helped him a lot. Maxie was the front man at Slapsie Maxie's, but Mickey Cohen actually owned the place.

The guest list would include everyone Cohen knew in Los Angeles. His friends would either have money or know how to get it. Mickey said it would be his pleasure to pick up the tab. He was true to his word. Two weeks later we entered the enormous room, jammed with scary types who were not about to offend our new friend, Mickey Cohen. Among the guests was notorious mob figure Benny Siegel—better known as Bugsy—and his girlfriend, Virginia Hill. It was only a couple of months after our fundraiser that he was gunned down at Hill's home. They seemed like a nice quiet couple, and Benny made a generous pledge for the cause. I honestly didn't know who he was until Harpo explained things to me on the way home. Zeppo and Marion joined us for the evening and arrived a little after we did. I was surprised to see Zeppo cruise around the room greeting many of the scariest looking of Mickey Cohen's pals as if they had been lifelong friends. I asked Harpo about it and all he said was, "Yeah. That's Zep."

Lou Holtz, a headline comedian of vaudeville and Broadway musicals who had done several USO shows with Harpo, elected himself master of ceremonies. After a speech by Ben Hecht, Lou would entertain a little, then open it up for pledges. No problem, he assured Harpo. He had done this many times. I was nervous. Having been in *Manhattan Mary* on Broadway with Lou twenty years earlier, I knew he was not a fast-paced comic like Milton Berle. Lou was not one of those who can search around in their bag of one-liners until they find what their audience will laugh at. Lou was a storyteller. Eventually he would get to a punch line, but his audiences laughed hardest at the buildup and his marvelous mimicry, spiced with dialect. Would this hard-faced bunch know what he's talking about? No, they wouldn't. After a quiet five minutes, Lou signaled for help and, bless him forever, Mickey Cohen jumped up on the stage, saying, "That was great, Lou. Now I'll take over."

Taking the microphone, he said, "First, I'm gonna tell you why you're here, and then, what we're gonna do about it." Mickey had murmured to me, "These mugs don't know nothin' but they'll come up with the money if I don't give them time to think of an out." For two minutes he described the urgency in Palestine, then in full command he looked around the room. Pointing at a fearful-looking man, he started his pitch, "Okay, Joey, what are you giving to send the first plane to Palestine?" Joey reluctantly offered three thousand dollars. "That ain't enough, you're giving fifteen grand." Joey just said, "Okay." He didn't really care. Mickey went from table to table like that, getting more and more forceful as his pride in demonstrating his success grew. The take was enormous, and Mickey Cohen made sure that it was all collected. I'm not saying they provided an air force that night. Only beat-up planes were available, and a lot of them disappeared south of the border on their circuitous journey as they were smuggled from somewhere near Los Angeles into Palestine. But that was to be expected. Those that did get across helped in a war that governments pretended didn't exist.

Harpo never seemed the least bit nervous about his involvement in this crazy plan to ferry planes from the United States through an underground network in South America to a secret air force in the land that would soon become the state of Israel—all funded by the organized crime community of Los Angeles and a bunch of Hollywood movie stars, writers, and comedians! Ben Hecht was already in trouble because of his outspoken support of Palestine's independence from Great Britain. In England, Ben's credit was removed from any of the films he'd written when they played there. Why Ben and Harpo weren't arrested for sub-version was a mystery to me. Spies were looking under every bed in those days. My guess is that some people in high places approved of what Ben and Harpo had done. Around a year after our night at Slapsie Maxie's, the British withdrew from Palestine, and the United States officially recognized the newly formed state of Israel. Harpo was justifiably proud. He'd picked a winner. The American League for a Free Palestine was dissolved, and Irgun became a political party in Israel. At a celebratory dinner in New York, Menachem Begin toasted Ben Hecht, saying, "You are the man most hated by the British. We are two of a kind."

Ben and Harpo became very close during their days as international covert operatives. Ben was one of the best story men in the business, and Harpo mentioned to him that he might want to try making a movie without his brothers. Word got around that Harpo might be available, and Burt Lancaster offered him a part in a project he described as a combination of Robin Hood and William Tell. I don't recall the discussion going very far, but the film turned out to be *The Flame and the Arrow*, a box office hit for Lancaster. Around the same time Gregory Peck called with an offer for Harpo to appear in a play at the La Jolla Playhouse. Harpo didn't take these offers seriously, although it wouldn't have been so bad for him to play a supporting role in a hit film at this point. But Harpo's discussions with Ben Hecht continued, and he was very serious about the opportunity to get a film scenario out of him.

We took a Florida vacation and stopped in New York on our way to Miami so Harpo could meet up with Ben. They came up with an idea called "Bryant Park" about an old vaudeville rehearsal hall. I don't think Ben ever actually wrote it, but it somehow got into the press that they were cooking up a project together. Later on, Ben asked if Harpo would consider a speaking role; maybe something without his traditional costume. Harpo felt it might be time to move on and try something new—after turning down an obscene sum of money for uttering one word in *A Night in Casablanca*. Ben had an idea that he thought would be perfect for Harpo. A few weeks later a package arrived from Nyack, New York. In a small notepad, written out in longhand with a pencil, was a scenario that Ben called "Please Die!" Harpo and I were puzzled by the title, and I began to read it aloud.

It was the darkest of dark comedies and concerned a struggling playwright who can't get his play produced. He's on the verge of a breakdown and becomes ill. His devoted wife contacts an old boyfriend who happens to work for a famous eccentric producer. The idea is developed that the playwright is dying and the producer would have a huge hit if the play opened after the playwright died. But the writer's failing health doesn't pan out. Learning of the plan to produce his play, he makes a miracu-

With my parents, Bill and Bunny Fleming, around 1910.

My first professional photo shoot for
Ziegfeld's Palm Beach Nights, 1926.

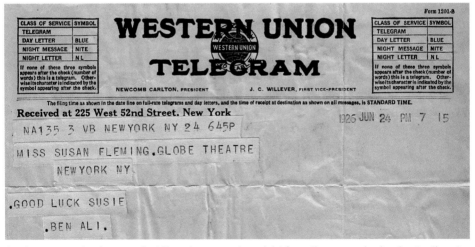

A telegram received on my first Broadway opening night from the man who inadvertantly set
up my first movie opportunity.

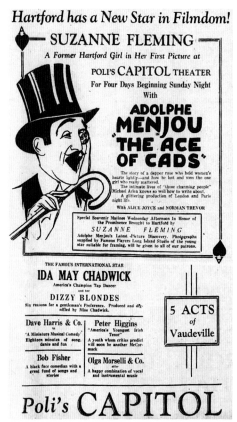

We did not live in Hartford long enough for me
to have deserved this.

With Adolphe Menjou in *The Ace of Cads*,
my film debut, shot during the Broadway run
of *Ziegfeld's American Revue*, 1926.

With Paulette Goddard in Ziegfeld's *Rio Rita*,
1927.

The Broadway stars of *Manhattan Mary* as seen by *New York American* caricaturist Ken Browne, 1927.

A modeling job for Lord & Taylor during the Broadway run of *Manhattan Mary*, September 1927.

Near the end of the Broadway run of *Manhattan Mary* in 1928, I became a "cover girl."

Around the time of *George White's Scandals*, 1929.

At RKO with Edna May Oliver in *Ladies of the Jury*, 1932.

At Paramount with W. C. Fields in *Million Dollar Legs*, 1932.

The cast of *Million Dollar Legs*: Ben Turpin, Jack Oakie, Lyda Roberti, Susan Fleming, W. C. Fields, and Hugh Herbert.

At Paramount on the set of *He Learned about Women*, with Alison Skipworth and director Lloyd Corrigan, 1932.

'HE LEARNED ABOUT WOMEN'

STUART ERWIN-ALISON SKIPWORTH
SUSAN FLEMING *a Paramount Picture*

For a brief period at Paramount, I was considered a star on the rise, but I managed to fight my way back to bit parts pretty quickly.

Shortly after meeting Harpo in 1932. The rest of the gang includes Fredric March and his wife, Florence Eldridge, at the upper left. The others are a faded memory.

Caught by a newspaper photographer during one of our early dates.

Harpo living it up in Leningrad in the fall of 1933 while I toiled away in Hollywood wondering if he would ever come home.

A golf outing with Groucho and Ruth, around 1934.

Out on the town with Harpo, around 1935.

From the hastily arranged M-G-M photo shoot to announce our September wedding in November 1936.

If Louella Parsons says we got married on September 26, it must be true. But we did it again on the 28th just to be sure.

Harpo samples the water at the Biltmore Hotel, Santa Barbara, California, 1936.

At a movie premiere in 1937 with M-G-M publicity head (and lyricist extraordinaire) Howard Dietz, his wife, Tanis, and M-G-M costume designer Gilbert Adrian. Note Harpo's cigarette. This is just before he quit smoking.

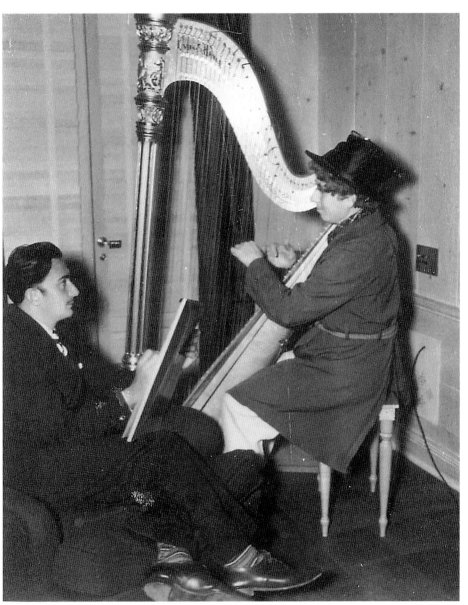

Salvador Dali sketching Harpo, February 1937.

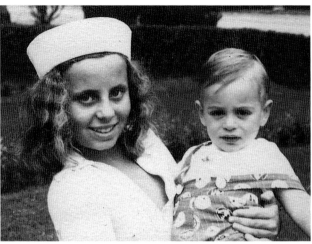

Billy's favorite babysitter, Groucho's daughter Miriam.

Billy makes us a trio, 1938.

Visiting the set of *At the Circus* in 1939 with my father, who ended up in the film as an extra.

Bucks County, Pennsylvania: Moss Hart, George S. Kaufman, and Harpo in *The Man Who Came to Dinner*, July 1941.

Marblehead, Massachusetts: Harpo in *The Yellow Jacket*, August 1941.

With Alexander Woollcott at Neshobe Island, Vermont, summer 1941.

Harpo teaching Billy the tricks of the trade.

Doing my part for the war effort, May 1944.

Our first Christmas as a sextet—Jimmy, Alex, Minnie, and Billy, 1944.

On the set of *A Night in Casablanca*: Chico, Alex, Groucho, Jimmy, Billy, Harpo, and Minnie, fall 1945.

On the set of *Love Happy* with Billy, director David Miller, and Ben Hecht, 1948.

Chico and Harpo met the press at the train station in London before we even checked into our hotel, 1949.

A publicity photo for Chico and Harpo's four-week engagement at the London Palladium, 1949.

Chico conducts and Harpo plays "I'm Forever Blowing Bubbles" at the London Palladium, 1949.

Harpo's 1950 tour program.

Christmas 1952: Billy, Alex, Minnie, and Jimmy.

Heavyweight champion Rocky Marciano takes a punch from Harpo. That's Mary Dee with Chico.

Harpo takes a lunch break during the construction of El Rancho Harpo.

I don't know what's going on here, but I'm sure it wasn't my idea.

At Tamarisk Country Club in Palm Springs around 1958.

Harpo and Rowland Barber, coauthor of *Harpo Speaks!*

Harpo spent most of his time painting after a couple of heart attacks cut back his performance schedule.

Harpo in his only dramatic role, as a deaf-mute in *A Silent Panic*, 1960.

The 1962 graduating class at Palm Springs High School included Alex, Jimmy, and Minnie. I can't explain why Minnie is the only graduate in this photo.

A celebratory graduation dinner with Jimmy, Minnie, Alex, and Harpo's new toupee. Jack Benny and George Burns brought their wigmaker to lunch and Harpo didn't want to be impolite. He wore it only a few times and concluded that wearing a wig on stage was enough.

Cowboy Harpo and his gang at El Rancho Harpo.

Erle Krasna (wife of Norman) helps Harpo with his golf swing.

Mary and Chico finally got married on August 22, 1958—after a seventeen-year courtship. I have no explanation for the photo.

Harpo and Bill in a jam session at the bay window of El Rancho Harpo.

Harpo crowns me with a Harpo wig at the *Harpo Speaks!* pubication party at the Algonquin Hotel, 1961.

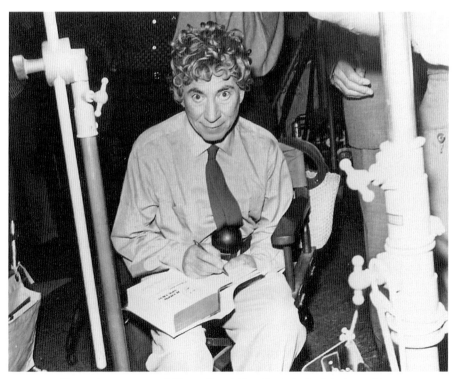

Harpo signs a copy of *Harpo Speaks!* on the set of a televison show.

Harpo sent this photo of himself at the Harry S. Truman Forest near Tel Aviv to President Truman.

The record of the trees Harpo and I planted in Israel.

A beautiful portrait of Harpo near the end of his life.

Bill and I presented Isaac Stern with a donation in Harpo's honor at the International Harp Festival in Israel, 1965.

1965: Bill and I retracing the steps I took with Harpo two years earlier.

MOM and DAD

IN THE PEOPLE'S CORNER
INTRODUCING . . .

SUSAN MARX

"SUSAN MARX
WILL BE THE BEST ASSEMBLYWOMAN WE WILL EVER HAVE!"

- BILL MARX
- JIM MARX
- MINNIE MARX
- ALEX MARX

- We know because she raised us, fed us, wiped our noses, put us through school and loved us.

BILL, JIM, MINNIE and ALEX

URGE
YOU
TO

VOTE NOVEMBER 3, 1970

| SUSAN MARX STATE ASSEMBLY | |

YOUR NEXT ASSEMBLYWOMAN FROM THE 75th DISTRICT

"She is truly the champion of the people."
—U.S. Congressman
JOHN V. TUNNEY

Jimmy was my campaign manager, and Harpo made a posthumous appearance on this flyer.

On the campaign trail in 1970 with former vice president Hubert H. Humphrey.

The gang visiting their mom in 1996: Minnie, Bill, Jimmy, and Alex.

lous recovery and puts the whole enterprise in jeopardy. Ben hadn't told Harpo which character he'd play, but it was pretty clear that he had the eccentric producer in mind for him. It certainly would have been interesting, but Harpo decided to remain silent and hang on to the iconic costume for his next film. This did not surprise me. What surprised me was that he also ended up hanging on to Groucho and Chico.

Ben took it in stride when Harpo didn't feel that "Please Die!" was the right vehicle for him. Ben was so prolific that I'm sure he quickly forgot about "Please Die!"—which, to my knowledge, never progressed past Ben's handwritten notepad. (I had certainly forgotten it until I found it many years later.) Harpo had a story idea of his own that Ben liked and agreed to write. They formed a partnership for the production, which had many different titles, but was called *Diamonds on the Sidewalk* early on. It was lovely on paper, but this project would cause Harpo so much aggravation that I encouraged him to drop it entirely on more than one occasion. This had nothing to do with Ben, who actually saved the project by convincing Harpo that the story could still be what they had envisioned as outside forces conspired against the original idea of a Harpo Marx film without his brothers.

The source of Harpo's trouble was mostly producer Lester Cowan, who was brought on board by Gummo. Cowan started floating the idea of getting Groucho and Chico involved almost from the start. This idea was planted in Cowan's head by Gummo, who decided that he would become a producer when he heard that Ben Hecht was writing something for Harpo. Cowan apparently got the financing for the film from his new production partner Mary Pickford, one of the owners of United Artists. Mary thought from the start that she was getting a Marx Brothers picture. Harpo seemed to be the last person to know that the Marx Brothers were reuniting—again.

CHAPTER TEN

London, 1949

Once Chico heard that Harpo was going to make a movie, the game was on. Harpo had trouble saying no to Chico, and Gummo was pushing Harpo to include him in the project. Chico had recently suffered a heart attack—or at least we thought he had. A reporter called our house to ask about it and Harpo, having not heard the news, was puzzled and worried. We soon learned that Chico had taken ill after his opening in Las Vegas, but Gummo cleared it all up, explaining that Chico wanted to get out of his contract for the Las Vegas engagement—probably for gambling reasons—and faked the heart attack. Harpo was furious. This was the last straw—until it wasn't. I would have thought Gummo, our medical expert, would be the most upset since he also got Chico the Las Vegas booking. But he just acted like faking a heart attack was perfectly normal. Harpo, the avowed hypochondriac, thought Chico was crazy for tempting fate with something so serious. But pretty soon Lester Cowan and Gummo were negotiating to get Groucho on board so they could turn Harpo's movie into a Marx Brothers picture.

Harpo realized that Cowan had planned this all along, correctly figuring that there was more money in three Marx Brothers than one. But Harpo's original contract with Ben Hecht called for the project to star Harpo Marx, and Cowan was bound by that deal if he wanted to use Ben's script. So, the plan was to have Chico in a supporting part and Groucho as the narrator, appearing on camera only briefly at the beginning and end of the picture. Harpo was not pleased but still thought it might work, mostly because Ben felt that Groucho and Chico could be easily worked in without sacrificing the story. A couple of additional writers were brought in and one of them was Frank Tashlin, who had worked with Harpo on some gags for *A Night in Casablanca*. Harpo felt better about it with Tashlin and Ben Hecht in his corner. Press coverage of Chico's "heart attack" complicated things for Cowan, but he figured it all out somehow. Maybe Chico just told the production's insurance company that it was a fake heart attack and nothing to be worried about.

They started shooting in the summer of 1948, and Harpo was soon disappointed that the sweet film he and Ben had envisioned bore no resemblance to what they were shooting. Harpo, in a rare display of anger, made it clear to Lester Cowan that he knew he had lied to him. But amazingly, Cowan told the press that he was starting another Marx Brothers picture soon, and it would be their life story. One look at Harpo's face when this topic came up made it clear that this film would be made with Cowan only after the freezing over of hell. They were having enough trouble finishing *Love Happy*—as *Diamonds on the Sidewalk* came to be titled. For close to a year, we wondered if it would ever be released. Cowan screened it for some United Artists executives, and he was told that it needed more Groucho. Cowan reedited the film to spread the Groucho segments throughout it, and he added a few unused bits. Harpo reminded him about the contract calling for Groucho and Chico to be only supporting players in the picture. For some inexplicable reason Cowan told the press that Harpo and Groucho were feuding over the amount of screen time Groucho should get. If they had asked Groucho, he would have simply preferred not to be in the picture at all. He was already starring on radio in *You Bet Your Life* and was no longer interested in Marx Brothers movies. He'd even made his own film, *Copacabana*. It wouldn't surprise me if Chico tried to get into that one, too, but Groucho was much better at saying no to Chico than Harpo was.

By this time Groucho, Harpo, and Gummo had been handling Chico's income for several years, doling out what he needed but making sure Betty and Maxine were not financially ruined by his gambling. (Zeppo was not involved in this scheme—probably because he was just as likely as Chico to blow the money at the racetrack.) Maxine had gotten married a few years earlier, so she was less of a concern by this point. They also set up an allowance for Mary, who lived with Chico in a modest apartment while Betty—still refusing to grant Chico a divorce—continued to live in their house in Beverly Hills. Chico should have been well off and able to cover the normal expenses of two homes, an estranged wife, and a girlfriend, but with the *Love Happy* mess, he really forced Groucho and Harpo to lay down the law with regard to the Marx Brothers. There would be no more Marx Brothers movies. Chico would have to find another way to make a living. For me it was a relief. I never wanted to see Harpo that upset again. But Chico's selfishness had no limits. It clearly never occurred to him that his behavior caused his brothers a lot of pain and anguish. And at least one sister-in-law was thoroughly disgusted by Chico's refusal to behave like a responsible adult.

The end of the Marx Brothers would not be the end of Chico's endless need for money. He was perfectly capable of working without his brothers and could make a very comfortable living doing so. After Chico finished shooting his last scenes for *Love Happy*, Gummo and the William Morris Agency booked a tour of theatres in England and Scotland for him. He also did some shows for the servicemen still in Germany. The reports were that audiences loved him, and the tour continued for around four months. Gummo let us know that there was interest in Harpo playing the British circuit. My suspicion was that this was an attempt to get more bookings for Chico by getting Harpo to work with him. Sure enough, the agency in London offered a healthy guarantee if Harpo and Chico would play the London Palladium together. Harpo was unreservedly delighted, but I kept to myself the feeling that even if there were a lot of money and publicity to be had, one shouldn't jump off the Eiffel Tower unless someone was there to catch him. I couldn't imagine Chico being much of a catcher, but Harpo didn't hold a grudge over *Love Happy*, which was finally scheduled for release that summer. Harpo considered the offer and concluded that British audiences adoring him might be a nice break from the relative chaos of our house full of kids.

Show business was Harpo's business, and he didn't need me to burst the soap bubbles he liked to blow out of his clarinet. Besides, it would be great to trade southern California in July for what we assumed was a London cooled by breezes off the surrounding ocean waters. However, this cheering section was not going to England to sit in a dressing room for ten weeks. Because of this unique opportunity for him to visit a foreign country, we were taking Billy, who at the age of twelve was absolutely thrilled at the prospect of becoming his father's property man. Backstage would be a new world for him. Needless to say, his mother would then be free to indulge a lifelong fascination with English history. And Alex, Jimmy, and Minnie would get their opportunity to break down Mother's resolve and see if they could get away with things I never could. But surely Father would spoil them behind her back as he had done with me. Agnes would really have most of the responsibility in our absence, and I pleaded with Mother in advance not to be too difficult with her.

Every square foot of Great Britain is historical, and I wanted to see it all. I promised to do the necessary nightly laundry and see that supper would be served in our hotel room after the show. My trusting husband smiled optimistically. Contracts were signed and Harpo agreed to play a week in Leeds and a week in Glasgow to get his material in shape before the London engagement. The original contract called for Harpo to play two weeks at the London Palladium by himself and then pair with Chico for another two weeks. Somehow that got changed to a four-week engagement with Chico. Harpo laughed at the suggestion they hire a British writer to work with them, asking, "Doesn't Chico have proven material?" Harpo had a pretty well-honed act from his years on the USO circuit. Just shuffle them together. It seemed simple enough, and we hit the road.

We spent a few days in New York visiting with old friends and taking in a game at Yankee Stadium. (The Giants were out of town, to Harpo's dismay.) The next night we took Billy to his first Broadway show. I suppose the original cast performing *South Pacific* was a nice introduction to musical theatre. We sailed on the *Queen Mary* on May 20, 1949. On the eve of our departure, I told Harpo to go to the party being thrown for us without me as I was feeling strange. The next morning it was clear that I had the mumps. We were due to board the ship early, and knowing I wouldn't be allowed on if anyone knew, I tied a scarf around my swelling glands, adopted a haughty air so no one would try to speak to me, and left it up to my husband (one of whose talents was deception) to smuggle me on board. From their accounts, my two men had a wonderful voyage, but I didn't care. I spend the entire trip in our cabin. Anyone who has ever had mumps will understand why.

When we reached Southampton five days later, I was still a little out of sorts but feeling better. We arrived in the morning and took the train to London, where Chico met us at the station for some press interviews and photos. We checked into the Savoy Hotel, where we all promptly went to sleep. The next afternoon there was a luncheon at the Prince of Wales Theatre given by Val Parnell, the head of the Moss Empires music hall and variety circuit. He was in charge of all of the important British theatres, including the London Palladium. Harpo was anxious to talk to Chico about putting their act together, but before he could get a few moments with him, Chico was gone. He had a show that evening. They'd figure it out somehow. Harpo decided to catch Chico's act at the Hippodrome in nearby Golders Green that night, and what he saw made him nervous. After the show he came back to the hotel almost in tears. "It's blue! All his jokes are dirty! It won't work at the Palladium. Now, here's the best part, he says he hasn't time to rehearse with me. Can you believe this? How can we coordinate the two acts?" Getting no answers from me, he fell asleep. Such a sensible man. Harpo was a realist and a man of action. Somehow, he set about casting his own act with two delightful English actresses as foils.

We had a week off in London before Harpo's opening, and he had been under the impression that Chico would be available to work up the act for their upcoming joint engagement. But Chico had been booked at the Chiswick Empire for that week. Harpo tried to arrange some time for them to rehearse, but Chico just told him not to worry so much. I asked the kind and gentle Mary Dee to help, and she was able to convince Chico to set aside some time. Harpo was concerned that they were unprepared, but Chico was supremely confident that it would all work out and that they'd be great. We tried to relax in London before we had to hit the road for Harpo's two weeks of solo shows. Val Parnell invited us to the Palladium to see Danny Kaye. Harpo thought Danny was wonderful and mentioned that after seeing his magnificently produced show, London audiences might not appreciate Chico's haphazard approach to his craft. After a few more days in London, we arranged for the Savoy to store our trunks, and Harpo, Billy, and I headed off to Leeds and Glasgow, where Harpo would work out his material before the London opening with Chico.

Val arranged for us to travel "British-style"—which meant staying at boardinghouses when trying out new material before a London engagement. The host at the hostel in Leeds was pleasantly accustomed to accommodating the eccentric hours of his theatrical guests. The bathing facilities were startling to Americans expecting hot and cold running water in even the most modest accommodations. Here, bathing was accomplished in an iron tub of ancient design, standing on four sturdy lion's paws. (My grandmother's bath had such a tub, and I used to fantasize about the tub running down the hall with my grandmother in it.) Cold water ran from the only faucet in the tub, but for those who wanted the luxury of hot water, they provided a tank called the "geyser," suspended five feet over the tub, from which hot water would flow if fed a shilling. Harpo explained to us that in his small-time vaudeville days, this setup would have been considered a luxury.

Neither Harpo nor I liked to sit in dirty, soapy water, but creating a shower bath was tricky. The absurd solution was that the one to be cleansed stood in the tub, fed the shilling, and hurried to wash while the partner stood at the faucet trying to splash cold water into the descending hot before it hit the body. It was exciting and funny at first, but when we were moving on to Glasgow for our second week, Harpo asked the theatre manager to reserve rooms for us at a hotel. We had risen to the shower challenge, but Harpo thought he needed all his creativity for the show. The hotel in Glasgow also had its memorable moments. At the check-in desk, when I insisted on a private bath, the clerk was incredulous. "Madam, each floor is equipped with two bathrooms that have always serviced our guests quite adequately." However, when Harpo backed me up, he reluctantly gave us two huge bedrooms with a lovely big bathroom between and marked the hall door "out of order." Of course, we were careful not to be seen entering it. We had won that round, but the clerk won the next one. Harpo flung open a window for fresh air, only to receive a blast of black smoke. Our window opened into the railroad station, and the coal-burning engines were directly below us. There was no talk of changing rooms. We had our bathroom, so we had to keep quiet.

Harpo's act was delighting audiences, allowing us to enjoy the wonders of England and Scotland without him worrying about the show. We were captivated by the sheep on the hillside and cows grazing in the deep grasses among the ancient ruins. It's a beautiful part of the world. Harpo agreed to hire a car so we could get out of Glasgow and see where we really were. The day was so successful that the three of us explored Scotland every day. We drove across to Edinburgh, to climb up to the castle and have tea and scones and load up on cashmeres.

Glasgow was delightful but as we neared the end of the week, Harpo again became restless about Chico and the Palladium. A couple of days before closing, Chico finally called. He was suddenly free. He and Harpo would have some time to pool their acts once we were back in London. But Harpo now knew better than to trust Chico and made a call. After he had initially rejected the idea of outside help, Harpo accepted the offer of the British writer just in case Chico needed material. No act would dare open cold in a big city without polishing in front of an out-of-town audience first. How could they get away with it at the London Palladium? Maybe a bit of direction from someone in the English theatrical world would help. I could see my fatalistic one was resigned to a disaster. At that moment I hated Chico for what he was doing to my beloved.

While we were in Leeds and Glasgow, Chico had those two weeks off in London before the Palladium opening. Mary had her hands full keeping him away from the racetrack. She tried to convince him to visit us in Glasgow, but he wasn't interested. Chico had trouble finding anything to gamble on at some of the stops on his tour, and Mary told a story about him spotting some kids pitching pennies in an alley behind the theatre where he was playing. Naturally he got himself into the game and lost more money than one would think possible at pitching pennies. Sure enough, those kids showed up every day for the rest of Chico's engagement. We got back to London the day before the Palladium opening. Mary and I stayed out of the way by dragging Billy to antique shops and other places guaranteed to bore a twelve-year-old, while Harpo and Chico refined their act. In the evening Billy worked with Harpo on his props—even though he'd been thoroughly drilled with the exact way to set up each prop. Anything to keep down the rising anxiety. Finally, the calendar told us it was June 20—the dreaded opening night in London.

The day began with a phone call from Hillcrest. It was Groucho, Jack Benny, George Burns, Lou Holtz, and Danny Kaye—recently returned from his own London trip. They wanted to wish Harpo luck and congratulate him. He told them they were crazy to spend so much money on the long-distance call, and Groucho assured him that they had reversed the charges. We headed over to the theatre with Chico and Mary. Ticket sales were good, and it would be a full house for the opening. It was the hottest July anyone could remember, so that cool ocean breeze we were expecting never came. The Palladium was not air-conditioned, and I suddenly had a new role. Billy was working well with the props, but every time Harpo came off stage looking like he had been rained on, I had to be there with a towel and a dry wig. I didn't really get to see the show on opening night. His three wigs and the curling iron kept me busy backstage. Finally, it was over, and Harpo was back in the dressing room with an amazed grin on his face. "Whadda-ya-know, we were a smash!"

Harpo and Chico really whipped their show into shape after a few performances, and Chico was quick to say, "See? I told you there was nothing to worry about." But it was infuriating to watch what he put Harpo through leading up to the opening. Once things had settled down and the shows were going well, we could all relax a bit. Some afternoons Mary and I searched the antique shops. And I enjoyed sightseeing around London with Billy when Harpo preferred an afternoon nap to being a tourist. We visited Stratford-upon-Avon—where we attended a performance of *Macbeth*—Madame Tussaud's Wax Museum, and the Tower of London. Harpo joined us for a boat ride on the Thames. We usually had breakfast or lunch with Chico and Mary, and the London experience was suddenly altogether pleasant.

London turned into a great trip for each of us. Our son discovered heaven backstage. By helping his dad, he became a member of the troupe, and by being a nice kid, the magician on the bill taught him card tricks. I put the wigs under the control of a stagehand with a hair dryer and enjoyed the rest of the engagement from the front of the stage. The relief of success relaxed Harpo to the point where he became interested in where he was. He enjoyed lunch in the dining room of the House of Parliament, visiting old friends, or, some days, just exploring the mazes of London with Billy.

One afternoon their walk took them to a burlesque theatre. When I suggested that this might not have been appropriate, Harpo said, "He's old enough. Burlesque is a legitimate form of show business. It's the audience that perverts it." Billy told me that as they left the theatre, Harpo said, "I'm sorry, that wasn't a good show." Billy mumbled something like "That's okay, Dad." But Harpo said, with the authority of a professional, "No, the girls didn't take off enough clothes." Then, with the air of a father preparing his son for following in his footsteps, he delighted Billy by sharing the secrets of the business. "The British are good at low comedy, and I'd rather you watched a fifth-rate burlesque comic working hard with bad material than a star performer giving 50 percent of himself. If you go into show business, remember, keep a watch on your ego. If you have thirty minutes of good material, do twenty-five and get off while they're still applauding. Leave them asking for more." Billy asked, "How much applause do you need for a good night's sleep?"

Some days Harpo just wanted to relax in the hotel room, so I was free to do my own exploring. One morning I called the desk for a car and took Billy to visit one of the racetracks outside London. At the recommended time we went to the entrance to find the hotel had provided us with a town car and a chauffeur. I had a worried moment thinking of the cost, but ostentation won out. The infield looked more like a county fair than a racetrack, with a Ferris wheel and merry-go-round, and crowded with family picnickers. Nearing race time, we went off to prowl among the bookies, intending to pick a long shot. Harpo, not being a racing man, had no interest in seeing it for himself. However, when Val Parnell offered his box at Ascot, that was different. Chico and Mary accepted immediately, and Harpo didn't hesitate. Ascot, the showplace of the racing world, the playground of royalty, where commoners could gawk at high society in their most brilliant plumage. To Harpo this was not just horse racing, it was theatre.

We were transported to that fabled place in a chauffeured Rolls-Royce, with the Savoy's finest lunch basket, to sit in a box overlooking the track. Billy, underage for betting, was picking winners by the jockey's colors. Mary and Chico were circulating among the touts for questionable inside information, and Harpo and I were leaning on the rail of the box fascinated by the activity in and around the small fenced-off area reserved for VIPs and special guests. Chico, sitting down and grabbing a sandwich, asked, "Is there any form on these horses? Billy, what colors do you pick to win the next race?" Then Chico sent Mary to make a bet on Billy's colors, correctly concluding that Billy's system was as good as any he could come up with. It was probably better, because when we left Ascot, Chico actually still had some money in his pocket. Harpo laughed when I suggested that if Chico left the track with money, he probably felt like he hadn't gotten his money's worth.

Harpo and Chico did some publicity for the show, and one afternoon there was a photo shoot at the London Zoo. Glynis Johns, the lovely British actress, took them on a tour of the zoo, and a picture of the three of them with a pair of chimpanzees ran in the local papers. Chico was very interested in animals, and he had many questions for the gentleman from the London Zoological Society who served as our liaison. Another publicity stunt didn't go as well. American tennis champion Ted Schroeder was competing at Wimbledon while we were in town. Someone came up with the idea that Harpo and Chico would appear courtside as Ted's ball boys. They arrived in tennis shorts and sneakers and started clowning around with Ted. This did not sit well with the stodgy Wimbledon officials, who promptly asked Harpo and Chico to end what the London papers called their "undignified intrusion" on the proceedings. Ted Schroeder got the last laugh when he won the tournament a few days later.

One night as we were leaving the Palladium, we encountered two young women at the stage door. But these were not the usual autograph seekers. They were harp students, and they were wondering if they might get a look at Harpo's harp. Harpo was tired after having just finished a show, and he would have loved nothing more than to get his supper and go to bed. But he invited the two women to come into his dressing room, where he allowed each of them to play his harp and then decided to give them a few pointers. This late-night harp class could have gone on for quite a while had I not pointed out to Harpo that his chance of getting something to eat at the Savoy was getting smaller as it got later. Another night Harpo's dressing room was visited by royalty. Princess Margaret and a few of her friends came to the show. But one particular visitor at the Palladium would become a dear friend.

Hannen Swaffer was respectfully called the dean of the London critics. Hannen liked to have supper with us after the show, at first in a small cafe he habituated in Soho; but after a night in the Palladium steam bath, Harpo preferred to dine in his room at the Savoy. Only after showering and putting on his pajamas would he feel sociable enough to be entertained by this chain-smoking eccentric, whose cigarette never left his lips until he lit another from it. It was a sort of permanent flame from which dropped ashes in a constant shower over his shirt and jacket. Harpo's favorite moment with Swaffer came one evening when he was sitting back in his chair gossiping. Hannen leaned forward to make a point and said, "Do you feel them?" "Feel what, Hannen?" "Fairy fingers." "How's that again, Hannen?" "When I leaned forward, I could feel them press against me." Of course, when he leaned forward his jacket tightened, and he felt it pulling. Those islands have more superstitions than they really need, and Hannen was a true believer. Anyway, Harpo found this endlessly amusing.

Hannen persuaded us to visit his wife, as she hadn't left their apartment for many years. Entering the building, I looked at Harpo—no elevator. He shrugged, so we started climbing the stairs. This was atypical of my boy, as he hated stairs. The Marx Brothers had once had a second-floor office in Hollywood, reached from the street by a steep flight of stairs. When Harpo needed to attend to business, he stood on the sidewalk below and whistled. Their secretary, waiting at the window above, lowered a basket, and Harpo signed whatever he needed to. She then raised the basket and, after inspection, signaled that business was over. We reached the second floor of Hannen's building. Leaning against the railing Harpo gasped, "Just what floor do you live on?" "Fourth," replied Hannen. "No way," said Harpo. "Unless you move down a few floors, I'm afraid I will never meet your wife." Back on the street again, Harpo had just one question. "Why a fourth-floor walkup?" Hannen answered with all the dignity of one who is conscious of an ancient heritage, "Where else could I live in a building that's three hundred years old?"

Hannen had an air of egotism and self-importance that immediately brought to mind a sort of British Alexander Woollcott. He was a complicated man, but we really didn't know much about him at first. We later learned that he led the fight against capital punishment in England. But we also learned that he had been accused of trying to ban black actors from the theatre. He also was known in some circles as being quite anti-Semitic, although he later renounced his early views in that department. It was difficult to reconcile the many sides of Hannen Swaffer. But Harpo found him amusing, and they never discussed the disturbing things in his past. It was Hannen who recommended a book that greatly impressed Harpo—*The Memoirs of Joseph Grimaldi*, the great nineteenth-century British clown. Actually, the book was not entirely the work of Grimaldi, who left a mess of a manuscript when he died. A young novelist named Charles Dickens was hired to finish the book. Harpo was so taken with Grimaldi's story that he decided he wanted to play Grimaldi in a filmed version of his life. He asked Hannen if he thought this Dickens fellow might be willing to work on a script. Harpo was having a bit of fun with him, but he was unable to keep a straight face, and Hannen immediately knew he was being put on.

Near the end of our stay in London, Hannen brought Harpo a beautiful tribute: the two-volume edition of *The Memoirs of Joseph Grimaldi*, published in 1838. He inserted a note that read, "Hearing that I wanted a copy of this work for Harpo Marx, the firm of W. & G. Foyle Ltd. found these two volumes for me, and then, most generously, insisted on making no charge for them, although they are first editions and therefore rare. Foyle and I, therefore, present the story of Grimaldi, Britain's greatest clown, to Harpo, the greatest clown in America. —Hannen Swaffer, July 15, 1949."

CHAPTER ELEVEN

After the Last Marx Brothers Reunion

URING OUR TIME IN LONDON, LESTER COWAN'S NAME BEGAN appearing in the press frequently—usually in connection with his new Marx Brothers film, *Love Happy*. As much as Harpo detested Cowan, he was committed to promoting the film, and Cowan arrived in London to start working the press in advance of the premiere. But what infuriated Harpo was Lester placing items in the press that suggested he'd be working with the Marx Brothers in the future. If you believed what you read in the papers, Lester Cowan would be producing a biographical film based on the lives of the Marx Brothers. (The boys were certainly talking about this project, and Lester had purchased the rights to a magazine article Woollcott had written about the early years of the brothers, but that had come and gone a year earlier. If Lester Cowan was still involved, he certainly wouldn't be after *Love Happy*.)

Lester had also somehow gotten wind of Harpo's desire to make the Grimaldi film and announced that he'd be producing it in France with Glynis Johns starring alongside Harpo. (Poor Glynis Johns went to the zoo and posed for a few pictures with Harpo and Chico and now she's making a film in France with a producer she's never heard of!) Lester kept at it, also announcing that he would be making a film with Groucho as a Scotland Yard detective. Then he announced that Groucho would be flying to London for the premiere of *Love Happy*. (It was hard enough to get him to drive fifteen minutes to the studio to shoot his scenes. He wasn't coming to London.) Just to cover all the bases, Lester also announced that he'd signed Chico for a straight role in a western. (This he might have really done, since Chico would certainly have accepted such an offer if the pay was good.) The important thing to understand about all of this is that none if it ever happened because Lester Cowan was lying about all of it.

To be fair, Lester was really trying to arrange a London premiere for *Love Happy*. During some of the Palladium shows, Chico promoted the film, and this managed to catch the attention of the press well after the papers had reviewed the show. In our scrapbook from the trip, I have this item from the *Daily Herald* dated June 22, 1949:

> In his act at the Palladium, Chico Marx has a lot to say about the last Marx Brothers film, *Love Happy*. We mustn't miss it, he says. But we shall miss it, all of us. Part-author of the film, who says he has a share in the profits, is Ben Hecht, hater of the English, who did so much (from a safe distance) to get British soldiers killed in Palestine, and publicly boasted that he rejoiced in their deaths. British cinemas, advised by their trade association, have refused to show any future Ben Hecht films. *Love Happy* is the first to come under the ban, which is unlikely to be lifted. Doesn't Chico Marx know this?

If Chico didn't know, he soon found out. Lester quickly pivoted to premiering *Love Happy* elsewhere. Harpo and Chico each went on to separate solo bookings after they'd closed at the Palladium, and Harpo gave his final performance of the trip at the Birmingham Hippodrome on July 23. It was a special show and Harpo was so moved by the wildly appreciative audience that he made a curtain call and delivered a little speech, sending the audience home with a special memory of the evening. As if to give Harpo one more reason to despise him, Lester scheduled the *Love Happy* premiere in Detroit—four days later. Chico had two more weeks of shows booked, so he couldn't attend the premiere. Groucho was probably even less likely to attend a Detroit premiere than one in London. But Harpo decided it was worth going to help promote the film, so the morning after the last show in Birmingham, we took the train back to London and flew to Detroit the following day.

There were a few other screenings around the Midwest, but *Love Happy* was barely released when United Artists pulled it from theatres almost immediately. The Ben Hecht controversy kept the film from screens in England, and now we had a separate controversy to keep it from screens in the United States. Lester had concocted a rooftop chase scene for the film's finale and made deals with several companies to advertise their products with billboard signs visible throughout the scene. Exhibitors revolted against the notion of not being paid to show what essentially amounted to a sequence filled with commercials. Thanks to Lester, we flew four thousand miles to promote a film that was not playing anywhere, instead of following our original plan to visit Paris. In addition to the controversies, Lester also ran into financial trouble and was unable to get prints of the film made. It took a while, but *Love Happy* was eventually released in the United States and England to a lukewarm response. Any remaining interest Harpo may have had in making movies vanished.

Shortly after we got home, news came that my father had been diagnosed with thyroid cancer. It didn't take long. He had an operation in November, and when the call telling me that he was gone came on January 28, 1950, I was not surprised. Billy was practicing at the piano, and I stopped him to break the news. It was Billy's first real experience with death. He was too young when Woollcott died for it to have had much of an impact. He was thirteen when Father died, and he had grown up around him. The other kids were old enough to understand, but they were so young that they hadn't had much of a chance to get to know Father. Mother was predictably stoic. Father was seventy years old, and he'd spent forty-four years taking orders from Mother. He was a sweet, gentle man, and it pained me to think that Alex, Jimmy, and Minnie would not get to know him the way Billy had. Harpo pointed out that Bill Fleming had a lot in common with Frenchy Marx. Minnie ordered Frenchy around a lot too. My father devoted his life to a woman who could most charitably be described as difficult. When the kids were discovering Marx Brothers movies a few years later, I took some pride in pointing their grandfather out in the background of the scene in *At the Circus* when Groucho sings "Lydia the Tattooed Lady." (They can see their other grandfather in *Monkey Business*, by the way.)

I'm not sure if it was because of my father's death, but I was becoming restless. After several years of luxuriating in our world, I'd had it. I resented being limited to playing a social role as Harpo's wife while all of the household duties were handled by a bevy of experienced incompetents. I didn't know until after I got married that I hadn't been trained for anything but uselessness. Consequently, when I had my own house to run, I was just that—useless. It was humiliating. Faced with having to hire a staff, I was lost. It took me only one visit to an agency to interview and hire three incompetents. Their references had been checked, and I was assured they were of the highest caliber. They had no police record, so what else could I ask? I took the agency's recommendations and assumed they knew what they should know. But our staff could be temperamental and quarrelsome among themselves, and it was clear that the most incompetent member of the household was me.

I was fed up with the tyranny and well-deserved contempt of our staff and called for a family conference. "We're not doing this right," I said. "This is what I'd like to try." Cheered by a hopeful husband, who at least was going to save some money, I fired the cook, the butler, and the upstairs maid. Then I set about learning how to run a house. To start our independence, Harpo claimed to know how to broil a steak. Agnes volunteered to prepare all the children's food and to teach me the magical formula for making a baked potato come out of the oven as if it had been in a bonfire—"mickies" to those who were children in lands where gardeners burned leaves and children threw potatoes into the fire.

The children were given chores that children would be able to do, just so they would be taking part in the great adventure. Then, I went off to cooking school. It was scary. Most evenings I was in a state of collapse. Too often Harpo would have to pound the table, saying, "You eat your dinner. Your mother worked all day in the kitchen to make it." He wasn't exaggerating. My day started at six. I had mastered breakfast, and Agnes would take care of lunch. Harpo had lunch at Hillcrest, so at least he was assured of one good meal a day. The big question was dinner. Everyone was interested and helpful except for Mother, who, when I telephoned to ask questions, would laugh and say something like, "Oh, darling, I don't remember," or "Susie, dear, I never made it." She knew. Mother was a fine cook, but she didn't approve of my doing it. The greatest help came from the milkman. I'm sure he thought we were in financial trouble. His morning deliveries were always good for a sympathetic inquiry and a bit of culinary enlightenment, like, "Cooking onions, are we? Be sure to burn them." He was right. And this was such an important ingredient in a meat loaf or over Harpo's endless steaks. A few months of this intensive training and I felt equal to directing a staff with efficiency and some economy. The house was now in order. The children were in school, and I felt all grown up and competent.

My reward came one morning when a truck pulled up in the driveway and delivered to me a shower of boxes with a single card that read, "With the blessings of a grateful husband." This grateful husband was watching the opening of the cartons with a hopeful smile. When I asked why, his answer was to the point. "Zeppo says he never had any money to save until he turned the checkbook over to Marion. Mom, you are now the keeper of the family purse." He handed me a checkbook showing a deposit had been made in a local bank, to the account of Susan Marx. No more to be said. And the cartons? Pencils, pens, ink, erasers, stationery, adding machine, and large desk with filing drawers for the budding accountant. I didn't point out to him there might be limits to my competence. Silently I reviewed my history. At no time in all my years of being the wage earner did I ever have a dollar in my pocket. Mother took care of everything. I had no idea of the limited value of money. All I could say to myself was, "Courage, girl, he thinks you can do anything, so don't spoil it because maybe you can." Harpo's smile was becoming uncertain when I forced a cheerful "Thank you for the confidence, I'll do my best," then started to cry. He hugged me thinking it was for happiness, but I was just afraid I wasn't all that grown up and competent after all. But I recovered quickly because there would be much more to worry about than running the house.

The anxiety caused by *Love Happy* and working with Chico in London convinced me to break a promise I had made not to meddle in my husband's show business affairs. Harpo wanted to work, but only when he felt like it. And more significantly he wanted to work solo. I made this clear to Gummo, just in case he was thinking about ambushing us with Chico again. Pretty soon the William Morris Agency set up a two-week engagement for Harpo at the Flamingo Hotel in Las Vegas. And to put Harpo at ease, he would have an out-of-town tryout. We went to Long Beach for three days, and the new act Harpo had worked up went perfectly. He felt confident in the cast and the routines a solid month before we left for Las Vegas. He was completely relaxed. There would be no surprises and there would be a rehearsal whenever he felt he needed one. I could get used to this.

Shortly after the successful Las Vegas booking, Harpo announced, "I'm ready to book some dates, okay?" That was my signal. No longer an ordinary housewife, I would become valet, hairdresser, stagehand, and union negotiator. I was proud that he trusted and needed me, but there would have to be some limits. I assumed Harpo was talking about some dates around southern California, mostly on weekends. But it would be far more ambitious. We had met a very interesting man named Irwin Parnes, who would best be described as an impresario. He had been bringing unusual and seldom-seen multicultural and ethnic entertainment to Los Angeles, including such things as Indian folk dancing, the American Negro Repertory Players, a children's choir from Paris, and opera and ballet companies from around the world. Harpo enjoyed being exposed to different kinds of music and performance and mentioned to Parnes that he would be interested in working with him.

Parnes came back to Harpo with a six-week tour that would take him to some pretty remote places that fall—at the start of the school year. It became clear that I could not be a regular part of Harpo's touring entourage. Harpo and Parnes put their ideas together and came up with *Harpo's Concert Bazaar*, which would feature Harpo's act in a classical setting. Harpo loved the music, which included the works of Beethoven, Bizet, Debussy, Grieg, Chopin, and Puccini. One part of the act I could have done without was the dancer who did a wild number with a boa constrictor! But I had to hand it to Irwin Parnes; it was different. The tour was set to begin in Sacramento on October 13, 1950—Friday the thirteenth. But no one was superstitious enough to even notice this before we left for the show.

Harpo again got his pre-opening tryout the night before at an Army base in nearby Fairfield, California. This would turn out to be a very memorable occasion. President Harry S. Truman was stopping at this base to refuel his plane on his way to Wake Island to meet with General Douglas MacArthur to discuss the progress of the Korean War. But in Fairfield, the president met with Harpo to discuss the Marx Brothers, and they posed for a photograph that ran in papers across the country. Truman was excited to let Harpo know that he had seen the Marx Brothers in Kansas City several times during their vaudeville days. Truman loved vaudeville and had even taken a job as an usher so he wouldn't have to pay for tickets. Later they would each autograph a copy of the photo for the other.

I stayed out on the road with Harpo for the first few shows in the Bay Area and then headed home to the kids as he and his troupe traveled the way Harpo and his brothers had forty years earlier in vaudeville. This tour was no walk in the park, but Harpo was excited about it, and audiences loved every bit of it. He kept in touch from the road with phone calls and letters. I saved a letter he wrote from Owensboro, Kentucky, on November 18, 1950. It made me laugh then and it still does.

It is now 11:30 PM—after the show. The theatre was two miles out of town. Business was bad. I am sitting in the hotel lobby in the dark. I can't go to my room until I'm ready to go to bed as it is cold. A Victrola is playing a hillbilly record. I was driven around town and people looked like L'il Abner characters.

I made a mistake after I spoke to you and took a physic. I spent the entire day and night on the can. At four in the morning on one of my trips I took a swig of Kaopectate but it was Nivea. My heinie was sore, so I put some zinc ointment on. When I got back to bed, I smelled toothpaste. I realized my mistake, but even that felt good.

I played in Nashville last night in the dirtiest theatre I have ever seen in my life. The whole south is dirty. What it needs is a flood like New Orleans had, but longer—and the last ten days it should rain penicillin.

The tour was a success, but it wasn't perfect. Two shows in the South had to be canceled at the last minute, and press reports made Harpo look like the villain. The local promoters had all signed contracts agreeing that Harpo would receive a certified check before the performance, but in Mobile, Alabama, the promoter presented Harpo with a regular check that wasn't certified. The audience was in their seats waiting for the show to begin, but the promoter refused to pay by certified check. Harpo canceled the show, and the promoter was forced to issue refunds. The promoter in Jackson, Mississippi, for the following night's show also refused to pay by certified check, so that show was canceled as well. This story was in newspapers across the country within days. The disgruntled promotors made a point of telling the press that many other performers accepted their normal checks that had not been certified. What the press never heard was that these two promoters became very upset when Harpo objected to their segregated seating policy. They planned to punish him for asking that black patrons not be relegated to a separate seating area in the last rows of the balcony. They were going to stop payment on their uncertified checks after the performance had been given. It was the deep South in 1950. It shouldn't have been a surprise, but Harpo still found it appalling.

At home I had other pressing matters to deal with. The kids were growing up, and nursery days were over. The upper floor needed reworking to accommodate the maturing family. Teenaged Billy needed his own room, which had to be built on to the house someplace. Then Minnie and her hamsters could move into her own room, if a partial girl's bathroom could be framed in. If Alex and Jimmy doubled up in Agnes's room with their own bath, then Agnes could move to the guesthouse. Harpo agreed to everything once it was pointed out that he and I would be back in the master suite we had turned into a nursery, luxuriating in a regained privacy.

Parenting was fun in Beverly Hills in the forties and fifties. The residential area between Santa Monica Boulevard and Sunset Boulevard had a real small-village atmosphere. Everyone who had a child in one of the two elementary schools knew one another. I don't mean it led to backyard barbecues. It was parental involvement in youth activities. That small piece of Beverly Hills, attractive for its central access to the surrounding motion picture studios, had gradually become home to a mix of the many talents in the movie industry. The catalyst for parental involvement was Jack Gilbert, a genial survivor of polio, who was one of the best things that ever happened to the children of our town. Jack had a strong affinity with kids, and he added baseball to the Cub Scouts program, bringing the dads out to coach until the national scouting organization eliminated it. Undaunted, Jack formed a Little League, which soon became national in scope.

All three of our boys were into baseball, and Harpo loved to coach, but he eventually rebelled. After three games he came home disgusted. "Fathers should never be allowed near their sons' baseball games. I'm quitting before I take a swing at one of them." Harpo had eagerly offered to be a coach, so I asked, "What happened?" He said, "A kid named Mike was playing shortstop today. Now there is no reason to believe Yankee scouts are keeping an eye on a nine-year-old, but apparently Mike's father has this delusion, and he suddenly ran out to his son and started to bawl him out for dropping a pop-up. Can you believe it?" Again, I asked Harpo, "What happened?" Now almost laughing, Harpo told me, "Jack, in his wheelchair, rushed onto the field to stop the crazed father, but Mike ran off the field crying! When's the last time you ever saw a shortstop cry?"

We were blessed with warm and loving children—who were all pretty good little ballplayers—and who were concerned about one another. Each one was on a different time clock. Jimmy took the longest to crawl or walk as he wasn't going anywhere. Alex preferred to walk sturdily over to Jimmy, grab the toy he was playing with, and hit him over the head with it. This made no sense as they were always given duplicates, but Alex was a hoarder. The formula was always the same. The part Jimmy minded was being hit on the head. When he bawled his protest, his ally, Minnie, immediately scrambled over to Alex, grabbed back the toy, and hit Alex on the head with it. They seemed more like the Three Stooges than the Marx Brothers.

Being around Harpo was a lot of fun. He was an enthusiast—and a periodic enthusiasm was fishing. For him fishing wasn't about getting away from the pressures of work by restfully dropping a line in the water and communing with nature. I don't think Harpo ever felt the need to relieve the pressures of his work—or at least he didn't when he wasn't concerned with any offstage drama involving Chico. Chico could always cause anxiety. But Harpo generally lived in a state of equilibrium. He was the only performer I've ever known who was not in competition with other performers. No, Harpo was not a fisherman for peaceful contemplation or food to have frozen and sent home. It was a game.

Having read a glowing account of the fishing at the tiny Mexican village of San Felipe on the Gulf of California, he telephoned the fishing editor of the *Los Angeles Times*, who assured him that, although primitive, a motel there provided acceptably clean accommodations. Harpo hung up and telephoned San Felipe for a double room for a few days and reserved a fishing boat for the two of us. The drive down from the Mexican border was a bit unnerving. For 125 miles there were no signs of habitation or gas stations. Not wishing to dampen his pleasure, I didn't mention my concerns. Conditioned by the movies, I watched for brigands behind every rock south of the border. Of course, we arrived without incident, not having seen another car the entire trip. This road would have attracted only the stupidest of brigands. Arriving in San Felipe one wondered why a government would pave a road to get there. The motel was a lot less than I was prepared for. When Harpo's editor friend said primitive, he wasn't kidding. But Harpo was enchanted. This was no studio backlot reproduction of a sleepy village. This was real. Before we went in for our supper (which was to be a can of tomato soup and a doubtful hamburger), Harpo thought we should stroll through the village and savor the simplicity of this native scene.

I was skeptical of the amount of goodwill that people living with their livestock in huts made of packing crates can possibly feel toward people arriving in Cadillacs for a bit of fun. But we strolled through the dust. There were no happy sounds of children at play. The people were quiet. They didn't stare at us as we stared at them. We returned to the motel for dinner and went straight to bed. We had to. There was absolutely nothing else to do. After an early breakfast we were escorted to our fishing boat, which turned out to be a rowboat. The owner of the boat would row while we trolled. He said we would have to work to keep the fish from jumping into the boat. This was understandable as we were floating on a sea of jellyfish so dense our hooks couldn't pierce the water. If we were to catch any fish, they would have to jump in the boat to get at the bait. It must have been revolting to swim around under that mess.

It finally dawned on us that we had missed the point. This was an adventure designed for a gregarious group of drinking buddies who needed a weekend away from home. We didn't drink and we had come alone. It had nothing to do with fishing. As this became clear, Harpo pointed out that if we left, we could still catch the early show at the Fox Wilshire. We made our peace with the manager, who was not surprised, and drove off. About ten miles out of town, Harpo asked casually, "Have you noticed that car behind us?" I said, "Yes, it was parked off the road and pulled out when we passed." He said, "What do you think?" I said, "I've been wondering where they were when we came down. How fast will this car go?" That little sedan had been waiting for us. It took more than an hour for a Cadillac at top speed to shake it, but my fisherman was not discouraged.

Harpo read a newspaper account of great salmon fishing on the Campbell River in Vancouver. He went to Hillcrest Country Club and had no trouble infecting our dear friend Norman Krasna, a fellow fisherman, who was eager to leave immediately and would telephone his wife to pack. Krasna had recently gone through a divorce, remarried, and moved to Palm Springs. His new wife, Erle, was the widow of Al Jolson, and she was always up for an adventure. (I suppose being the tempestuous Jolson's fourth wife was pretty adventurous!) Erle suggested we get together for dinner and work out the arrangements. Such a level head was going to be a great addition to our party. Harpo was all for making immediate reservations, but I held out for a more organized trip. I can be levelheaded too, in a pinch. Cadillac limousines didn't seem very sporty, so we would rent a touring car with a convertible top. Norman would arrange for the car, and Harpo and I worked out the itinerary. Erle and Norman recognized us as experienced travelers because we had once driven across the South from Miami to Los Angeles in a borrowed car that ran out of oil at least once a day. My experience on that trip made me indispensable. When a tire blew out, I managed to change it in a drizzle of rain on the side of a hill with a broken jack while my hero stood next to me playing his harmonica to keep my spirits up. I attribute my resourcefulness to several years as a den mother with various scouting organizations, which is also terrific training if you're going to be married to a Harpo.

Harpo again called his friend the fishing editor for some hints, and I conferred with our gas station attendant. He gave me a free map, pointed out mileage numbers, and warned about motel reservations. Our leader sneered at this good advice, being blessed with a strange ability to find a parking space in front of any door he wanted to enter. No matter how heavily trafficked an area, cars seemed to move aside for him. Naturally, this gift would apply to motels having rooms available whenever we arrived. Our first day took us as far as San Francisco, where ignorance and Harpo's faith allowed us to dine in Chinatown and then move out of the city to look for a pleasant country inn to stay the night. At that time the country closed down early, and after an hour of driving through the darkness, the back seat rebelled. Either we go back to San Francisco or pull over and sleep in the car. Harpo, the map reader, assured us there was a town just ahead where soon we would be snug in bed. Sure enough, rounding a bend, there was a dim light hanging outside a barely visible building.

"Always trust me," exulted Harpo. Taking one look at the place, I said I'd rather sleep in the car. Harpo ignored this, and we climbed a narrow uncarpeted stairway to the sounds of heavy snoring to face a man behind a window who offered us a room with two double beds at three dollars each. We were in a flophouse. Exhausted and furious with Harpo, we all laid down on a pair of beds fully clothed and turned out the lights. Then, in the darkness and over the din of the snores from down the hall, we heard Harpo's harmonica. We could barely control our hilarity. In the morning the washbasin was used for other than its designated purpose, and Harpo promised it would never happen again, but we didn't achieve separate rooms until Vancouver Island.

When it was finally time to go fishing, I was not at all surprised that we'd again fish from a rowboat piloted by our guide. Almost immediately Harpo hooked a fish. It was a big salmon, but after battling to reel it in for nearly an hour, he'd had enough; and I was ready to shoot both Harpo and the fish. If we had been alone in the boat, we could have cut the line surreptitiously, but our oarsman kept shouting "Tyee" and other unintelligible instructions to Harpo. Other boats milling around in the crowded river started to notice his catch. Apparently, the boatmen had some sort of ongoing contest. I was swinging between utter boredom and spasms of laughter, and Harpo was exhausted and furious at not being able to land his fish. Eventually, an exhausted salmon swam over to the boat and climbed in—at least that's my story.

Harpo then turned graciously to me and said, "It's your turn, Mom." In rowing up and down the river, we had passed Erle and Norman in their rowboat many times but hadn't seen them hook anything. I suggested we row over and ask if they thought it was time for lunch. We did, and they agreed eagerly. Of course, we still had to weigh the salmon and have Harpo photographed standing proudly beside it. Only then did we learn what "Tyee" meant. We thought it had something to do with warning other boats to stay out of the way, but it means "a big one." Harpo's salmon, which had ruined his morning, weighed around forty-five pounds, making him a life member of the Tyee Club with a signed document to prove it. Harpo was so pleased to receive the document that he left it in the lunchroom. We now faced a serious situation. Harpo never wanted to be hooked to another salmon, and it didn't appeal to me either. The Krasnas's sole action had been to watch Harpo doing battle, and they'd had enough too. However, in discussing fishing with their boatman, Erle and Norman had learned of excellent trout fishing in Campbell Lake. After Harpo paid the guides and gave his big salmon to our boatman, we checked out. As we drove off, our boatman was being photographed with Harpo's salmon.

Vancouver Island is beautiful, wooded country to drive through. Free of fishing pressures, our spirits soared. Harpo pulled out his harmonica, and we sang whole scores of Gilbert and Sullivan to the residents of thatched cottages, out pruning their roses and waving as we passed. The unpaved roads reminded us of how smart we were to have rented a car. Arriving at the lodge we had the choice of rooms as there had been a forest fire, so the usual complement of guests (which they said would have filled their rooms) had sought other accommodations along the Campbell River—where we had just come from. It had taken a disaster, but we had a nice, clean lodge to ourselves. In the morning we were escorted to the landing, where each one of us was given a small rowboat and offered a variety of suitable tackle. It seems there are many ways to catch trout, depending on the day and the mood the trout are in. Although I'd never tried it, I opted for fly casting, as impaling a wriggling worm on a hook, no matter how appealing to the trout, was something I wouldn't do.

Two days of this peace and contentment was about all we could take. Besides, the blackened trees were beginning to look eerie, and the loons' cries were sounding melancholy, as if the terrible devastation of the fire had brought death to too much of their world. It was time to move on. There were other areas to explore. We didn't fare much better with motels on the return trip, but at least we knew what to expect. Norman, the avid fisherman, fell asleep as soon as the car started moving. With me taking my turn at the wheel, out came Harpo's harmonica to provide the soundtrack for the long drive. For Harpo, working was easy. Vacations were a mess.

CHAPTER TWELVE

Growing Up with Harpo

THINGS AT HOME COULD REMAIN RELATIVELY UNEVENTFUL FOR months at a time, but I could always count on Harpo to surprise me with some kind of adventure to break things up. He was still in show business, but only when the mood struck him. In a careless moment of greed, Harpo accepted a lucrative offer to appear with a rodeo at the International Amphitheatre in Chicago. My first surprise was that they held rodeos in Chicago, but there would be several more. The arena was built right next to the famed Union Stockyards, the meatpacking center of Chicago. This was very convenient if you liked the odor created by thousands of animals waiting to be turned into steaks. Taking a deep breath, we made it through the doors of the arena and were stunned by the size of the facility. This was not the perfect setting for the close intimate act that Harpo had been delighting theatre and club audiences with. I was a worrier, so, just for reassurance, I climbed to the upper gallery, but I could barely see him down in the arena.

The setup was interesting. The stockyards were just outside the walls of the dressing room. The animals kept up a constant bellowing, and the thin walls were no match for the smell. I know he spent many years in small-time vaudeville, but this had to be the dampest and smelliest dressing room of Harpo's career. Harps are affected by humidity, and even in dry conditions, they don't stay in tune very long because of the tension on the strings. While trying to tune up before the performance, the din and the dampness had Harpo attempting "Stardust" in a key never heard before. The full absurdity of our situation hit us when the stagehands got to work covering the cement floor with hay and dirt for the livestock show. We took a look at the program for the evening. It read, "Chicago International Rodeo Starring the Clown Prince of the Cowboys, Harpo Marx." Harpo had been on some strange bills in vaudeville, but I believe this was his first time working with a steer-wrestling exhibition. I kidded him about the comedy mule act listed in the program, but he assured me he had appeared with a legendary act called Fink's Mules years before. He added that those mules got paid more than the Marx Brothers.

One thing they don't usually need at a rodeo is a stage, and no one thought of getting one when they booked Harpo. It was decided to put him and his harp on a flatcar drawn by oxen and pulled to the center of the arena for the best positioning. Maybe it would have worked on a firm surface, but during the livestock show, the untidy animals had done their business with impunity and turned the floor into an aromatic ooze. Harpo was trundled out on the flatcar, which lurched through the lumpy mess. The possibility of both Harpo and his very expensive harp being tossed into the mire to the uproarious laughter of the observers was very real. Somehow the oxen did their job, and Harpo made it to the center of the arena. He was assisted in his act by a lovely soprano named Merri Fenn. She always came on after a musical number for the comedy bit. When her cue came, like a good trouper she pulled up her beautiful gown and waded through the muck to get to Harpo. The oxen, however, hadn't seen a script and began pulling the makeshift stage around the arena with the gallant Merri chasing them and Harpo hanging on to the harp for dear life. The audience was in hysterics, and no one laughed harder than I did. Everyone thought it was a planned comedy routine. With the help of a few sympathetic cowboys, Merri and Harpo managed to finish the act. Harpo was booked for eleven days, and on a few of them there would be matinees. He wasn't going to be this lucky fifteen times. The rodeo people worked out a more efficient plan for getting Harpo and Merri in and out of the mess, but there was nothing they could do about the smell.

Another of Harpo's memorable misadventures came when tax shelters swept the world of show business. A new form of income had been introduced. Show people trying to hang on to their salaries suddenly had the help of some creative financial advisors. Hillcrest Country Club must have become known as the pigeon coop of the West. Salaries were out. Capital gains were in. Oil wells had supplanted cattle breeding in Montana as the hot investment when Glenn McCarthy, the newest glamorous oil baron, built the luxurious Shamrock Hotel in Houston, Texas. McCarthy was known as the "King of the Wildcatters," and Edna Ferber used him as the basis for the character Jett Rink in the novel *Giant*. James Dean would play the fictional version of McCarthy when the book was turned into a film. There was no resemblance.

McCarthy lured the top names in show business to Houston to perform at the Emerald Room, the nightclub attached to the Shamrock. The stars would also appear on McCarthy's radio broadcast that originated there. Instead of cash, the payment was in oil leases for a percentage interest in McCarthy's oil fields, payable to the stars' newly formed oil companies. The income would not be subject to the normal income tax. This money would be considered a business investment and taxed at a much lower rate. It sounded fishy to me, but Burns and Allen, Frank Sinatra, Dinah Shore, Danny Kaye, Humphrey Bogart, Jack Benny, Harpo, and Chico were among the stars who fell for this deal. Harpo agreed to a two-week booking with Chico, mostly because he thought Chico would have a hard time gambling away McCarthy's oil leases. Chico might have been the only skeptical participant in this crazy enterprise. Chico was strictly cash and carry. Oil leases were not accepted at racetrack betting windows.

We were received in Houston with a great show of hospitality. Our suite was the size of our home in Beverly Hills. The living room had been filled with flowers, food and drink, and assorted well-wishers. Soon the crowd started drifting off and Harpo asked, "Where's McCarthy?" I replied, "When you find him, ask how big a percentage of how many oil wells he's giving you." We had been over this before, so he merely went off to take a nap. Why should he listen to my negativity? The investment counselors at Hillcrest had described this as an opportunity of a lifetime. I rarely found myself in agreement with Chico, but this just seemed ridiculous. Mary and I enjoyed our luxurious accommodations and had a front-row seat for the coming disaster. Chico was willing to bet that we'd never get paid. If he could have found any takers, he'd have cleaned up.

Harpo looked a bit unsure himself after we had a cocktail with McCarthy the next afternoon. His secretary had called to apologize for his not being at our reception, "as he never goes among crowds." Would we join him in the bar of the hotel at five o'clock? Of course, we would be delighted. At five o'clock we were groping our way through a darkness like in a theatre just before the movie goes on. Harpo suggested we stand still and maybe someone would come and get us. There was a light at the far end of the bar, and the bartender was moving toward us. No, we were not in the wrong bar, just follow him. We were led to a table where a slender man, wearing the huge dark glasses of a blind man, was sitting with a woman. We introduced ourselves and sat. He said nothing, just waved his hand at the barman to ask what we would like to drink. Another wave of his hand brought a guitarist. By this time, we had become accustomed to the dark and could see there wasn't another soul in the place. We learned later that if McCarthy was to be there, the bar was closed to anyone else. The guitarist was on a chair facing us and launched into songs extolling the greatness of McCarthy; telling how this mere youth had set the old Texas tycoons on their ears. He smeared lies all over our host, who was acting as if he were accepting the plaudits of a vast populace. My disgusted boy described it later as "jerking off." A half hour of this and Harpo nudged me, so I reminded him of an early dinner date, which we didn't have, and, apologizing to the guitarist, we left McCarthy to his trance.

We should have known what to expect for opening night in McCarthy's spectacular nightclub. By this time Harpo and Chico had their London act pretty well set and could pull it off without much rehearsal. Any trouble in the Emerald Room would not be caused by Chico. Except for one empty table, center front, the place was packed. The show had been on for close to an hour, and Harpo was well into his harp solo, when the spotlight left him in darkness and slid over to the entrance to pick up our host and friends. Harpo, not being able to see, stopped playing and watched the spotlight hold on the McCarthy party while they slowly moved to the empty table. He waited while they were fussily seated. The audience wondered how Harpo would take this insulting pretentiousness. The spotlight then moved back to find Harpo laughing helplessly. For a while there was pandemonium. The club rocked with laughter; then Harpo started to play softly, which never failed to control the rowdiest groups. Harpo certainly wasn't going to start the solo over for that egomaniac. Harpo and Chico finished their two weeks in Houston, and we never saw Glenn McCarthy again. We went home to wait for the checks to roll in.

Finally, the day came when an envelope arrived from Glenn McCarthy Enterprises. Of course, Harpo himself had to open it. I could hardly wait to see his face when he did. Harpo made the opening very ceremonious, carefully pulling up the flap with a "you didn't believe me" smile. Drawing out the check slowly, he held it out to me and collapsed with laughter. One dollar and eighty-six cents. So much for tax shelters.

A rodeo and a failed tax dodge, while at the top of the list of Harpo's strange decisions, paled in comparison to the all-time champion in that department, *The Yellow Jacket*. But I laid the blame for that one squarely at the feet of Alexander Woollcott. What then was I to make of Harpo's decision to revive *The Yellow Jacket* nearly a decade after Woollcott's death? Amazingly, the limited run of the show at the Pasadena Playhouse in the fall of 1952 was well reviewed and sold out every night. I think the whole thing was a joke in honor of Woollcott. That was the sort of thing that shouldn't have surprised me, but it somehow did.

During those years, Palm Springs was the weekend retreat for those of us in the movie colony who just wanted to lie in the sun, play tennis, and not answer the phone until Monday. Charlie Farrell ran a restful lodge at the Palm Springs Racquet Club, which he owned in partnership with actor Ralph Bellamy. The place was always so full of celebrities that no one stared. In fact, Charlie himself was a popular leading man in the twenties and thirties. He moved to the desert in the thirties, and, as his movie career slowed down, he retired and became the mayor of Palm Springs. Television revived Charlie's career in the early fifties, and he was simultaneously starring on *My Little Margie* and serving as the mayor. The main entertainment after dinner at the club was a walk down the three blocks of the main street to inspect the wares of the drug store. Visits to this cluster of old Indian spas were so healing of the week's stresses and free of fears induced by the big city that no one blinked when

Red Skelton's wife, Georgia, emptied her purse on the drug store counter looking for change to buy some postcards, and enough diamonds fell out to buy the main street. No one, that is, except me.

The desert changed when hotels moved in to catch the stream of tourists who had read the town's promotional material and wanted to see for themselves how movie stars looked without their makeup. To preserve some privacy for our increasingly frequent weekend getaways, Harpo and Gummo made a deal with the owner of a small hotel, a short distance from Palm Springs, to let us buy enough property for two small bungalows. These would be serviced by the hotel and have the use of the pool. A contractor was found, and our houses were started with the stipulation that they be ready in six months for Easter vacation. That seemed a reasonable length of time to us.

Reasonable or not, we were readying for the great Easter vacation when we learned the contractor had disappeared, leaving a pair of unfinished houses and howling creditors across southern California. Harpo and Gummo had paid the contractor's monthly bills, but apparently the subcontractors had not seen a dime of the money. But we would not be denied our Easter vacation, so with an accountant in charge of the creditors and a sympathetic young carpenter willing to work over the holiday, we went camping in our new house and learned a lot about living together. It was awkward having the carpenter using the living room for his workshop, but Alex swept paths through the sawdust every evening with a great display of responsibility. Minnie volunteered to make up the bunk beds, Jimmy posted himself with his bow and arrow outside to guard the house against a wave of caterpillars, and Harpo supplied creative plumbing. No fixtures in the showers? No problem. The weather was hot enough for cold showers, and since we had no hot water yet anyway, he attached a hose to the cold-water faucet in the kitchen sink and hung it out the window for showers to be taken standing in the dirt. We had no grass yet either. With this minimal form of cleanliness, we soon were asked not to use the hotel pool, but we were too busy anyway.

As we were planning our escape to the desert, we couldn't help but notice that Billy was suddenly a couple of feet taller than his sister and brothers. While we were dealing with Little League, Cub Scouts, and

Brownies, we also had a young man trying to figure out his future. Music seemed like the obvious path, but Billy wasn't sure. He'd been working out arrangements for Harpo by this point, and the work was certainly of professional caliber. But he wondered if he got the opportunity only because his dad was Harpo Marx. Billy lacked confidence and we were probably guilty of sheltering him from things like competition for a job. After brief flirtations with college and the Coast Guard, we shipped him off to New York. He'd work it out somehow, we hoped. We had friends in New York ready to help him. Max Gordon, the legendary producer and longtime friend of the Marx family, took up the challenge of helping Billy get on his feet in the big city. After a few weeks of Max trying to find Billy a job to no avail, this letter came in the mail:

October 26, 1955

Dear Harpo,

Raise the flags! Bill got a job at Gimbel's for $45.00 with a chance of getting $70.00. He did this all himself. I deserve no credit for it. I know one thing—if he gets rich, we're in on it.

Love to you and Susan.

Sincerely,
Max

Bill? Who was Bill? In Max's letter from only two days before he was still Billy. Our little boy had grown up. Working in a department store apparently made him realize that he was a musician because in a matter of only a few months in New York, Bill had managed to get himself into the Juilliard School of Music as a composition major. This he did completely on his own—Bill indeed!

We'd have to build our desert home with a slightly depleted crew, but Harpo was as proud of Bill getting into Juilliard as he was of anything that he'd ever accomplished himself. The rest of us adopted the attitude that building our home was pretty high-class camping, and we were having a wonderful time, especially due to the young carpenter who was delighted to have the kids help hang doors and pick up nails. Except, he drew the line at Alex, at the ready with a broom and a dustpan, trying to catch the sawdust before it hit the floor. And Harpo? His harp was in front of a sliding glass door, shaded by a striped, green awning; and he had an audience. The first morning as Harpo tuned up, a big yellow cat slid down the awning and laid there with his head hanging over the edge, listening blissfully until Harpo went off to experiment with his golf game. Then the cat disappeared. The next morning, as Harpo was tuning up, there was the cat again. From then on, whenever we came to the little house, at the sound of the harp, the yellow cat appeared in his balcony seat to enjoy the concert. I don't know which of the two of them enjoyed it more, Harpo or the cat. No offers of the traditional saucer of cream could lure the cat into friendly relations with the rest of us—only the harp.

The carpenter and the kids had the house put together before we had to go home for school, and we started looking forward to weekends in the desert. But it wasn't working out that way. The weekends were getting longer. Harpo wanted to be on the first tee early Saturday morning, which meant taking the six-hour drive (before the freeway came along) on Friday and returning on Monday. But the children had to be in school Friday and Monday. As an experiment, Harpo was encouraged to try it alone for a long weekend. If it worked for him, the family would just go down on holidays. Confident in his ability to survive alone, off he went. This worked for a little while, but one Monday evening at dinner Harpo said, "Let's talk. The smog here is so bad it's hard to breathe. The air in the desert is so clear, they keep windows open day and night. We've changed this house so often we might as well just build a new one. Traffic is getting horrendous; crime is moving in. Right?" Heads nodded.

Seeing he had our interest, Harpo continued. "Instead of living on a city lot, we could have a ranch of four acres—I just happened to see it across from the golf course—where you could have horses, and all the other pets you could think of." Minnie's eyes were glistening, "Horses, really?" I had only one question. "Wouldn't you miss Hillcrest Country Club?" Harpo answered, "They all belong to Tamarisk now." Tamarisk Country Club was the Palm Springs alternative to Hillcrest, and all of

Harpo's cronies had weekend places in the desert. The vote was unanimous. (Bill, being in New York, didn't get to vote, but he enthusiastically supported the plan.) The next day our home of twenty-one years was put on the market. Our new task was to design an appropriate ranch house for El Rancho Harpo. The timing seemed to be right as we were promised the new house for the following September, when Alex, Jimmy, and Minnie could enter Palm Springs Junior High School.

Predictably, the promise proved to be a bit optimistic, and I refused to move into a house with another carpenter. But with Harpo, anything that was unavoidable was not to fuss about. We had our little weekend house to wait in anyway. Harpo wasn't going to give me time to get restless, so he suggested we plan the design and landscaping of the four acres and think about doing the planting ourselves, as if we were putting down our new roots with those of the plants, like the early pioneers. Chain-link fencing already ringed the property against the pack of yelping coyotes prowling the area, so armed with a do-it-yourself book on landscaping, we set about putting down the Marx roots with oleander cuttings snipped from the hedges marking the perimeter of Tamarisk golf course. Having the extra virtue of saving a bunch of money by not buying rooted stock in cans from a nursery, Harpo kept assuring us that we would feel the joy of creativity when they leafed out. There's not much to be said for backbreaking work, except for the heavenly relief when it's over. But Harpo was right, we were enjoying making it ours—every leaf, every blade of grass. In the rich minerals of the desert sands our roots would grow as deep as the Tamarisk trees probing the earth for water.

Growth in the desert is fast, and it seemed as if overnight the little sticks were putting out leaves. It was time for us to take the next step in promoting a lush growth. The family crew went out to designated areas, directed to "sparingly spoon" a chemical fertilizer between the plants. No one was paying any attention to Harpo until suddenly Alex called out, "Dad, what are you doing?" "More is better," shouted back our gentleman farmer, who was happily shoveling the hot chemicals into his strip of trench. I ran to grab his shovel, yelling, "Mother Nature will get you for this." The kids tried to scoop the chemicals away from the squirming plants, but we had put in a system that sent water dripping into the troughs, and it was already carrying the chemicals to the burning new roots. That took care of Harpo's efforts at immortality via oleanders.

The day finally came to wave goodbye to the yellow cat and settle into our new permanent home. The very first morning I was lying in bed looking out through a wall of glass at the blackness that precedes the desert's dawn. Then, the hint of a red line spread across the edge of the horizon signaling the rising sun. I watched with awe as the color grew more intense, spreading across the skyline. This was impressive for a city girl who grew up with a skyline filled with skyscrapers. Harpo's special welcome came just a few mornings later. From his perch at the harp, he called excitedly, "Look who's at the window." Relaxing on the deep sill was the yellow cat. Harpo's audience had followed him the two miles across the desert.

We settled in and started thinking about how to celebrate the approaching Christmas in our new home. In Beverly Hills we had been accustomed to moving the furniture to make room for a ten-foot pine tree. In our new Spanish hacienda with a ceiling height of more than twenty feet, a ten-foot tree would be dwarfed. Never mind that a ten-foot tree cost only ten dollars in the city, while in the desert a tree cost ten dollars a foot. The kids suggested to Harpo that if he could find some ladders of different sizes—from four feet to about seven feet high—we could make a snowy landscape by throwing sheets and blankets over the ladders with little trees to fill up the vastness. Harpo's new buddies at the small country store he had adopted as his local hangout came through with the ladders, and Harpo promised to invite them to the dedication ceremony for the Marx Mountain Range, complete with eggnog. We put up an inexplicable sign at the foot of our mountain range: "Seattle 10 Miles."

While Harpo, Jimmy, and Alex drove to the nearby Indio Fairgrounds for our forest, Minnie and I draped the ladders with sheets and cotton batting, creating our mountains with Mt. Harpo at the summit, indicated by his clarinet and a little car horn. It was to be the family mountain range, so we scattered photos of the kids growing up among the trees. This was turning into the ultimate creation, and Harpo was having as much fun as his children. It was finished only when we ran out of room. I noticed someone had placed a photo of me peeking warily from behind a tree. Only one person would have put it there. I can't say it looked much like an Alpine landscape. Not many people have ever seen red and green cows with gold tails except on our Christmas trees, or laughing gnomes on sleds flying down a ski slope. It was our own fairy tale that Harpo wouldn't allow to be photographed, as it should never be duplicated; but it still lives in my memory. We hung Christmas balls on the harp, and Cathedral City came for eggnog.

Meanwhile, concerned that Bill couldn't be with us over the holidays, his father was busily spreading the family arms by readdressing to him, in New York, all the greeting cards from friends as we received them. With the snow on the New York streets and the deluge of greetings from our show business friends added in, Christmas 1957 was one he'd never forget.

I wondered how we could make this first desert Christmas even more special for the kids, who had risen to the occasion of building two houses and were all such good sports about our new pioneer lifestyle. It couldn't just be something in a gift-wrapped box sitting under a tree Christmas morning. I put it to our house genius at the harp, then sat back and waited while he strummed a few of his special arpeggios for problem solving. When the smile lit up, I knew my rational man had it. "There's too much for one day, right?" "Right." "So, let each person have their own day. Get a pencil and I'll lay it out for you," he continued. "Let's say the first day is Alex's day because he is the eldest of our three youngest. Minnie's day comes next, and then Jimmy's. Christmas Eve is for you and me for only one gift for both of us." We kept the gifts under ten dollars, and for Christmas day Harpo gave Alex, Jimmy, and Minnie each fifty dollars to fill the stockings that we'd hung by the fireplace.

To make Alex's day, we had a tractor with a mowing machine delivered. He went out of his mind with delight, and the other two didn't sleep that night wondering what would happen for them. The next day Minnie got a horse and plans for a stable. Then Jimmy got a tool shed for gardening stuff, delivered complete. It wasn't complicated. Sears outfitted Alex, and the local nursery, Jimmy. Minnie had joined a riding club when we first moved down to the desert, so we conferred with the ranch owner and bought Spots, her special horse. We arranged to have him walk in on Minnie's day. Our first Christmas in the desert was a very memorable Harpo-style affair.

CHAPTER THIRTEEN

Hypochondriacs Do Have
the Occasional Heart Attack

Y THE 1950S HARPO DIDN'T NEED TO WORK, BUT THE IDEA OF A complete retirement was unthinkable to him. He was still selective about club engagements and did team up with Chico every now and then, but suddenly there was a new alternative. Radio had essentially put Harpo on the nightclub circuit, but television had possibilities for a silent comedian. For a lot of stars, radio had been a restful interlude. Standing at ease in front of a microphone without makeup reading lines from a script seemed too good to be true. Soon rumors started to spread. "I hear Texaco has signed Milton Berle for a television show." "Agencies are talking to Burns and Allen, Jack Benny, Eddie Cantor, George Jessel, and Red Skelton." "Soon we'll see Edgar Bergen and Charlie McCarthy instead of just hearing their voices."

After some initial hesitation about television, reality set in and radio stars put their makeup back on. One of the first was Groucho, who brought *You Bet Your Life* to television in 1950. It had already been a top-rated radio show for three years. Chico also got a show that year, but it didn't last. Harpo didn't care for the pressure or the responsibility of a weekly show of his own, so when NBC offered a contract that would require him to appear on the network about once a month it seemed perfect. This would allow him to appear on different shows as a featured guest. His first guest shot was on the *Colgate Comedy Hour* with Donald O'Connor in 1951. He did several others in the early days, but he found it difficult to see the studio audience through all the cameras and equipment, which worried him because he couldn't gauge the audience's reactions. He eventually asked to be let out of the NBC contract. He'd still perform on television, but as with the nightclubs, he'd be selective. One offer that was just too good to turn down was from Lucille Ball, who had worked with the Marx Brothers in *Room Service* early in her career, several years before she became a star. She asked Harpo to appear on *I Love Lucy* in 1955, and that show turned out to be one of his most famous performances. Incidentally, Harpo performed Bill's arrangement of "Take Me Out to the Ball Game" on that show.

One of Harpo's television appearances remains indelibly connected to a sad memory for me. This has nothing to do with Harpo's performance or the show. Just before we were to fly to New York for Harpo to appear on *The Martha Raye Show* in 1956, Harpo overheard my mother make a horrible anti-Semitic remark at his expense. It went something like this: "Susan could have married into royalty or been married to a member of the Nobel family of Nobel Prize fame, but instead wound up marrying a kike." Harpo was crushed but said nothing to Mother. I knew it was still on his mind a few days later when we arrived in New York. We visited Bill at his apartment near Juilliard, and Harpo told him what Mother had said—mostly because Bill could see that something was troubling his father. The broadcast with Martha Raye went well, and Harpo was excited that several members of the New York Giants and Brooklyn Dodgers baseball teams appeared in a sketch with him; but Mother's bigoted remark cast an ugly shadow over the trip.

Harpo was never one to hold a grudge, but I'm sure he never felt any sort of closeness to Mother again. She was full of contradictions. As awful as she could be, she was also capable of being kind and thoughtful. Harpo wanted to take Alex and Jimmy on a weekend fishing trip, but they were each responsible for their paper routes. Mother told them to go with Harpo and enjoy themselves. She would handle it. She got on a bicycle and delivered all of the papers on both routes that weekend. It took her several hours. She was in her seventies, and it was very hot, but she got up at the crack of dawn and got to work; and of course, she had to deliver the heavy Sunday edition. But she could also say the worst things imaginable.

In January 1956, a few months after Bill left for New York, Harpo agreed to have the family participate in a television salute to Beverly Hills. The crew set up right in front of our house and Minnie, Alex, and Jimmy put on Harpo wigs. I didn't wear a Harpo wig, but I did act as Harpo's interpreter. Except for home movies I hadn't been in front of a camera in about twenty years. I wasn't surprised to learn that television was no more thrilling for me than the movies. The one thing about it that appealed to me was that it was over very quickly. Bill was still in New York at Juilliard, so he blew his chance to wear a Harpo wig on national television. By this time Bill had become an accomplished musician, so when he finally did appear on television with Harpo it was as his accompanist. Bill had worked on record albums with Harpo as both pianist and arranger.

In January 1958, after we'd settled into our new house in Palm Springs, the family made another television appearance, and this time Bill managed to be home. Edward R. Murrow's popular program *Person to Person* was famous for bringing television cameras right into the stars' homes. Harpo was eager to show off El Rancho Harpo. Once again, I'd get to be Harpo's interpreter, but this time it was a little different. I think Murrow expected Harpo to actually speak, since he was talking up a storm while the crew was setting up the cameras. Murrow was completely flustered when show time arrived and Harpo became his usual silent self. Murrow was visibly relieved when the time came for Harpo and Bill to play a selection from *Harpo at Work*, the new album they had recorded for Mercury Records. Harpo and Bill developed a close relationship because of their musical interests. The previous year they had collaborated on Harpo's first Mercury album, *Harpo in HiFi*. As a small boy, Bill would sit on the floor next to the harp, taking in Harpo's morning practice sessions with complete fascination. He would try to figure out how the difficult instrument worked as he enjoyed the sounds. It amazed him that his father could work his hands and feet simultaneously without falling off the stool.

Once, at a children's concert presented by the Los Angeles Philharmonic Orchestra, Bill whispered to me, "I know that music. It's Prokof." He was close enough. I knew he meant Prokofiev, but he was about five years old at the time, so I didn't correct him. Instead, I asked, "How do you know it?" He said, "Daddy plays it. It's *Peter and the Woof*." I couldn't wait to get home and tell Harpo, who wanted to start him on piano lessons immediately. Harpo's theory was that it's never too early to develop a musical talent. Perhaps early instruction would have changed the course of his own life. He might have been a concert harpist. I couldn't believe my ears. I asked, "Why would you want to change your wonderful life? Why would you want to be a concert harpist anyway? You can't be dragged to a harp concert. Why would you want to perform one?" He looked at me and said, "Well, if you're going to put it that way, I guess I'll never regret it again." I convinced Harpo that recognizing *Peter and the Wolf* (or in Bill's case, *Woof*) and having a good ear didn't necessarily make our son a musical genius. Piano lessons would wait—but not for long.

Years later there would be an interesting catch to Bill and Harpo's musical relationship, and it gave Harpo fits. His son wouldn't let him play in the key of C anymore. This man, who imagined himself as a concert artist, rebelled against having to work in unfamiliar musical forms. "It's too much," he would gasp to me in frustration. "I wouldn't do this for anyone but Bill." Harpo hated the discipline, but he loved the new sounds and soon became very comfortable with what Bill was showing him. When Harpo decided to make those albums for Mercury Records, it was only natural for Bill, with his special understanding of the harp, to do the arrangements.

Bill had taken an apartment in Hollywood to be close to the recording studios and nightclubs where he was often working in those days. When they started to work on Harpo's albums, they had world-renowned harp makers Lyon & Healy send a harp to Bill's apartment so they could rehearse at their leisure. They both loved this setup so much that the harp at Bill's place became permanent, and whenever he changed residences the harp followed. Harpo and Bill had a special bond. Bill had progressed from Harpo's twelve-year-old prop man to his nineteen-year-old musical collaborator, and nobody loved the idea more than Harpo. When Bill began to make his own albums a few years later, a very proud Harpo was pictured on the cover of one of them along with the line, "Bill Marx's Father Presents . . ."

I was thrilled to see Bill and Harpo working together, and those albums still sound beautiful to me. Unless it's played by Harpo, though, the harp is not my favorite instrument. Harpo could produce lovely warm tones that skilled harpists couldn't achieve. Some of the most renowned harpists in the world urged him to show them how he got certain effects, but Harpo's magic was all his own. It couldn't be taught. It was all in his fingertips and his soft touch. Highly trained players were taught to pull the strings hard which, to my ears, sounds tinny in the upper register. You can't go wrong in the lower register, that's sonorous no matter who hits it. Harpo, in the upper register, was as light as a bird's trill, but then he wasn't trained at any academy. Being self-taught, he played because he loved the sounds he could produce. Harpo's dear friend Mildred Dilling, a concert harpist, used to claim that she was Harpo's teacher. There was nothing anyone could teach Harpo about the harp that he hadn't learned by himself, but he would say to me, "If she needs it, let her have it."

I can remember when the Marx Brothers had just finished filming *Go West* at M-G-M. Harpo's harp solo was "From the Land of the Sky-Blue Water." He'd worked strenuously with the music department, finding a suitable arrangement, and then had to play it several times for the cameras. I thought he'd just about had it with "From the Land of the Sky-Blue Water." A few weeks later Harpo called me to hear a new piece he'd been working on. He launched into a big introduction, and then, varying tempo and volume, which was his particular style, he started to play some beautiful harmonies over a vaguely familiar melody. When he was finished, he smiled at me and asked, "What do you think?" What could I say? He had just played "From the Land of the Sky-Blue Water." Apparently, he had never noticed the melody, only the succession of chords. Playing different harmonies, he didn't notice he was playing them to "From the Land of the Sky-Blue Water." Harpo could fool with harmonies for hours without bothering to find a melody to go with them, playing softly for his own pleasure, or for the pleasure of a small child or a yellow cat. Harpo at the harp was like no other harpist. He seemed as if he was playing *to the* harp, bringing different emotions out of the instrument. If he played a sentimental ballad, the harp purred with pleasure, if in a mood for jazz, he and the harp would take off as if his fingers were tickling the nerve strings of a giggling harp. The harp was not an instrument to display Harpo's talent. It was more like they were into every piece together.

Harpo's health began to be a concern by the mid-1950s. The hypochondriac had finally progressed to having some real issues with his heart—or, as he called it, his ticker. A series of mild heart attacks should have permanently stopped him from performing, but he managed to convince the doctors that a carefully selected small schedule of performances wouldn't kill him. I'm not sure they really went along with the idea, but Harpo just couldn't completely stop working. That would have killed him before another heart attack could. As a compromise with his doctors, Harpo came up with an unusual idea. He attached a small box to the frame of his harp that would not be visible to audiences. It became Bill's responsibility to make sure the little box contained some of Harpo's nitroglycerine tablets. If he felt any chest pains during a performance, he would take a pill. He practiced removing a pill from the little box and taking it imperceptibly while playing the harp. I wasn't thrilled about this plan, but I suppose it was better than him being onstage without the pills.

The timing of Bernie Geis asking him to write *Harpo Speaks!* was a blessing. And I'm not so sure it was a coincidence. Groucho, well aware of Harpo's health situation, was a partner in Bernard Geis Associates and was finishing up his own book for Bernie. Groucho and Bernie encouraged Harpo to tell his story at the perfect time, knowing it would be just the right therapy. I loved the idea because it was something he could focus on instead of a show in Las Vegas or a television appearance in New York.

There were shows that Harpo insisted on doing, such as the annual benefits for the Palm Springs Police Department and the occasional booking with Chico, which usually put Chico on his feet financially—or at least paid off his latest round of gambling debts. But he really did scale things back. The book idea took shape in between Harpo's second and third heart attacks. In the fall of 1958, Bernie set up a meeting at our house with Rowland Barber, and Harpo liked him immediately. Rowland had coauthored boxer Rocky Graziano's autobiography, *Somebody Up There Likes Me*. Harpo was acquainted with Rocky—they'd appeared together on *The Martha Raye Show*—and he liked the book very much. Rowland suggested they get started with Harpo recording some of his memories on tape. Harpo tried this but didn't really like to have his voice recorded, so it lasted only a few days. Once they figured out a good process, the book came together quickly. Rowland would take notes as Harpo told him stories during his morning harp sessions at the bay window. Once it was clear that this was going to work, Bernie issued a press release about the book. At that point Harpo had been mostly inactive for around nine months, so he was pretty well rested in January 1959 when he went on the *Kraft Music Hall* television show with Milton Berle.

The show with Berle was followed by a half-hour television show with Chico for the *General Electric Theatre* series. Groucho made a quick cameo appearance in *The Incredible Jewel Robbery*. Chico looked terrible, and I spoke to Mary about his health. Neither of them should have been working. Chico needed to, but Harpo should have just stayed home talking to Rowland. To my astonishment, Gummo convinced Groucho, Harpo, and Chico to shoot a pilot for a weekly television series after *The Incredible Jewel Robbery*. It was called *Deputy Seraph*. Harpo and Chico would have been the stars and Groucho would have appeared occasionally. But by this point Chico was obviously too ill to work. They started shooting it but had to stop because the producers couldn't get insurance for Chico, who not only looked very sick, but also had trouble remembering his lines. I tried to talk Harpo out of *Deputy Seraph* and almost did, but Gummo convinced him that it would be good for Chico to work. I couldn't convince him that it would be bad for Harpo to work.

Another job I couldn't talk Harpo out of was the annual police benefit at Palm Springs High School a few weeks after *The Incredible Jewel Robbery* aired. Chico did the show with him, and all of the brothers gathered at our house to celebrate Chico's birthday. Harpo seemed up to the task for the benefit, and it was local, so I didn't push too hard on this one. But I really tried to stop a booking for Harpo and Chico at the Eden Roc Hotel in Miami in April 1959. This was purely an example of Gummo setting up a lucrative booking to keep Chico solvent. I was assured it would be all right, and for good measure Harpo squeezed in a couple of benefit shows before the Miami trip. I wasn't going to tag along this time, and I left Harpo in the care of Chico and Mary. I trusted Mary to take good care of Harpo but had mixed feelings about the whole thing. I tried not to let Harpo see how concerned I was, but I had a premonition that it wouldn't be okay.

The plan was for Harpo to spend the night before the flight at a motel near the airport in Los Angeles. Chico and Mary would pick him up in the morning, and they would be on their way. But in the middle of the night, Harpo had chest pains and called for a doctor, who gave him painkillers and nitroglycerin. At seven in the morning, Harpo called Chico and told him to cancel the Miami booking, but Chico was unable to reach anyone in Florida. Chico and Mary headed to Harpo's motel to take him back to Palm Springs, but by the time they got there the medicine had taken effect and Harpo felt much better. He decided to go to Florida. Had I made this trip, he would have been on his way home immediately. With all of the confusion, Chico didn't pick up the plane tickets and they almost missed their flight.

Chico and Mary had left their luggage at home thinking the trip was off, so Mary stayed behind to retrieve their bags and caught a later flight. She met them in Miami the following day. The plane Harpo and Chico were on was scheduled to stop in St. Louis but had engine trouble and had to make an emergency landing in Kansas City. Harpo called me from the airport when they eventually reached St. Louis and told me how the trip was going. I was furious. Why were Gummo and Chico putting a seventy-year-old heart patient through this? They arrived in Miami and the shows went on as scheduled. I wasn't sure Harpo would survive the week, but somehow, he did. Once again, Chico could say, "See? I told you it would be okay." Harpo celebrated when they got home by immediately having another heart attack.

Now I was going to take charge. I called Gummo and asked him why he was trying to kill his brother. Harpo and Chico were scheduled for a benefit with Mahalia Jackson in Chicago in May. We immediately canceled, and they got Mike Nichols and Elaine May to fill in. With no other bookings on the schedule, I put my foot down. Harpo was lucky this time. He just needed to take it easy and rest—no performing. He could paint and tell Rowland his stories, but I wasn't going to let him near a stage or a studio. I had wondered when my hypochondriac would actually understand that his doctors were telling him that working would kill him. This time it seemed to be clear. He painted almost every day, and he and Rowland made such great progress on the book that Bernie announced that it was finished in the fall. It wasn't, really, but Harpo had done his part. Now it was up to Rowland to put it all together. Harpo had the idea of calling the book *No Use Talking*, but Bernie eventually convinced him that *Harpo Speaks!* was a much better title.

After a year and a half of professional inactivity, an offer came that Harpo very much wanted to accept. He had considered taking a straight role, or even a speaking role in movies for years and never did it. Now came an opportunity to do it in a half-hour film for television. I was opposed to it not only out of concern for his health but also because I didn't want to see Harpo do anything on screen that was not natural to him. What he did in the movies was all very real. That was who he was. His own personality was in the character he created. I worried that he might not be able to do something so different, but he convinced me it would be fine. After much discussion we were able to arrange a relatively stress-free workload and a light shooting schedule. We also got Bill a bit part so he could stay on the set and keep an eye on Harpo. The film was called *A Silent Panic*, and Harpo was terrific as a deaf-mute witness to a murder. He could have said, "I told you it would be okay," but he was gracious about proving me wrong. It ran on the *Dupont Show with June Allyson*, and the reviews were so good that Harpo started talking about a career revival. I gave him a pretty stern look and he said, "Well, maybe not."

I couldn't keep him down too much longer. He was feeling rejuvenated and promised to take only very special jobs. A television show with Louis Armstrong couldn't be passed up. Harpo had to skip the 1960 Palm Springs police benefit, so he had to make up for that and perform at the 1961 edition. We were also about to see the publication of *Harpo Speaks!* and he had promised to do publicity for the book. We would just be careful and watch for any signs that he was having trouble. In the spring of 1961, it seemed like you couldn't turn on a television set without seeing Harpo. He was on with Ed Sullivan, Merv Griffin, Art Linkletter, and he even turned up with Groucho on *You Bet Your Life*. In New York he filmed a silly stunt for *Candid Camera* and went on the *Today Show*. The big press party at the Algonquin celebrating the publication of the book was featured in a *Life* magazine photo spread.

He held up so well that I started to fear that Harpo would start booking some shows. But he took the summer off and only committed to a couple of benefits and one television show in the fall. In October we flew to New York, where Harpo was to star in *The Wonderful World of Toys* with Carol Burnett. It was to be shot in Central Park. Almost as soon as we arrived, the news came that Chico had died. It was not entirely unexpected. He had been in failing health for some time and was bedridden for several weeks. Mary and I had often compared notes about our frequently ailing Marx Brothers, and it was clear that Chico was not going to get well. It pained me to see such extreme sadness in Harpo when he got the news.

We immediately flew back to California. The next day we drove from Palm Springs to Beverly Hills for the funeral with Zeppo and his second wife, Barbara. He and Marion had divorced several years earlier. Groucho was on his third wife by this time and Eden, a lovely, quiet young woman, was with him at the funeral. Harpo was mostly silent for much of the long drive from the desert. For all of the aggravation Chico caused, he and Harpo had shared a special bond since they were kids. The four surviving Marx Brothers looked ashen at the funeral. They wondered aloud about which of them would go next, but by the end of the day they were sharing their favorite Chico stories and trying to laugh while facing their own mortality head-on.

CHAPTER FOURTEEN

Israel, 1963

HARPO WENT RIGHT BACK TO WORK AFTER CHICO DIED. WE
flew back to New York, and Harpo began shooting the show
with Carol Burnett as originally scheduled. He got through it,
but Chico's death was a blow Harpo found it hard to recover from. They'd
been inseparable since childhood, and, in spite of whatever trouble Chico
caused, Harpo could never stay angry at him. Chico had that effect on
many people. I somehow managed to remain immune to his charms as he
constantly got himself out of trouble with those closest to him. I probably
witnessed too many "what will we do about Chico" meetings with Harpo,
Groucho, and Gummo over the years.

Harpo was now telling reporters and friends that he was semiretired.
It was an important step because he was starting to feel his limitations,
and he was telling people about it. For the first time he was saying that he
was tired and preferred to stay home and paint. He relaxed for a couple
of months before we made a trip to New York for a pair of shows that
had special meaning for Harpo. Bill came along on this trip as his father's
arranger. Harpo had become a big supporter of symphony orchestras and
loved performing with them. Just before Chico died, Harpo had played
two benefit concerts for the Riverside Symphony. On January 16, 1962,
he appeared with the Symphony of the Air at the Waldorf Astoria, and
a few days later we headed south to a benefit for the Philadelphia Symphony Orchestra. Harpo worked with Leopold Stokowski and Eugene
Ormandy for that one. A reporter asked if he was nervous about playing
with these giants of classical music, and Harpo said, "Sure, but you have
to admit I've got plenty of guts." Harpo loved that phrase and used it

when he was asked about playing the clarinet at the London Palladium just before Benny Goodman was scheduled to play there.

In New York the phone in the hotel room started ringing the moment we checked in, and it seemed to never stop. There was a young woman desperately trying to get an interview with Harpo. He gracefully declined but she kept calling, and after not answering the phone for a couple of days, he picked it up and she was still trying. So, he agreed to do the interview. The woman turned up at our room for the interview and as they were speaking the phone started ringing. Harpo ignored it. The woman asked, "Aren't you going to answer that?" Harpo replied, "No. It's probably you."

The symphony performance at the Waldorf was a benefit for the America-Israel Cultural Foundation. Although he'd raised money for Israel with total commitment, Harpo had no desire to go there. But he couldn't resist an invitation from the State Department to be a guest of the Israeli government. In 1963 the Israeli Ministry of Culture reached out to prominent artists from around the world, hoping these people would visit and promote their emerging country. In March, I accompanied a slightly reluctant Harpo, and we joined a group of distinguished people traveling to Israel for a week. As soon as we took off, Harpo's escape system went into action, putting him to sleep for the entire flight. We were received by two delightful men. Moshe Pearlman was an Englishman who seemed to be connected with the military. Moshe had the local distinction of looking like Groucho. Teddy Kollek was an aide to the prime minister and later became the mayor of Jerusalem. They would be our hosts and guides.

One afternoon, invited to the Kolleks' for tea, we realized that their small apartment was representative of an economy that put strict priority on public services like schools, hospitals, and, of course, defense. Luxury was not only morally questionable because of the shortage of money, it was dangerous. Historically, the nonaggressive Jews relied on prayer as a means of defense. But their religion couldn't create a peace with another religion teaching their destruction. The world was generous, but the need for armaments was enormous. To quote Golda Meir, "We Jews have a secret weapon in our struggle with the Arabs; we have no place to go." Harpo's initial thought was that Israel didn't have any problems that money couldn't solve, but seeing the complexities of the political climate in the Middle East up close made him realize there was much more needed than money.

Harpo decided to go along with me to see the antiquities and local crafts that he wasn't sure would interest him. A car and a guide were assigned to us, and after lunch in an old Arab market, we drove to Nazareth to see marvelous tapestries being made. There was much creativity in Israel to show the tourists, along with the ruins of cities built and destroyed by a stream of conquerors. But there was more. Our guide offered to show us an Israel that the usual visitor would never see. When a wary Harpo asked "How?" our guide said, "Carefully." Harpo was in. Early the next morning, Harpo told me to take my toothbrush and we took off for the Lebanese border. I wasn't crazy about exposing myself to the trigger-happy Lebanese, but we had done my tourist stuff, now it was time to see the real Israel. Driving in Israel was a sociable experience. There being few cars, and fewer buses, the roads were lined with pedestrians who expected to be picked up by any car going in the same direction. Eventually we came to some thin wire stretched across the hilltop that wouldn't stop a loose cow from ambling through. "Where's Lebanon?" Harpo asked. Our guide pointed and said, "It's in the valley below, simmering in hatred." Harpo sneaked a cautious look beyond the fence and reported that it looked quiet. I stayed in the car thinking that perhaps they didn't start target practice until evening. As we drove away, Harpo confessed he had felt terror for the first time in his life.

In a small dusty village, we were invited into the home of an Arab teacher, who fortunately spoke excellent English. He proudly showed us his library, which included a large supply of *Popular Mechanics* magazines sent to him by a friend in the United States. He explained that by using them as textbooks, he was able to teach the boys of his village a fairly basic academic program. He said, "The text supported by pictures is essential, as my students need the visual picture of what they are reading about. If you have never seen a cup, it's only a funny sound." He was thrilled when Harpo promised to send him a subscription to *National Geographic*. He wrote later of the delight of his students in discovering the exotic places the magazine described. This dedicated man had only one wooden chair in his two-room house. His table was a plank supported by local handmade bricks, his bookshelf the same. His students sat on the floor. But he felt he was one of the fortunate. His village was proud to have a distinguished educator among them.

We spent that night at a kibbutz and shared a supper of the local bounty in the community dining room. Harpo and I listened in awe as the communal society was explained. Back at the hotel, Harpo said, "In all my years of being wrapped in defense against the contempt of small-town people for vaudevillians and Jews, I never realized how personally I had taken anti-Semitism until tonight. Sitting among these people, laughing and chatting, I now understand that none of that anti-Semitism from those small-town people had been directed at me personally. It was wonderful. It has made me feel light-headed." He knew I understood; women have to absorb a lot of contempt to be able to hang on to self-esteem. Harpo now wanted the total experience of these people.

What unified them apart from survival? Powerful pagan nations who appeared in history along with the emerging nation of the Jews have totally disappeared. Why not the Jews? We found the right book. It was right there in *Jews, God, and History* by Max I. Dimont: "They have had a continuous living history for four thousand years. They have survived three thousand years without a country of their own yet preserved their ethnic identity among alien cultures. They have expressed their ideas not only in their own language, but in practically all the major languages of the world." This single passage contained all the information Harpo could absorb before he fell asleep.

An early priority of the Jewish National Fund was reforestation. When we arrived, the project was well under way, but getting water to hillsides was still a problem. Men and women daily carried cans of water to dribble sparingly in the trough of every tree, and it was working. The mineral-rich sands were bringing back the forests. We were introduced to a ceremony in which visitors planted their spiritual roots in the land.

Jew or Gentile, it all started here. For a few dollars one is given a spade, a paper cup of water, and a tiny fir tree, then shown a prepared hole in which to plant the tree and sprinkle its roots with the few drops of water. Harpo and I planted our trees side by side, feeling that we were taking part in something eternal.

While manning their defense posts, Israelis were also building cultural centers. Under the direction of the great violinist Isaac Stern, the Mann Auditorium was built in Tel Aviv to house the superb Israel Philharmonic Orchestra. This magnificent concert hall was packed for every performance. One memorable evening, Harpo and I were taken to the opera. We didn't care what opera. Knowing my husband, we would probably leave during the intermission anyhow. From our box we watched the buzz of the arrivals, visiting, greeting, and finally finding seats in high anticipation. It was interesting to watch the effect it was having on Harpo. He was absorbing the excitement and pleasure of a people he was feeling a kinship with. Harpo had become a Jew among Jews and was enjoying it.

A familiar overture started. Harpo looked at me and broke into a big grin—*Il Trovatore*. Had our hosts known that the Marx Brothers destroyed *Il Trovatore* in *A Night at the Opera*? In the film, Harpo and Chico break up the scenery in a wild chase before popping up in the orchestra pit throwing a baseball to the rhythm of "Take Me Out to the Ball Game." I worried that Harpo might feel sad remembering Chico, who had died a year and a half before. I needn't have. The audience was well aware that a beloved member of the tribe was in the house. Marx Brothers films played constantly in Israel. We were enjoying the music when it happened. Some of the singers stepped to the footlights to join the orchestra ringing out "Take Me Out to the Ball Game." There was pandemonium. The audience beat out the rhythm with their hands, and a young man jumped up from his seat and pretended to throw a ball to Harpo. Of course, Harpo caught it and threw it back, but convulsed with laughter and tears. There was no doubt, Harpo was family. We saw as much as we could of this land of rich cultural contrasts. Harpo loved it all. He now had some historical perspective.

Another member of our group, the novelist James Michener, whole-heartedly received the inspiration the Israeli government had hoped for when inviting him. Nightly, at dinner, he was reporting on daily visits to the archaeological dig at Tel Megiddo, the site of the ancient city of Megiddo, King Solomon's stables, and the biblical Armageddon. He was feeling a growing excitement in finding a new environment in which he could weave a modern story into the deep perspective of Biblical history. Jim's work would eventually result in the historical novel *The Source*, which told the story of the Jewish people and the state of Israel. A careful researcher, Jim liked the factual evidence of geologic time as opposed to ecclesiastical speculation on ancient documents. To absorb the cultural clues, Jim planned to move into the area. This meant that he and his wife, Mari, would return home and repack for a year's stay in Israel. Mari and Jim were going home via Turkey and Greece, and Harpo had been talked into doing the same.

To our great surprise the customs people in Greece recognized Harpo, and he was instantly lauded as a national idol and a great hero. He was certainly not accustomed to the tremendous enthusiasm and the grand welcome he received strolling thought the airport in street clothes. It was a brief glimpse into the normal routine of other stars who had to accept that sort of thing every time they ventured out in public. Unexpectedly, Athens became the perfect finale to our trip. In just one day and night, Athens provided us with the contrast of holiness versus grandeur. In the afternoon we visited the Acropolis, awed by the marble beauty of the remains of once glorious buildings desecrated by time and plunder. Athens' belated effort to provide a small museum for the few sculptures remaining added to our sense of the remoteness of classical Greece. How different it was from Israel's biblical durability.

Before leaving Israel, an enchanted Harpo had volunteered to enter-tain for a year at fundraisers for the United Jewish Appeal in American cities, playing some harp and talking about what he had seen and felt in Israel. As for me, the short visit had allowed us only a brief sense of this modern miracle of survival. My lasting memory is of the narrow road from Tel Aviv to Jerusalem, winding through wooded hills, lined on both sides with wrecked jeeps and small tanks. On each one hung a wreath. There is no more solemn cemetery.

Home again, Harpo looked back on Israel with a new feeling of lightheartedness. No longer was he just in sympathy for a foreign people in distress. Jews were not just denied membership in restricted country clubs; they were produced of a deep thrilling history. Harpo had been absorbed back into the Hebrew race, a people proudly exhibiting their respect for one another in achieving a freedom to be themselves. This had eased a pain long buried. Harpo loved the feeling of being a part of this rich history. But he would have only a year and a half to enjoy it. 1964 was waiting.

CHAPTER FIFTEEN

The Widow Marx

I T MAY HAVE BEEN A GOOD YEAR FOR THE GRAPES IN NAPA VALLEY, but 1964 was a lousy one for me. In July I had to cope with the trauma of a mastectomy; and on September 28, Harpo died. Not only did I feel my femininity had been damaged, but I felt useless. I could have sat in a dark hole forever, but the reality was that I had to crawl out and get going. There was still Minnie and Jerry's wedding to be planned, and Minnie wanted it to be in our home. We had plenty of room, so I didn't mind as long as the caterer brought everything in and set it up. Minnie needed a wedding outfit and so did I, having dropped from a size sixteen to a size twelve—and not in a healthy way. Bill would play "The Wedding March," and we could have the minister stand by the silent harp for the ceremony. That ought to break everyone up.

It was a lovely affair. Groucho was honored to take Harpo's place to give the bride away, but he was in shock. When it came time to place Minnie's hand in Jerry's, he clung to her. Minnie kept whispering, "Let go, Uncle Groucho. Sit down, Uncle Groucho." A deeply emotional man, the silent harp paralyzed him. Bill, still sitting at the piano, knew by the silence that something was going wrong, so he started playing "The Wedding March" again. Groucho came out of his trance, let go, and the ceremony proceeded in a state of suppressed hysteria. Jerry's family came out from Ohio, and all our relatives and oldest friends came down from Beverly Hills to share our mixed emotions. Later, Harry Tugend's wife, Jean, said to Gummo's wife, Helen, "I kept watching Susan. If she didn't cry, I certainly wasn't going to let myself lose control." I wouldn't have liked it if she had. To cry would be to turn away the day from Minnie. The emotion was there. Everyone felt it. To release it would have destroyed its depth and permanence.

Understanding Harpo had been like a literature course I once took from a wonderfully eccentric professor. He would try to explain the underlying symbolism in even the most straightforward story. With Harpo there was no symbolism. My boy was not one to explore his psyche. I had Harpo down pretty well, but there were occasionally times when I blew it. Bill always teased me about one such incident. When Bill was very small, there was a local children's radio program called *Uncle Whoa Bill*, and Harpo would often skip a bridge game at Hillcrest to hurry home and listen to it with him. The two of them had a standing date in front of the radio every day at 5:30. The show was fairly silly even by Harpo's standards. Uncle Whoa Bill would announce the names of children listening in who were celebrating birthdays. He would then, with a little help from the child's parents, tell the kid where to find a surprise birthday present. That, and the sound of a toy piano comprised most of the show. Otherwise, it was a radio show with puppets. Of course, if the kids wanted to see these puppets, they could be purchased from Bullock's department store, *Uncle Whoa Bill's* sponsor.

Harpo's birthday came on November 23, and he passed another milestone. After that day's installment of *Uncle Whoa Bill*, Harpo and Bill just looked at me. It was clear. I had failed. My fifty-four-year-old child had expected Uncle Whoa Bill to announce little Harpo's birthday. He had listened that afternoon waiting for Uncle Whoa Bill to give him clues so he could find his hidden birthday present. More than fifty years later, I still regret not thinking of it. When Bill brought it up recently, I feebly defended myself. "That show was so moronic I couldn't imagine even your crazy father listening to it." But Bill would have none of that. He liked *Uncle Whoa Bill* too. But of course, he was only five at the time.

Harpo had been his mother's favorite, which was a great start in life for anyone. Some have concluded that Chico was her favorite. But the brothers agreed that while she indulged Chico more than the others because she couldn't resist his charm, Harpo was the most special to her. Minnie Schoenberg Marx was unique. She invented the Marx Brothers in her own image. Each of the brothers had a piece of her, but Harpo had the most. To me, he also got the best: her calm, her kindness, her sense of the absurd, her loving acceptance of error (if indeed she ever saw it), her directness of purpose, and her sanity. The bond was closer than he was aware of. From old photos it amused me to see the curly blonde wig that Minnie wore was the same as the one worn by Harpo when he developed his mute, puckish character.

When we married, Harpo wore the gray three-piece suit complete with starched-front shirt, gloves, and cane that I recognized as the outfit Frenchy had worn on the few occasions when we had met at Harpo's beach house. I wondered where Harpo had kept them during the years after his father's death. I also wondered why. This was no comic disguise. Harpo's instinct was unerring in everything he did, so it would be characteristic of him to do something that might add a bit of solemnity to our offbeat wedding ceremony. Harpo may have been thumbing his nose at Hedda and Louella with our elopement, but our marriage was being taken seriously by at least one of us. Whether by intent or not, Frenchy's outfit became a solemn reaffirmation at every one of our twenty-eight anniversaries, except the last. I buried the complete costume finally, with his ashes, in a ceremony just for the two of us.

Before I had a chance to even realize how alone I was, Bill moved in with me. He pretended that he wanted some quiet time in the desert to write music, but he needed as much help as I did. Bill called me a role player, meaning I am what I am, by popular demand. Name your needs and protean Susan will attend to them. But where there is no demand, do I cease to exist? Important question. Could I fill up this void with new experiences and have the sum total be me again? After we married, I wore Harpo's name and put aside the one I had been using. It was a strange dislocation at first. It took many years to discover how to play the new role assigned to me. After he died, I wondered if I should look for a new part to fit myself into. Or perhaps it was time to find out who that other half really was. I had to be more than a leftover wife.

I spent the next year virtually sleepwalking. People were astonished and impressed at my seeming grasp of legalities. I could sit through a business conference, asking appropriate questions for clarification, but what I didn't let on was that, as I walked away, I didn't remember a word.

For protection I never went to a meeting without Bill. He was able to repeat the important points to me later on. The most difficult thing for me to handle was the financial advice coming at me from all directions. To the consternation of a few friends, and my lovingly anxious brothers-in-law, my confident husband had named me sole trustee of everything. Groucho, Zeppo, and Gummo could see me blowing it all at the final fadeout, with me and the four children huddled at a street corner, piteously holding out our tin cups.

I didn't like the advice I was getting, as it was more of the same that had plagued our personal economy for years. I had never understood how all of our money being tied up in deductible investments was advantageous if it left us without cash. Besides, the investments were only deductible if they lost money. Harpo had been especially attracted to deals controlled by the unscrupulous. He felt that being with the smart money was insurance against loss. Nothing crooked—just the percentage of the house, to use a gambling term. I was usually critical of these deals. It seemed to me that when you're let into a deal for a percentage, it saves the dealer from borrowing money and paying interest and you carry the risk.

Now it was my turn to be the decision maker. No more investing for tax write-offs. My mother believed in blue chip common stocks, through which she had acquired a comfortable income with the money inherited from her mother after my parents' years of financial ups and downs. Harpo had looked at the stock market like a drowning man being thrown a rock. He came by that feeling naturally. He and Groucho had each lost a small fortune in the crash of 1929. I thought the choice was obvious, so I stepped out of the treacherous seas of tax evasion and told my broker not to call me. I would call him. I was determined that our four children and I should be the ones responsible for our combined destinies. I was well aware that I didn't know much about high finance; but I was also appalled at how easily Harpo had been sucked into some strange, and obviously losing, investment opportunities by financial giants who got to be financial giants by using the money of gullible friends. Bill has a little of that gullibility. A used-car dealer has an edge over him every time.

One enterprise that I promptly dumped, in spite of threatened lawsuits, had been costing us forty-five thousand dollars a year to support.

Harpo had never lost confidence in this deal. I never believed in it, but Harpo was in charge of investments then. Now, however, I was family caretaker. The family income was going to go in five different directions, and I needed to be careful. I also needed help. So off I went to the bank holding the loan to the primary shareholders in this dubious investment. The bank president listened to me quietly and then phoned our lawyers and authorized them to threaten my partners in the deal with cancellation of their loan if they continued to make trouble for me. He said, "Harpo Marx has died, and we are in sympathy with his widow." Al Hart was an unusual banker who had started City National Bank in Beverly Hills with friends and stayed with them. Al's scrupulous honesty might have surprised people who knew he got started as Al Capone's beer distributor during Prohibition in Chicago.

My big problem was the Brotherhood. They were lovingly concerned that the witless widow was going to blow the inheritance unless they were counseled with. It was a little tricky to keep from being thought ungrateful and irresponsible when I was being counseled by Gummo, the family advisor, who was considered informed because he subscribed to the *Wall Street Journal*. He recommended a railroad stock that the *New York Times* business section showed in bankruptcy. Zeppo managed to sell his share of a family-held citrus ranch just before a statement was issued showing that the rest of us were stuck with a loser. Harpo had followed Zeppo into a few deals, having faith in his ability to outsmart his competitors. Unfortunately, Zep also outsmarted his partners.

A strange man who even his brothers never completely understood, Zeppo could entertain a party of friends with uproariously funny anecdotes. He had style, taste, and good looks, but there simply hadn't been room for a fourth comic Marx Brother, and Zep had to settle for the humiliation of straight roles. The funniest Marx Brother off screen couldn't get a laugh on screen. He left the team to become a highly successful agent, representing some of the biggest names in Hollywood, but his lack of success as a member of the Marx team was a psychological problem he struggled with to the end. Zeppo's agency also represented many top screenwriters, and there was a time when he was trying to get Norman Krasna to sign with him. They were in a restaurant in Hollywood, and Zep was really pressing him. Norman kept telling him that he already had an agent. During the course of the dinner, a nearby drunk had started pestering Norman. As they were leaving, the drunk tried to throw a punch at Norman, but Zep intercepted him and knocked the drunk out with one punch. Before the guy hit the ground, Zep turned to Norman and said, "Yeah, but does your agent do that for you?"

A heavy gambler, Zep made a point of feigning big losses. This was a game he played with other gamblers. He always pretended the other fellow had the edge. In his later years, Zep managed to convince Gummo, who wasn't a gambler, that he was having financial trouble. Gummo persuaded Groucho, who was frugal to the point of miserliness, to give Zep an allowance! When Gummo proudly told me how he had taken care of his baby brother, I could only wonder if he knew he'd been had.

My interactions with Groucho, Gummo, and Zeppo became less frequent after Harpo's estate was settled, but I did remain friendly with Chico's wife, Mary, for many years. Groucho's third wife, Eden, was also a dear friend, and we became even closer after she divorced Groucho. Eden convinced me to take a writing course with her, which turned out to be the impetus for me writing my memoirs. Eden was saddened by the sight of Groucho, in his eighties, trying to work on television and even doing concert appearances after suffering a couple of strokes. While I had been against Harpo performing once doctors expressed concerns about his heart, I would have really put my foot down and stopped him if he was embarrassing himself with poor performances. By this time Gummo was in roughly the same shape as Groucho and had long since stopped handling Groucho's bookings. He died in 1977, shortly before Groucho did. Groucho's condition was so precarious that he was never told about Gummo's death.

Eden had kept in touch with Groucho and visited with him occasionally right until the end. But she was in no position to tell him the truth about what he was doing to his reputation by working. She would have been kept from seeing him if she said anything critical. I was relieved that even in his compromised state Groucho was always complimentary to me in interviews. I gave one in which I was probably a little too honest about Groucho's performing capabilities in his old age. I was truthful, but in retrospect I should have declined the interview. Eden was very troubled by Groucho's final years. A crazy young lady, coincidentally named Erin Fleming, had taken over his life and was abusing him. This led to a lengthy series of circus-like courtroom dramas concerning Groucho's competence, his medical care, the appointment of a conservator, and ultimately his estate. Eden loved Groucho to the end, but, as he had twice before, he drove away a loving wife. Sadly, she died of cancer in 1983 at the age of fifty-three. Zeppo had died in 1979, and suddenly the Marx Brothers were all gone.

CHAPTER SIXTEEN

Rediscovering Susan Marx

AFTER HARPO'S DEATH THERE WAS A LOT MORE THAN FINANCES to reorganize. What does one do with two very valuable Lyon & Healy harps? The answer came unexpectedly, before I had even considered the problem. Included in the flood of condolence cards and letters I received from around the world was one from A. Z. Propes, the chairman of the Israel Harp Festival Committee. The summer of 1965 would be the time of two major events in Israel. The Seventh Maccabiah Games—the International Jewish Olympics held every four years for Jewish athletes from around the globe—was scheduled at several facilities, including Ramat Gan Stadium in Tel Aviv. But more to the point, the Third International Harp Contest—which was not limited to Jewish artists—would also take place that summer. First prize for the contest was, most appropriately, a harp, donated by Lyon & Healy. Mr. Propes wrote asking if I would like to come as their guest and be a judge.

I explained that I was far from qualified to judge a harp contest, but my son Bill was a graduate of the prestigious Juilliard School of Music and had worked very closely with his father as an arranger and pianist. He could function very well as a judge. Propes was delighted to invite Bill, and it was decided that I would present the second prize of two thousand dollars, which we donated in honor of Harpo. It would be wonderful to share with Bill a little bit of what Harpo had found so rewarding on our trip to Israel in 1963. Bill and I would also be special guests at the opening ceremony of the Maccabiah Games. In further correspondence with Mr. Propes, I learned that there were only two harps in Israel for students learning the instrument. These harps were also used by the philharmonic orchestras in Tel Aviv and Jerusalem and were often unavailable to students.

Isaac Stern was the president of the America-Israel Cultural Foundation, and with his help I was able to cut through a lot of international bureaucracy and donate both of Harpo's harps to the Rubin Academy of Music—one each for their campuses in Tel Aviv and Jerusalem. It had been suggested that I put them in a museum. But harps must be played, or they lose their tone. I was not offering a work of art to be hung on a wall. The tension of the strings on the soundboard shortens the life of the instrument, so there was a practical reason to get people playing these harps as soon as possible. And most importantly, the beauty of a Lyon & Healy harp is the quality of its sound, unequalled by any other, and, unfortunately, that sound does not improve with age, unlike the sound of a violin. I wanted these harps to be played, not viewed. And Harpo would have loved his instruments being used by students. Subsequently, Bill and I visited both campuses of the Rubin Academy of Music and had the pleasure of seeing students playing Harpo's harps, with a long list of them signed up for practice. The harps were silent no more. Harpo would have been thrilled.

We had arrived in Israel a couple of weeks before the start of the Harp Contest, so we had a chance to explore Tel Aviv and attend the Maccabiah Games. Our seats for the opening ceremony were high in the stands at Ramat Gan Stadium, giving us a superb view of everything. I can't remember ever being so interested in the audience at a spectacle at home. I was glad to be there to share their excitement. It was a celebration of Israeli pride, a warm, humble pride in hosting athletes from around the world. We attended a basketball game at the Yad Eliyahu Arena, which was still under construction when the games began. I thought Bill was getting bored when he excused himself for a moment. He returned giggling and said, "They haven't put in all the toilets yet, so the men are peeing out of the upper concourse." Adaptable people. Harpo loved the absurd, and I was sorry he missed this.

The harp competition was to last twelve days. Some of the world's finest harpists would go head-to-head. It was understood, that with the scarcity of instruments, there were no Israeli harpists who could qualify to enter. But we were pleased that the donation of Harpo's harps would help change that for the future. Being part of this experience was exciting and stimulating. This was at the height of the Cold War, and even the three Russian harpists—kept socially separated by their KGB-agent chaperones to the point of not even being seen except at performances—were respected for their superb playing. Fortunately for the Russians, there were no points for charm; although one Russian player received a big hand for her aplomb when she broke a string and had to stop playing to replace it. I had become infected by the general excitement in the air. I don't remember anything spectacular about the evening of the finals. It was a marvelous evening in Tel Aviv, and I'm sure there was a banquet somewhere, but my anxiety at the expected disappointment of those who wouldn't win first place spoiled any pleasure I might feel in the joy of the only one who would win. Stupid I know, but I'm a rooter. I wanted everyone to win.

Bill and I came home from Israel shortly before the first anniversary of Harpo's death. The hardest year was behind me. Now the time had come for some self-examination if I weren't to become an alcoholic. While I did spend some time considering my situation with a vodka bottle at my side, I was determined not to follow the path of Groucho's alcoholic ex-wives. My brief flirtation with numbing the pain through alcohol accomplished nothing. When I mentioned this to Groucho, who loved me dearly, he said predictably, "No one has a better reason to drink." I could have copped out on that one, except I knew he was wrong. Groucho eventually saw all three of his wives take that course without ever wondering why.

Groucho didn't treat those he loved any differently from the contestants on his quiz show. The difference was that if he missed a chance to insult a contestant on the show, the contestant could walk away with a feeling of survival, but this relief was not available to those who lived with him. Sooner or later Groucho would get them. His lack of sensitivity bordered on sadistic. It was not an intellectual impatience with a fool. No matter who it was, if Groucho saw weakness, he compulsively let fly. Gummo was actually one of his most frequent targets. Same parents, close brother relationships, and supporting environment, but Groucho was the exact opposite of Harpo. So, when I heard Groucho justify drinking away my problems, I thought of Harpo, who would have said, "You're not solving anything."

Listening to the wisdom of Harpo that had guided me through twenty-eight years of marriage, I set aside the past, accepted my new reality, and started to live alone. It was different. I still had our cat, Chandu, and our three nutty poodles—all named Charlie. Since they moved as a unit there was no sense in wasting any other names. We had a heavy turnover in Charlies, due to their flirtations with a coyote pack that nightly ran across the open desert behind our ranch. It sounded like fun to the poodles, who dug under the fence to join the gaiety. Even the lucky ones, limping home with only a few tears in their hides, never learned. So now it would be just me and the cat and the poodles. For twenty-eight glorious years with Harpo, I was intoxicated by love and encouragement. I lived for Harpo's approval. It was even apparent to those around us. I wasn't so sure I would be okay on my own.

I thought back to an incident from a few years earlier. Georgia Skelton startled me one day with, "Susan, you really are a bird in a gilded cage." I told her, you sure don't sound like my manicurist, who shook her head at the condition of my hands, exclaiming, "Your husband may be a very rich man, but these hands spell hard work to me." If that was how I was seen, I had made that bed for myself. And I loved every minute of it. But Harpo wasn't there for me to pamper anymore. All four children were out on their own, working on new relationships, and soon they'd all be married. If I had been in a gilded cage, the door to it had opened, and this bird had to learn to fly on her own. I wanted to know if I had an identity beyond that of Mrs. Harpo Marx.

It wasn't as if I hadn't ever done anything on my own or for myself after marrying Harpo. I had actually won an election in 1961, when I decided to run for a seat on our local school board. Alex, Jimmy, and Minnie were all attending Palm Springs High School at the time, so at first it just struck me as the next move of an involved parent, flowing naturally from being a den mother in the Cub Scouts and Brownies. Harpo cooked up such hilarious campaign press releases that the local newspaper tried to counsel us against them, thinking readers might get the impression I wasn't taking the election seriously. We believed the public would accept a humorous campaign ad from the Marx family when they wouldn't from a lawyer or a banker. They might even see it as a refreshing expression of modesty in contrast to the often-exaggerated claims of qualification and high purpose by the other candidates.

Political Ad Paid for by Harpo Marx:

Harp and politics don't mix. This was proven some years ago in Beverly Hills when I was campaign manager for Jimmy Gleason, who was running for the City Council. Unaccountably, he lost by the largest plurality ever known. After the election I decided to relax from all my hard work and drove to Palm Springs for a rest. On the way a tire blew. Opening the trunk to get out the spare I found the reason for the voter apathy. Three thousand stamped and sealed envelopes containing campaign appeals which I had forgotten to mail. Undaunted, I am returning to the political scene. I have been hired as stamp licker for my most favorite candidate since William Jennings Bryan. My candidate for the Palm Springs Board of Education has independence of mind and a dedicated, concentrated interest in school problems. My candidate cannot be reached by pressure groups. My candidate will bring enthusiasm, vigor, and good judgment to a demanding job. My candidate is Susan Marx . . . my wife.

Privately, I felt I was more than qualified, having come up through the ranks via PTA, Cub Scouts, Girl Scouts, Little League, and all the other "Mom" things one does to steer four children in varying degrees of reluctance through public education. Susan Marx—or perhaps Mrs. Harpo Marx—was entrusted by the voters with the education of the children of Palm Springs. But which one was it? Questions did seem to pile up. First, who was I? Second, who did people think I was? I became the first woman president of the school board in 1965, reaching the unreachable dream of every woman who has ever served on a board with four men. I was also the second woman president. I only accepted the second term to show off. I ended up serving for twelve years, so eventually it became clear that the woman on the school board was indeed Susan Marx, not Mrs. Harpo Marx.

I became totally immersed in the work of education and was too busy to feel sorry for myself. But living alone with three dogs and a cat gave me the opportunity to make the worst mistake of my life. After my father died, Mother had lived a pretty barren life among the lobby sitters in a small Beverly Hills hotel. Thinking it would give her contentment, I brought her to the desert to live with me in 1967. But it was too late. By summer her irrational behavior had started to frighten me. Once we were working on a jigsaw puzzle, her favorite pastime, when she suddenly stood up and said, laughing nastily, "I'll get even with you. You think I don't know what you're up to. I'll tell the world about you." Hoping it was a joke, I said, "What's up, Ma?" Her laughter turned to cold hatred as she stalked off.

I really knew I was in trouble one morning after taking Mother for a ride in a golf cart. I parked it in front of its stable, got out and bent down to lift the metal door when the cart lurched forward, smashing me against the door. The cart rolled back on the slight incline, fortunately preventing me from being pinned against the door, but, while I tried to get up on my hurting legs, the cart again smashed me against the door. I was terrified and too badly hurt to do more than roll out of the way of a possible third assault. I yelled for my housekeeper, who helped me to bed, where I stayed for three days wondering what to do. It wasn't clear to me why it had happened. Obviously, Mother had stepped on the accelerator pedal, which could have been accidental, but why twice? Would she have finished the job if I hadn't rolled out of the way? It was clear my home was not bringing peace to Mother, who was scaring the hell out of me.

The desert summer heat helped me persuade Mother that she should spend some time in Santa Monica. Thinking I was taking the first step in separating us, I leased an apartment overlooking the ocean and hired a companion for Mother. But then the really bad times started. Mother was not enjoying the sea air. Her horror stories of bodies being thrown out of the window above her were creating such consternation among her neighbors that before the week was out, I was called to cancel the rest of the lease and remove her. Mother laughingly claimed she made the stories up to get rid of her companion, to whom she had taken a dislike. I moved her to a hotel where she could resume lobby sitting, but by this point she was experiencing significant hallucinations. Again, within a week I was asked to remove her. Three nursing homes later she had her first noticeable stroke and was in a Santa Monica hospital.

I couldn't handle it myself any longer and, in the spring of 1968, I called on my daughter for help. She provided the miracle I knew she was capable of. Minnie arranged for an ambulance to carry her sedated grandmother to a remarkable place in the city of Orange, not far from where she lived, so she could keep an eye on this batty lady she had loved since infancy. There came a time when Mother recognized Minnie but had shut me out of her consciousness completely. Then one day a call came saying she was at peace. I'm still sad at the waste. I can't believe that indomitable spirit isn't out there someplace waiting for another chance. In some future incarnation, she could be so valuable. We're all products of our environment and experience. In retrospect, I wondered if perhaps some of the nasty things Mother had said in the past were indications of mental illness way before it became obvious.

Alone again, I resumed my self-evaluation. Through her erratic behavior, Mother had knocked out my anger and hurt over losing Harpo. Perhaps I should thank her. Her dying had broken the final ties with the past. I had coped with death; now I would cope with life. An inventory was called for. We would soon know if I was thinking for myself or still trying to fit into Harpo's world. For starters, I was curious to know the limits of my education. Before going on the stage, I'd had heavy doses of history, English, and math, along with French, German, and Latin. I was a collection of miscellanies that could use some organization. I needed to look at the educational opportunities offered by our local community college. At the outset it sounded a little discouraging. Without my missing high school transcripts, they would allow me to take only remedial classes, where they identify student qualification for placement. In this class I would be among the happy illiterates who pour out of our educational institutions. At least there was no discouraging competition for a student of my advanced years.

I wasn't thrilled with this situation, and I wasn't interested in their two-year degree. I wanted it all. I was the president of the school board, and it was necessary to pull a little rank. So, off I went to the dean. To avoid embarrassment, they let me into the regular freshman classes, but they had their revenge. The first semester had me carrying eighteen units, with a double major in art and anthropology. What did I know? I'd never been to college. No one told me that for each hour of class time a student was expected to put in four hours of study. I thought the reason my kids took all night to do their homework was because they kept one eye on the television set. My first semester put me in the hospital for two weeks. When I crawled back to college it was to only sixteen units then back to the hospital again. Eventually, my academic load was adjusted to a realistic twelve units, and I finally graduated without further mishap. I'd proven my point, but I settled for the two-year degree and took some time to travel before going on for my bachelor's degree.

Harpo would rarely go anyplace unless he was working. Which meant my view of the world, whether in Chicago or London, was often from a dingy dressing room backstage, helping with the props, supper in the hotel room after the show, breakfast at noon, lunch around four, doing laundry in the bathroom, and sleeping the rest of the time. Except for an hour or two walking in the fresh air, the theatre was our entire world. Or should I say his world? It certainly was no longer mine. It was time to find a world of my own. To start I would journey through foreign lands to see how people had been living. Not with friends who would want me to share their interests, but alone with people who shared mine. I joined an artist workshop and headed for Spain and Portugal. Later, shortly after Eden and Groucho were divorced, Eden accompanied me for a three-week trip to Japan with a group from the Aspen Institute for Humanistic Studies.

During his college years, our son Alex had been around the world on the MS *Seven Seas* for a semester offered by the University of the Seven Seas, an experience I had envied but never dreamed was available to me until I met the dean of the ship at a political rally in Palm Springs. By the time of this meeting, the program had been renamed World Campus Afloat and was chartered by Chapman College in Orange County.

They offered international studies through travel and higher education to students of all ages. Through this wonderful program I was able to visit South Korea, New Guinea, Singapore, and Tahiti. Seeing the world in the company of artists, social anthropologists, and a shipload of young people was a definitive experience. Life with Harpo had been maturing, but seeing the outside world through the eyes of youth gives perspective. It was finally, while sitting under a thatched roof in Tahiti, listening to the rain making sounds like mice running about on the thatch, that it burst on me like the glare of car headlights in an empty house. I am what I am. I behave out of my nature. No one imposes anything on me. Harpo had said this a long time ago.

CHAPTER SEVENTEEN

Peace through Selfishness

OME AGAIN, WITH MY IDENTITY FIRMLY IN PLACE, I SOLD EL
Rancho Harpo in 1970. I traded in the home that we had built
for a family of six near the Tamarisk Country Club for a condominium in the same vicinity. It would better fit me and the new life I had
every intention of making self-indulgent, best arrived at by eliminating
the demanding responsibilities of acreage—although my new place was
actually a fairly spacious freestanding house. It was a condominium in
name only because it was part of a group of eight similar homes. When
Alex protested, "You've sold our home," he understood my answer. "No, I
haven't, we don't live there anymore. You live in Vallejo, Bill lives in Los
Angeles, Jim lives in San Luis Obispo, and Minnie in Orange. I haven't
sold our memories of seven wonderful years." When we left Beverly Hills,
none of us looked back, although it was there that we had established the
unity of our family. Roots, as I explained to Alex, are not in places, they
are in relationships.

Alex's security is in the confidence that his world will be unchanging.
He comes unglued at any sign of inconsistency. Alex was into a comfortable second marriage with a fondly understanding woman, who brought
him two daughters and instant fatherhood. When he called me about
a coming Christmas family gathering at Minnie's, clinging to what he
saw as an established tradition, he was profoundly concerned that what
he was proposing might be seen as the disintegration of the family. He
hoped that we would understand that his little family wanted to start
their own traditions in their own home. Would we mind if they came
down only every other year? Here we were again. "Alex, Christmas is not

for adults to renew family ties. It's for a moment of mystery and magic for children. What you want to do is right. It will unify your family, whether you sing carols by a Christmas tree or dance the hula around your television set." He got it. Alex never minded a lecture if I kept it short.

I decorated my new home with a combination of the art I had acquired in my travels and Harpo's paintings. We had both been painting for a while, but when Harpo began devoting much of his time to it, I quit and focused on carving ornate wood frames for his creations. I surprised myself with the quality of my frames, but it was hard to keep up with Harpo. Carve faster. He's finished another one! Harpo first dabbled with painting through his friendship with Neysa McMein years before he started to have heart trouble, but when he had to cut back on performing, he became a prolific artist. For several years it seemed that every charitable function in the Coachella Valley featured an auction for a Harpo Marx painting. I'm occasionally asked how many Harpo paintings there are, and I have to say I have no idea. He loved giving them to friends and raising money for good causes with them. I would occasionally spot one in a friend's home, not remembering even carving the frame. I decorated my living room with some of my favorite Harpo creations, including a few inspired by our trip to Israel, and resumed my solitary life in much smaller quarters.

I was fifty-six years old when Harpo died. I had been married to him for exactly half of my life. I was not oblivious to the whispers among friends and family that I should consider getting married again. I'd spent my entire life playing a series of roles—the dutiful daughter, the Broadway showgirl, the up-and-coming movie starlet, and ultimately Mrs. Harpo Marx. It had become time for a new role. I would now be Susan Marx, an independent widow with no interest in the various suitors searching the desert for a wife. I'd had the best. There was no point in marrying again after having been Mrs. Harpo Marx for twenty-eight years. I was perfectly content to go it alone for the rest of the ride.

In 1969 I had been elected to my third four-year term on the school board and by that time had also served for two years on the board of the Cathedral City Chamber of Commerce. (Our family home and my new condominium were actually in a section of Cathedral City that would be incorporated into Rancho Mirage in 1973.) I enjoyed playing an active role in the community, and maybe I let that get the better of me in 1970 when some friends convinced me to run for a seat in the State Assembly. The kids all campaigned, and Jimmy was my campaign chairman. We ran a good campaign, but, alas, Susan Marx was not to be the assemblywoman from the 75th district. I can't say I was upset about losing that election. I still had the remainder of my term on the school board to serve, and I would have needed to resign had I won. There were also still some other things I wanted to do for myself, and the time was right. In 1973 I decided not to run for a fourth term on the school board. Instead, I enrolled at the College of the Desert and studied art and anthropology.

My interest in education remained strong, and I was occasionally frustrated by the operation of the school district after I was no longer on the board. I kept myself involved in other ways and ended up on the board of trustees of the Coachella Valley Community College. I also joined the Rancho Mirage Planning Commission. But I couldn't ignore what I thought were serious problems in the Palm Springs school district. Kids were being shortchanged by the system. They were graduating high school unprepared for college. We were just giving them diplomas and letting the colleges worry about it. In 1981 I decided to stop complaining and took some action. I again ran for a seat on Palm Springs School Board and won. I was reelected for my fifth term in 1985 and served until 1990. It was the most satisfying work of my life, and I believe I made a real difference. During my years on the board, the Palm Springs Unified School District grew from a small PTA-type group to an organization with a $50 million budget.

I had finally settled in. I had come to terms with myself and established a life of my own after years of just floating along. Fate is such an inexorable pressure. Struggle as I might I was never able to take charge of my life. It was as if I was hurtling into the unknown, directed purposefully by an intelligence that had it all mapped out, and I was not to interfere. I didn't want to be a movie star. Even so, I went dutifully to singing lessons, drama, and dancing classes because in my world of ambitious young people, I needed to be a part of some group that could let me

feel there was a place for me. It was an accident that I was on Broadway.
I didn't know that I wanted anything until I met Harpo.

Only in recent years, when self-evaluation could be faced with
diminished embarrassment, do I muse over the crooked trail that led to
peace. Crooked, because of the roadblocks stopping me from my endless
dashes in the wrong directions. I must have given my fate a hard time.
With marriage to Harpo, an emotional harmony set in. Harpo, no role
player, was a completely natural person in an unnatural world. At peace
with himself, he was an understanding observer. He never gave directions because that meant making judgments, which was not his way. He
could respect a person for just one redeeming feature, while I was used to
looking for a weakness to reject the whole. His creed was, "Do the best
you can and, with luck it will all come out right." Harpo was a supporter.
He was every performer's best audience. Unthreatened by the success of
others, he was first and loudest in his applause. He never questioned an
action of mine even when we both knew it should be questioned.

Our marriage was a success in a sea of Hollywood unions that
weren't. Our kids were normal and well-adjusted and turned into beautiful and kind adults. Some close to us were not so lucky. I'm sure whatever
I had to do with any of this came as a result of Harpo's effect on me. In
the years since he's been gone, I've found a different kind of happiness
after struggling to figure out life without him. I've received many letters
from fans asking me what he was really like. Interviewers have come to
me for the inside story because there must be something mysterious or
controversial about Harpo. I disappoint them with the plain truth that
he was exactly what you would hope he was. A simple, uncomplicated,
beautiful, funny soul, who loved and cherished his friends and family.
Of course, some people love to learn that, so I don't worry much about
disappointing the others.

He's been gone for a long time. I write this shortly after our children
surprised the hell out of me with a ninetieth birthday party. It wasn't just
the party that surprised me. I'm pretty damned surprised to have made
it to ninety! The day was overwhelming, but as I went to bed that night,
I could hear Harpo say, "What do you think of that, Mom?" Harpo
hadn't really gone away. He was still there, and he stayed with me all the

years after September 28, 1964—along with the bitterness of not being allowed to keep him just a little bit longer. He's there with me whenever our children call or do anything that would make him proud. Sometimes I just feel like he's keeping an eye on me. I can hear him laughing his head off when someone calls to tell me that *Million Dollar Legs* is on television and that I must put it on.

The truth is that in all the time he's been gone I've never spent a moment without him.

Afterword

A FEW YEARS INTO MY MORE THAN THIRTY-YEAR FRIENDSHIP with Bill Marx, I sent his mother, Susan, an anthology of lost writings by Groucho Marx that I edited, called *Groucho Marx and Other Short Stories and Tall Tales*. I was living in New York at the time and several months later drove to Rancho Mirage during a visit to Los Angeles for a lunch that Bill had set up for the three of us. I didn't expect Susan to say anything about the Groucho book, but I hoped that if she had even opened it, she enjoyed the stories about Harpo in it.

After only a few minutes, Susan said, "I liked your Groucho book. In fact, I liked it more than I liked Groucho." She also said something complimentary about the portions of the book that I'd written, the good majority of it having been written by Groucho. She mentioned that she had been struggling to complete her memoirs and asked if I would be willing to take a look at her work. Bill laughed, knowing that, as an obsessive Marx Brothers fan and researcher, there wasn't much I wouldn't have done for the chance to read Susan's manuscript. After lunch Bill and I took it—parts typed, parts handwritten—to a local copy center. I suppose I shouldn't have expected computer files from a writer in her eighties.

Her first draft was long, and it left me wondering about a lot of the things I expected to learn about Susan's life. In particular, she seemed to have no interest in writing about her own show business career. I called Bill and told him it needed a lot of work. He suggested I give Susan my honest assessment, and I did. I told her that I thought the manuscript was lacking key parts of her story and focused too heavily on her life after Harpo's death. She didn't flinch and immediately asked what I planned to do about it. That was how Susan asked me to collaborate with her on the book.

We agreed that I should start by editing and organizing what she had written before we could fill in the gaps. I sent her a new version with notations like, "I think we should mention that you were in three Broadway shows," and "tell me anything you can remember about being in two early John Wayne films." I was living in Forest Hills, New York, at the time, and I gave Susan my address so she could send me a few pages she was working on to answer some of my questions. She gasped when I mentioned Forest Hills. "Fate has brought us together. I lived in Forest Hills when I was a little girl." She described the street where she lived, and I mentioned the Forest Hills Long Island Railroad station. She remembered the sound of the trains filling the house. Later, when she found the exact address, I took a few photos of the house for her. She told me that it hadn't changed a bit, which was true of most of that particular neighborhood, with its lovely cobblestone streets that dated back to Susan's time there.

Once I had a reasonable edit and an outline, we made plans to work in person. In October 1995 I traveled to Rancho Mirage with a laptop computer and a tape recorder. When I told Susan that I had retyped her entire manuscript into a computer, she said, "I thought you might be a little crazy. Now I'm sure you are." She had invited me to stay in her house, and I promised to be as unobtrusive as possible. Upon my arrival, Bill, who was living nearby, took me to a local supermarket so I could pick up some food and supplies. I didn't want to get into trouble for raiding Susan's refrigerator, although I was told to help myself to whatever I wanted. I woke up very early my first morning in Rancho Mirage and quietly crept into the kitchen to make myself breakfast, having been told that Susan was not an early riser. A few minutes later she appeared. "You can cook?" she asked. "Just bacon and eggs. Nothing fancy," I assured her. She headed to the phone and I heard her tell someone, "You don't have to come today. I've got a guy here who cooks." She hung up the phone and asked, "Can you do over easy?"

I mentioned to Bill that I was going to find a place to watch the baseball playoffs, and he assured me that Susan would be watching every pitch. We became deeply involved in the American League Championship Series between the Seattle Mariners and the Cleveland Indians.

Susan was pulling for Cleveland, and I asked why. "Harpo always rooted for the underdog, and the Indians haven't won a pennant since 1954, so I'm for the underdog." With no real rooting interest—my team, the New York Mets, were light-years from the playoffs in those days—I jumped on the Harpo-Susan underdog bandwagon. She threw me for a loop during the sixth game of the series. In a scoreless tie at the Kingdome in Seattle, Mariners second baseman Joey Cora made an error that allowed the Indians to take the lead in what would ultimately be the deciding game of the series. As the crowd of close to sixty-thousand Mariners fans showered Cora with boos, Susan felt sorry for him and wanted the Mariners to come back so the fans wouldn't blame this poor guy for blowing the game. "Well, now *he's* the underdog," she explained.

In between ball games we did manage to work on the book. We recorded interviews each day, after breakfast, and Susan would occasionally become frustrated by my questions about working at Fox or Paramount and being in the chorus of a Broadway musical. "No one cares about that junk," she would insist. I would ask about a film she had appeared in, and she would reply, "If you say I was in it, I suppose I was." It was much easier to get her talking about her childhood and her parents, topics she had also neglected in her first draft. The Forest Hills connection certainly helped break the ice in this department. But I couldn't imagine telling Susan's story without getting her to talk about her work as a dancer and actress—and the events that would get her to Hollywood, where she would meet Harpo.

I made a call to Bob Birchard, a noted film historian, collector, and author. Bob managed to get some prints of Susan's films from a few collector friends, and I was soon driving to Los Angeles to borrow them and a projector. Susan again reminded me that I was crazy and told me to drive carefully. That evening, after the baseball game of course, I draped a bedsheet over Susan's large television and fired up the projector for a screening of *The Range Feud* starring John Wayne and Susan Fleming. Bill was certainly interested in seeing it, so Susan played along, warning us that it was going to be awful. It actually wasn't. It was surely not of the caliber of Wayne's later work, but as low-budget 1931 westerns go, it was pretty good. Within a few minutes, Susan was laughing hysterically at the sight of herself. She said she had never seen the film and asked, "Why the hell did they hire me with such a terrible voice?" When it was over, she called her daughter, Minnie, to tell her how ridiculous and silly it was. But she clearly enjoyed the screening. The next morning our interview session was very different. Susan suddenly shared a lot of details about her early days in Hollywood but made it clear that she thought it was all nonsense. We screened a few more films, including one that—in spite of what the research indicated—she was not actually in. When that one was over, she said, "There's my best work. Have you seen enough?"

After a week of movies, baseball games, and cooking breakfast—Susan was impressed by my cheese omelets—I had managed to get her talking about almost everything that she left out of her manuscript. I went back to New York confident that I could put it all together. A couple of months later, I sent a new version of the manuscript to Susan. She mostly liked it but wanted to rewrite some of the portions I had transcribed from tapes. She began mailing pages that, to my great surprise, included even more interesting new material. Bill was pleased with the progress, and we seemed to be moving toward a finished manuscript. But then Susan wanted to write some additional pages, which soon became chapters. We were getting the manuscript closer to the unwieldy length it had started at before I trimmed it. Months turned into years, and Susan began referring to my willingness to take on an impossible task. When I visited in 1998 for her ninetieth birthday, I mentioned that I was ready to complete the job. She expressed doubt that anyone would want to read her story. I assured her there was an audience out there.

During her last years, I also had the opportunity to interview Susan for a couple of television projects. On the last of these occasions, I told her, "Anything you say can and will be used against you in your autobiography." She said, "Whatever happened with that?" And just like that, she was sending me new pages. She also sent an occasional letter with interesting things that I would sneak into the manuscript. But what she never sent was her final approval of the book. Susan died on December 22, 2002, oddly enough on the same day as her dear friend Mary Dee, Chico's second wife. It made me think of another pair of people whose lives were intertwined and had died on the same day. John Adams and

Thomas Jefferson both died on July 4, 1826. I felt a strange bit of comfort that Mary and Susan didn't have to hear about each other's death.

Susan's unpublished manuscript, the recordings we made, and such things as the scrapbooks and photo albums she had given me, were boxed up and mostly forgotten. Several years after Susan died, I began writing *Four of Three Musketeers: The Marx Brothers on Stage*, a book that would be published in 2016. I quoted Susan's account of Harpo's marriage proposal and their elopement as she had told it in one of our manuscript drafts, and I cited Susan's unpublished memoir in the bibliography. It was the first public acknowledgment that the book, which Susan occasionally told people she would someday write, actually existed. I began receiving inquiries about how Susan's manuscript could be accessed. My response was usually not very helpful, but I would typically say that it may be published at some point.

In the fall of 2020, I was involved with Film Preservation Society's restoration and release of the 1925 film *Too Many Kisses*, which features a young Harpo Marx in its cast. Promoting the film's premiere on Turner Classic Movies, Bill Marx—who, incidentally, composed and performed the new score for the film—did a press interview in which he mentioned my collaboration with Susan on her autobiography. I began getting inquiries about the manuscript again. Bill encouraged me to do whatever was needed to finish it and get it published. Resurrecting the long-dormant project from 3.5-inch floppy discs (remember those?) reminded me that we had four different versions of the manuscript. None of the four were quite right. Susan was likely somewhere laughing at me for once again taking on that "impossible task."

But it was actually quite possible to assemble an entertaining and readable manuscript by taking the best portions of the last two versions and transcribing material that Susan didn't think was important from the tapes. Bill encouraged me to include such "unimportant things" as Susan's experiences working for Florenz Ziegfeld, social encounters with people like Howard Hughes and Bugsy Siegel, and what life was like for a low-level contract player in Hollywood in the 1930s. Bill was very clear: I was in charge and Susan couldn't push me around anymore. If I wanted the story of Harry Cohn trying to get Susan to go to bed with him in the book, it would be in the book. Susan uncensored was very entertaining. She was always honest about things like Chico causing Harpo all sorts of grief and Gummo constantly indulging Harpo's hypochondria. And she didn't hold back on the subject of Groucho's complex relationships with the people closest to him. I once asked her if she had anything nice to say about Zeppo and she said, "Let me think about it." When she read the first version of the book, which included some of this material, her initial impulse was to take it all out. I read her a few quotes from the interview she'd done for the 1973 book, *The Marx Brothers Scrapbook*. She was brutally honest about Groucho, and he was still alive at the time. She said, "Oh, Christ! You win. Leave it in."

Susan began her book project as part of a writing course she and Groucho's third ex-wife, Eden, took in the early 1980s. I suspect that she never envisioned publishing it when she started, and she abandoned it for years at a time. But as we worked on it together, it was certainly with the intention of the book being published. I know her children were anxious to read it because they all agreed that Susan and Harpo hadn't really told them much about their pasts. *Harpo Speaks!* was only half of the story. Sadly, their son Alex died in 2006 and daughter, Minnie, in 2020. Perhaps Bill recognized that it was time for Susan's book to see the light of day. Being given the opportunity to work on the book and get to know Susan was one of the great pleasures of my life. Finally getting the book finished has been another one. The process really brought her back to life. I could hear her in my head as I made editorial decisions. I'm sure she would be very pleased with how it turned out. But she would probably still take out the part where she was making movies in Hollywood. No one could ever convince her that people would care about that.

Robert S. Bader
Los Angeles, California
April 2021

Appendix I:
Susan Fleming on Stage

Ziegfeld's Palm Beach Nights / Ziegfeld's Palm Beach Girls / No Foolin' / Ziegfeld's American Revue
January 14, 1926–March 24, 1926—*Ziegfeld's Palm Beach Nights*
Club de Montmartre, Palm Beach, Florida

June 15, 1926–June 20, 1926—*Ziegfeld's Palm Beach Girls*
Apollo Theater, Atlantic City, New Jersey

June 24, 1926–September 25, 1926—*No Foolin'* (Title changed to *Ziegfeld's American Revue* in July)
Globe Theatre, New York, New York

CAST: James Barton, Greta Nissen, Arthur "Bugs" Baer, Louise Brown, Ray Dooley, Peggy Fears, Beth Beri, Edna Leedom, Moran and Mack, Claire Luce, Edna Covey, Irving Fisher, Andrew Tombes, Charles King, Polly Walker, Helen O'Shea, Yvonne Occent and Genesko, The Connor Twins: Thelma and Velma, George Baxter, Andrew Knox, George Moeser, Lew Christy, Noel Francis, John E. Hazzard, Anastasia Reilly, Evelyn Grieg, Lillian Smith, Katherine Burke, Dorothy Wegman, Helen Herendeen, Mabel Baade, Elsie Behrens, **Susan Fleming**, Paulette Goddard, Doris Lloyd, Stella Wooten, Margaret Langhorne, Evelyn Ware, Barbara Newberry, The Yacht Club Entertainers, William Murray, Hilda Olsen, Leslie Ostrander, Dorothy Patterson, Katherine Penman, Miss Shaw, Robert Shields, Biddy Somerset, Marion Strasmick, Miss Wayne, Miss Williams, Miss Wilson

[Morton Downey and Cliff Edwards appeared only in the Palm Beach production.]

Rio Rita

February 2, 1927–December 24, 1927 (Susan was in the cast from April to July)
Ziegfeld Theatre, New York, New York

CAST: Juan Villasana, Al Clair, Walter Petrie, Helen C. Clive, Bert Wheeler, Robert Woolsey, Fred Dalton, Vincent Serrano, Gladys Glad, Marion Benda, Dorothy Wegman, Peggy Blake, Myrna Darby, Marie Conway, Kay English, Ethelind Terry, Ada May, J. Harold Murray, Harry Ratcliffe, Donald Douglas, Alf P. James, Pedro Rubin, Alberto Carillo, Collette, Noel Francis, Katherine Burke, Albertina Rasch Dancers, Ziegfeld Dancers, **Susan Fleming**, Paulette Goddard

ENSEMBLE: Avis Adair, Mary Alter, Melba Alter, George Anez, Martha Ann, Alfred Arnold, Antonio Arreola, Mabel Baade, Margie Bailey, Anita Banton, Pauline Bartlett, Elma Bayer, Elsie Behrens, Carol Bergman, Jose Betancourt, Virginia Biddle, Victor Bragamonte, Alcides Briseno, George Butler, Camille, Suzanne Conroy, Peggy Cornell, Jean Crittenden, Audrey Dale, Agatha DeBussy, Naomi deMusie, Helen Derby, Dorothy Dickerson, Jennie Dolova, Rass Erickson, Carlos Estrada, Lucien Farland, Elaine Field, Janet Flynn, Helene Gardner, Margaret Godsworthy, Portia Grafton, Ann Hardman, Mignon Hawkes, Josephine Hayes, Gabriel Herrera, Owen Hervey, Charles Holly, Harriet Hughes, Yvonne Hughes, Theresa Hyle, Naomi Johnson, Ivanelle Ladd, Lavergne Lambert, Valerie Lennox, Mildred Lunnay, Cookie Lunsford, Lottie Marcy, Marjorie-May Martin, Earl Marvin, Robert Mathews, Dorothy May, Charles McClelland, Betty McHugh, Frances Mildern, Florence Miller, Alma Moore, Vivian Morgan, Franciska Mueller, Gladys Murphy, Vincente Murtado, Leo Nash, Henry Nelthropp, Bill Otero, Walter Palm, Dorothy Patterson, Molly Peck, Lillian Shields, Al Small, Jack Spinelly, Douglas Stead, Marion Strasmick, Norma Taylor, Morris Tepper, Edward Theopold, Jack Thompson, Raymond Toben, Francisco Torres, Peggy Udell, Manuel Valdespino, Bernice Varden, Richard Vernon, Rosemary Wallace, Florence Ware, Clarentine Wayne, Jean Wayne, Nondas Wayne, Maxine Wells, John Werner, Amy West, Marion Wilson, Ann Woods, Philomena Yvsocka, M. Zaharia, Frank Zolt

Manhattan Mary

August 22, 1927–August 27, 1927
Nixon's Apollo Theatre, Atlantic City, New Jersey

August 29, 1927–September 3, 1927
Sam S. Shubert Theatre, Philadelphia, Pennsylvania

September 5, 1927–September 17, 1927
Nixon Theatre, Pittsburgh, Pennsylvania

September 19, 1927–September 24, 1927
Sam S. Shubert Theatre, Newark, New Jersey

September 26, 1927–May 12, 1928
Apollo Theater, New York, New York

CAST: Ed Wynn, George White, Ona Munson, Lou Holtz, **Susan Fleming** (as Suzanne Fleming), Paul Stanton, Sue Elliott, Jimmy Scott, Adele Smith, Harland Dixon, Paul Frawley, Dorothy Walters, Doree Leslie, Victor Munro, Mae Clarke, Amy Revere, Harry Oldridge, Sam Ledner, Mary Farley, Vada Alexander, Serge Ury, Ray Hunt, Eva Lynn, Hazel Leming, John Plaza, Timothy O'Connor, The Scott Sisters, The George White Ballet, 24 Hudson Dusters, The McCarthy Sisters, The Embassy Boys: Messrs. Goff, Kerr, and Barth

ATLANTIC CITY ONLY: Francetta Molloy, Jewel La Kota, Marcel Rousseau, Elizabeth Hines, La Verta McCormick, Flo Brooks, Mary Coyle, Hazel Bofinger, The Williams Sisters

George White's Scandals

September 9, 1929–September 14, 1929
Sam S. Shubert Theatre, Newark, New Jersey

September 16, 1929–September 21, 1929
Sam S. Shubert Theatre, Boston, Massachusetts

(Susan was dropped from the cast after the out-of-town tryouts and did not appear in the Broadway production that opened on September 23, 1929, at the Apollo Theater in New York.)

CAST: Willie and Eugene Howard, Frances Williams, George White, Evelyn Wilson, Frank Mitchell and Jack Durant, Marietta Canty, Jack White, Carolyn Nolte, Ted and Sally, Florence Robinson, Ernest Charles, Jim Carty, Vada Alexander, Harry Morrissey, Fred Lyon, Arthur Cardinal, **Susan Fleming,** The Elm City Four, The Abbott Dancers: Florence Wilson, Pauline Bensinger, Marion Ford, Alice Fogg, Eleanor Gillespie, May Hass, Jessie Kassel, Amy McKay, Pearl McKnight, Myrtle Messer, Mabel Rickert, Rose Turman

ENSEMBLE: Joanna Allen, Nitza Andre, Kay Apgar, Stella Bayliss, Pearl Bradley, Ethel Britton, Pauline Brooks, Marion Dickson, Elsie Duffy, Sue Elliott, Elise Gernon, Dolly Gilbert, Julia Gorman, Mildred Green, Billie Hart, Theo Holley, Beatrice Jay, Renee Johnson, Alice Kerwin, Mildred Klaw, Gladys Law, Gertrude Lowe, Marilyn Mack, Margaret Manners, Ida Michaels, Leslyn Miller, Peggy Moseley, Patsy O'Day, Margie O'Shea, Lenore Petitt, Edith Pragan, Elizabeth Rapieff, Kathleen Reichner, Anna Rex, Peggy Schaber, Claire Scott, Elizabeth Scott, Jean Scott, Edwina Skorat, May Slattery, Etta Sparre, Lesley Storey, Elizabeth Sundmark, Marion Sweet, Youda Wood

Appendix II:
Susan Fleming on Film

The Ace of Cads
October 11, 1926 (Paramount)
Directed by Luther Reed

CAST: Adolphe Menjou, Alice Joyce, Norman Trevor, Philip Strange, **Susan Fleming** (as Suzanne Fleming)

Kings or Better
(One-reel short subject—*Eddie Buzzell's Bedtime Stories for Grownups* # 7)
May 5, 1931 (Columbia)
Directed by Eddie Buzzell

CAST: Eddie Buzzell, **Susan Fleming**, Oliver Eckhardt, Agnes Steele, Paul Power, John Winters, Nick Copeland, W. S. McDonald

Lover Come Back
June 5, 1931 (Columbia)
Directed by Erle C. Kenton

CAST: Betty Bronson, Jack Mulhall, Constance Cummings, Jameson Thomas, Fred Santley, John Mack, Kathryn Givney, Loretta Sayers, **Susan Fleming**

Men Are Like That (Originally titled *The Virtuous Wife*, retitled *Arizona*)
June 27, 1931 (Columbia)
Directed by George B. Seitz

CAST: Laura La Plante, John Wayne, June Clyde, Forrest Stanley, Nina Quartero
Uncredited: **Susan Fleming**

A Dangerous Affair
September 30, 1931 (Columbia)
Directed by Edward Sedgewick

CAST: Jack Holt, Ralph Graves, Sally Blane, **Susan Fleming**, Blanche Friderici, Edward Brophy, DeWitt Jennings, Tyler Brooke, William V. Mong, Fred Santley

The Range Feud (Originally titled *Border Law*)
December 1, 1931 (Columbia)
Directed by Ross Lederman

CAST: Buck Jones, John Wayne, **Susan Fleming**, Ed Le Saint, William Walling, Wallace MacDonald, Harry Woods, Frank Austin

Ladies of the Jury
February 5, 1932 (RKO)
Directed by Lowell Sherman

CAST: Edna May Oliver, Jill Esmond, Ken Murray, Roscoe Ates, Kitty Kelly, Cora Witherspoon, Florence Lake, Robert McWade, Charles Dow Clark, Helene Millard, Kate Price
Uncredited: **Susan Fleming**

Careless Lady
April 3, 1932 (Fox)
Directed by Kenneth MacKenna

CAST: Joan Bennett, John Boles, Minna Gombell, Weldon Heyburn, Nora Lane, Raul Roulien, J. M. Kerrigan, John Arledge, Fortunio Bonanova, Josephine Hull, Martha Mattox, William Pawley, James Kirkwood, Maude Turner Gordon, Richard Tucker, André Cheron, James Todd, Howard Phillips, Marcelle Corday, Louis Mercier
Uncredited: **Susan Fleming**

Million Dollar Legs
July 8, 1932 (Paramount)
Directed by Edward Cline

Cast: Jack Oakie, W. C. Fields, Andy Clyde, Lyda Roberti, **Susan Fleming**, Ben Turpin, Hank Mann, Hugh Herbert, George Barbier, Dickie Moore

Heritage of the Desert
September 30, 1932 (Paramount)
Directed by Henry Hathaway

Cast: Randolph Scott, Sally Blane, J. Farrell MacDonald, David Landau, Gordon Westcott, Guinn Williams, Vince Barnett
Uncredited: **Susan Fleming**
(Susan was originally cast in a lead role but was replaced by Sally Blane.)

He Learned about Women (Originally titled *The Book Worm Turns*)
November 4, 1932 (Paramount)
Directed by Lloyd Corrigan

Cast: Stuart Erwin, **Susan Fleming**, Alison Skipworth, Gordon Westcott, Grant Mitchell, Sidney Toler, Tom Ricketts, Claude King, Gertrude Norman, Irving Bacon

I Love That Man
June 9, 1933 (Paramount)
Directed by Harry Joe Brown

Cast: Edmund Lowe, Nancy Carroll, Robert Armstrong, Lew Cody, Warren Hymer, Grant Mitchell, Dorothy Burgess, Walter Walker, Berton Churchill, Inez Courtney, **Susan Fleming**, Luis Alberni, Lee Kohlmar, Myrna Kennedy, Harvey Clark

My Weakness
September 22, 1933 (Fox)
Directed by David Butler

Cast: Lillian Harvey, Lew Ayres, Charles Butterworth, Harry Langdon, Sid Silvers, Irene Bentley, Henry Travers, Adrian Rosley, Mary Howard, Irene Ware, Barbara Weeks, **Susan Fleming**, Marcelle Edwards, Marjorie King, Jean Allen, Gladys Blake, Dixie Francis

Broadway Thru a Keyhole
November 2, 1933 (Twentieth Century)
Directed by Lowell Sherman

Cast: Constance Cummings, Russ Columbo, Paul Kelly, Blossom Seeley, Gregory Ratoff, Texas Guinan, Abe Lyman, Hugh O'Connell, Hobart Cavanaugh, Frances Williams, Eddie Foy Jr., Dewey Barto, George Mann, C. Henry Gordon, William Burgess, Helen Jerome Eddy
Uncredited: **Susan Fleming**

Olsen's Big Moment
November 17, 1933 (Fox)
Directed by Malcolm St. Clair

Cast: El Brendel, Walter Catlett, Barbara Weeks, **Susan Fleming**, John Arledge, Joe Sauer

Now I'll Tell (Retitled *When New York Sleeps*)
May 11, 1934 (Fox)
Directed by Edwin J. Burke

Cast: Spencer Tracy, Helen Twelvetrees, Alice Faye, Robert Gleckler, Henry O'Neill, Hobart Cavanaugh, G. P. Huntley, Shirley Temple, Ronnie Cosby, Ray Cooke, Frank Marlowe, Clarence Wilson, Barbara Weeks, Theodore Newton, Vince Barnett, James Donlan, Leon Waycoff
Uncredited: **Susan Fleming**

Call It Luck
June 1, 1934 (Fox)
Directed by James Tinling

CAST: Pat Paterson, Herbert Mundin, Charles Starrett, Gordon West-cott, Georgia Caine, Theodore von Eltz, Reginald Mason, Ernest Wood, Ray Mayer, **Susan Fleming**

She Learned about Sailors
June 29, 1934 (Fox)
Directed by George Marshall

CAST: Lew Ayres, Alice Faye, Harry Green, Frank Mitchell, Jack Durant
Uncredited: **Susan Fleming**

Charlie Chan's Courage
July 6, 1934 (Fox)
Directed by George Hadden

CAST: Warner Oland, Drue Leyton, Donald Woods, Paul Harvey, Mur-ray Kinnell, Reginald Mason, Virginia Hammond, Si Jenks, Harvey Clark, Jerry Jerome
Uncredited: **Susan Fleming**

Elinor Norton
November 2, 1934 (Fox)
Directed by Hamilton MacFadden

CAST: Claire Trevor, Gilbert Roland, Henrietta Crosman, Hugh Wil-liams, Norman Foster
Uncredited: **Susan Fleming**

By Your Leave
November 9, 1934 (RKO)
Directed by Lloyd Corrigan

CAST: Frank Morgan, Genevieve Tobin, Neil Hamilton, Marion Nixon, Glenn Anders, Gene Lockhart, Margaret Hamilton, Betty Grable, Charles Ray, Lona Andre
Uncredited: **Susan Fleming**

George White's 1935 Scandals
March 29, 1935 (Fox)
Directed by George White

CAST: Alice Faye, James Dunn, Ned Sparks, Lyda Roberti, Cliff Edwards, Arline Judge, Eleanor Powell, Emma Dunn, George White, The Scandals Beauties
Uncredited: **Susan Fleming**

Break of Hearts
May 31, 1935 (RKO)
Directed by Phillip Moeller

CAST: Katharine Hepburn, Charles Boyer, John Beal, Jean Hersholt, Sam Hardy, Inez Courtney, Helene Millard, Ferdinand Gottschalk, **Susan Fleming**, Lee Kohlmar, Jean Howard, Anne Grey

Navy Wife (Retitled *Beauty's Daughter*)
September 17, 1935 (Fox)
Directed by Allan Dwan

CAST: Claire Trevor, Ralph Bellamy, Jane Darwell, Warren Hymer, Ben Lyon, Kathleen Burke, George Irving, Anne Howard
Uncredited: **Susan Fleming**

The Great Ziegfeld
April 8, 1936 (M-G-M)
Directed by Robert Z. Leonard

CAST: William Powell, Myrna Loy, Luise Rainer, Frank Morgan, Fannie Brice, Virginia Bruce, Reginald Owen, Ray Bolger, Ernest Cossart, Joseph Cawthorn, Nat Pendleton, Harriet Hoctor, Jean Chatburn, Paul Irving, Herman Bing, Charles Judels, Marcelle Corday, Raymond Walburn, A. A. Trimble, Buddy Doyle
Uncredited: **Susan Fleming**

Star for a Night (Retitled *The Holy Lie*)
August 28, 1936 (Twentieth Century Fox)
Directed by Lewis Seiler

CAST: Claire Trevor, Jane Darwell, Arline Judge, Evelyn Venable, J. Edward Bromberg, Dean Jagger, Alan Dinehart, Joyce Compton, **Susan Fleming**, Adrienne Marden, Frank Reicher, Dickie Moore, Chick Chandler, Astrid Allwyn, Hattie McDaniel

Gold Diggers of 1937
December 28, 1936 (Warner Bros.)
Directed by Lloyd Bacon; musical numbers created and directed by Busby Berkeley

CAST: Dick Powell, Joan Blondell, Glenda Farrell, Victor Moore, Lee Dixon, Osgood Perkins, Chas. D. Brown, Rosalind Marquis, Irene Ware, Wm. Davidson, Olin Howland, Charles Halton, Paul Irving, Harry C. Bradley, Joseph Crehan, **Susan Fleming**

God's Country and the Woman
January 16, 1937 (Warner Bros.)
Directed by William Keighley

CAST: George Brent, Beverly Roberts, Barton MacLane, Robert Barrat, Alan Hale, Joe King, El Brendel, Addison Richards, Roscoe Ates, Billy Bevan, Joseph Crehan, Bert Roach, Vic Potel, Mary Treen, Herbert Rawlinson, Harry Hayden, Pat Moriarty, Max Wagner, **Susan Fleming**

Acknowledgments

REVISITING SUSAN MARX'S MANUSCRIPT NEARLY TWENTY YEARS after her death was really a team effort. First and foremost, the readers of my book *Four of the Three Musketeers: The Marx Brothers on Stage* who expressed interest in the unpublished work listed in the bibliography were the catalysts that started the book on its journey from storage to publication. But it never could have happened without the enthusiastic cooperation and support of Bill Marx.

An important component of my work with Susan was fact-checking her recollections. By her own admission she was terrible with dates. She was able to recall the most vivid details of events, but she simply could not remember exactly when many of them happened and needed my help to put things in order. For example, she had no idea when Salvador Dali came to visit, but she could describe the time Harpo spent with him quite beautifully. In preparing the manuscript for publication, I called upon my usual suspects in this area for help. Robert Moulton and Paul Wesolowski were so detail oriented that Susan would have given them her signature declaration, "Oh, Christ. You two must be crazy." My longest-serving Marx Brothers buddy, Charlie Kochman, also deserves special mention for his words of encouragement and for patiently explaining the world of publishing to me. I have him do this every few years just to keep him on his toes.

Susan certainly would have acknowledged her children had the book been published in her lifetime. The encouragement she got from Bill, Alex, Jimmy, and Minnie while we were working together brought her joy. On my end, I must thank my wife, Tracey Goessel, who never got to meet Susan but fell in love with her while serving as my best proofreader. And of course, I owe a huge debt of gratitude to Susan for her faith in me and for trusting me with her very special story.

Index

Marx, Betty (sister-in-law), 50, 61, 62–63, 98–99

Marx, Bob (nephew), 62

Marx, Chico (brother-in-law), 31, 135, 180; Broadway and, 32; death, 144, 149; with *Diamonds on the Sidewalk*, 97–99, 110; at Emerald Room, Houston, 125–27; as father, 61, 80; gambling and, 50, 61, 88, 97, 98, 103, 106, 140; Great Britain tour, 99–106; with "heart attack," 97, 98; Hillcrest Country Club and, 50; as husband, 61, 62–63; Marx, Gummo, and, 63, 99, 114, 141–42, 145; personality, 99, 118; reunion and, 87–89, 95; on TV, 141

Marx, Eden (sister-in-law), 144, 158–59, 168, 182

Marx, Groucho (brother-in-law), xvi, 104, 109; baseball and, 51; with Bernard Geis Associates, 140; Broadway and, 32; Chaplin and, 45; Crawford and, 53; death, 159; with death of Marx, Harpo, 153; with *Diamonds on the Sidewalk*, 97–99; elder abuse, 159; at family wedding, 153; as father, 62, 80, 89; with finances and investments, 156, 158; *Groucho and Me*, xvii; *Groucho Marx and Other Short Stories and Tall Tales*, 177; Hillcrest Country Club and, 49–50; as husband, 61–62, 88; Marx, Gummo, and, 163;

Marx, Harpo, and, 33, 145; *The Marx Brothers Scrapbook*, 182; in Palm Springs, 128; parents, 25; personality, 31, 33, 49, 88, 156, 163–64, 182; with politics, 85; on radio, 63, 98, 135; reunion and, 88–89, 95; on TV, 135, 141, 144, 158; in *Twentieth Century*, 42; work ethic and retirement, 158–59; *You Bet Your Life* and, 98, 135, 144

Marx, Gummo (brother-in-law): death, 158; with *Diamonds on the Sidewalk*, 97; family wedding and, 153; with finances and investments, 156, 157, 158; as husband and father, 62; Marx, Chico, and, 63, 99, 114, 141–42, 145; Marx, Groucho, and, 163; Marx, Harpo, and, xii–xiii, xv, 182; in Palm Springs, 128; personality, 52; reunion and, 88–89, 95

Marx, Harpo (husband): with anonymity, 47–48; anti-Semitism and, 136, 148; atherosclerosis diagnosis, xi–xii, xiii; Broadway and, 7, 32; clarinet and, 99, 132, 145–46; commitment phobia and, 40, 56; courtship, 44–45, 46; Dali, Salvador, and, 56–57; death, xvi, 153–57, 161, 163, 172; with *Diamonds on the Sidewalk*, 95, 97–99, 109–11, 113; at Emerald Room, Houston, 125–27; as father, 58–61, 63, 78–83, 87,